NEW GEOGRAPHIES

edited by
**Daniel Daou &
Pablo Pérez-Ramos**

NEW GEOGRAPHIES 08
ISLAND

New Geographies 08
Island

Editors
Daniel Daou & Pablo Pérez-Ramos

Editorial Board
Ali Fard, Daniel Ibañez, Nikos Katsikis, Taraneh Meshkani

Founding Editors
Gareth Doherty, Rania Ghosn, El Hadi Jazairy, Antonio Petrov, Stephen Ramos, Neyran Turan

Advisory Board
Eve Blau, Neil Brenner, Sonja Duempelmann, Mohsen Mostafavi, Antoine Picon, Hashim Sarkis, Charles Waldheim, James Wescoat

Editorial Advisor
Jennifer Sigler

Text Editor
Nancy Eklund Later

Proofreader
Kari Rittenbach

Graphic Designer
Chelsea Spencer

Cover illustration courtesy of Studio Roland Snooks.
Project Team: Roland Snooks, Marc Gibson, Braden Scott.

"Boundaries" lettering for Mary Oliver's poem by Tania Álvarez Zaldívar.

New Geographies is a journal of design, agency, and territory founded, edited, and produced by doctoral candidates at the Harvard University Graduate School of Design. *New Geographies* presents the geographic as a design paradigm that links physical, representational, and political attributes of space and articulates a synthetic scalar practice. Through critical essays and projects, the journal seeks to position design's agency amid concerns about infrastructure, technology, ecology, and globalization.

New Geographies 08: *Island* has been made possible by grants from the Graham Foundation for Advanced Studies in Fine Arts and the Aga Khan Program at the Harvard University Graduate School of Design. The editors also thank Melissa Vaughn for her support.

All attempts have been made to trace and acknowledge the sources of images. Regarding any omissions or errors, please contact:
Harvard University Graduate School of Design
48 Quincy Street
Cambridge, MA 02148

**Harvard University
Graduate School of Design**

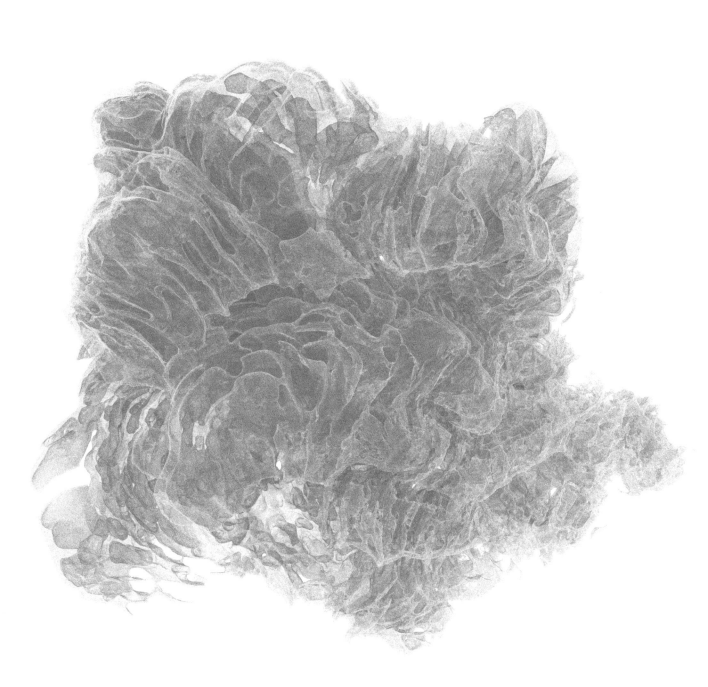

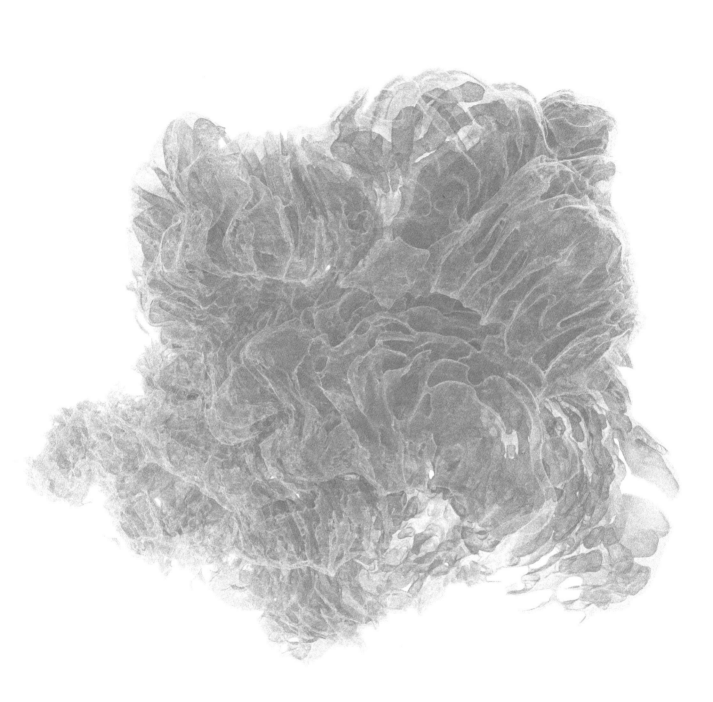

Island

Daniel Daou &
Pablo Pérez-Ramos

"There is no world, there are only islands," the French philosopher Jacques Derrida once declared. What he meant was that, despite the assumption that all beings inhabit a common world, no two share the same *Umwelt*, or experience of it. For him, the unity of the world is a construction, and therefore, we all inhabit incommensurably separate islands in a "world archipelago."[01]

In the wake of the 2016 Brexit vote, symptomatic of the growing political fissures within globalization, the image of Derrida's world archipelago [Wolfe] seems to defy one of the tacit yet most widely established catchphrases of our time: "Everything is connected to everything else." Borrowing from proto-ecologist Alexander von Humboldt's observation, *Alles ist Wechselwirkung* (everything is interconnection),[02] biologist Barry Commoner proposed this universal aphorism as the first of his informal laws of ecology.[03] Following Commoner's principle, today economists discuss globalization and the seemingly endless reach of the neoliberal market system; technologists talk about the ever-expanding technosphere that girds the globe with undersea data cables and envelopes the ionosphere with swarms of satellites; and environmentalists speak of "Gaia" and its biospheric metabolism encompassing every living being and process.

Resembling Commoner's law is another powerful image of our time: the rhizome. In their introduction to *A Thousand Plateaus* (1980), French philosophers Gilles Deleuze and Felix Guattari describe the rhizome as an image of thought where "any point . . . can be connected to any other, and must be."[04] Rhizomes can be entered anywhere, have neither a beginning nor an end, are always in the middle, and remain forever open as an endless series of "ands."[05] During the last two decades, this rhizomatic image of ecology has exerted great influence on design thinking, promoting a notion of territory characterized as an open, fluid, indeterminate, and interconnected field that privileges *process* over the legibility of form and objects [Allen].

If the Age of Enlightenment gave us the modern separation between the natural and man-made worlds, our present time of rhizomes, networks, hybrids, and assemblages might as well be named, as some have suggested, the Age of Entanglement.[06] In it, all boundaries seem to melt [Morton]; order and disorder are no longer conceived as opposites [Samuel]; human activity turns into a force of nature [Turan]; cities become inexorably linked to their planetary hinterlands [Topalovic]; pristine nature becomes an illusion [Ricciardi and Rose]; landscapes become infrastructure [Helmreich]; and the demarcation of boundaries becomes more relevant than ever [Felson]. And yet, as the global political climate becomes increasingly skeptical of the neoliberal narrative of the market system's limitless expansion and the liquid metaphors that enable it,[07] a revision of the figure of the island seems as pertinent as ever. After all, as Michel Serres reminds us, when systems extend and grow in complexity, they always have a tendency to produce heterogeneity and to form into subsets.[08]

Islands have a long tradition in science, art, and the humanities. One need only think of Charles Darwin and the Galapagos, J. G. Ballard's *Concrete Island* (1984), or Plato's allegory of Atlantis to realize the extent to which the figure of the island has been used as a master metaphor to derive insights and extrapolate them across fields [MacKay]. The prevalence of islands lies in their epistemological power as cognitive tools and their imaginative allure as vehicles for speculation.

Epistemologically, islandness addresses questions of identity and difference by sharply marking the edge between the territory of pure understanding and the "stormy ocean" of the unknowable.[09] On islands and imagination, Deleuze notes that, despite the generalized causal distinction that geographers make between islands—"continental islands" as detached fragments of larger landmasses, and "oceanic islands" emerging from the ocean's depths—the commonality that explains their speculative captivation is the possibility of disengaging from humanity and beginning anew.[10] Islands, then, possess a great capacity to frame and simplify the seemingly unbounded and complex, and to kindle different imaginaries that serve as settings for all kinds of real life and thought experiments [Staniscia].

In his 2008 paper "The Challenge of Nissology," hydrologist and geomorphologist Christian Depraetere argued that in the world archipelago, islands "are the rule and not the exception" [MAP Office], claiming that islands ought to be studied "on their own terms" and not as epiphenomena of larger continental trends. We agree with Depraetere's program and would like to extend it by releasing the island from its strict geomorphologic definition. In this regard, following literary critic Marc Shell, we are interested in revisiting not only the way we think *about* islands but also the ways we think *by means* of them [Shell].

***

New Geographies 08: *Island* bookends a trilogy that has been concerned with revealing the geographic dimension of flows and networks. *New Geographies* 06: *Grounding Metabolism* focused on the "imprints" of material and energetic flows proper to the metabolic metaphor, while *New Geographies* 07: *Geographies of Information* discussed the spatialization of cybernetic networks of information and communication technologies. Considering the ecological axiom of interconnectedness as the underlying premise for flows and networks, *New Geographies* 08: *Island* questions the co-optation of ecology by liquid metaphors (e.g., open-endedness, indeterminacy, interconnectedness) and revisits the figure of the island to recover and counterbalance the political imaginaries that these metaphors suppress or enable.

Under the guise of scientific neutrality, ecology has served as the ideal vehicle to introduce specific political ideologies bypassing critical scrutiny. Critical theory has shone light on the ways in which certain ecological metaphors help naturalize politico-economic processes, as if market laws were as inescapable as the laws of physics. Designers who embrace and attempt to replicate allegedly "natural" processes are therefore effectively partaking in the aesthetization of politics—laissez-faire disguised as self-organization, emergence, or bottom-up processes [Spencer].

Following Stéphane Mallarmé's maxim that everything comes down to aesthetics and political economy (*Tout se résume dans l'Esthétique et l'Économie politique*),[11] the present volume explores both the aesthetic and political implications of ecology's rhizomatic model. Politically, it has enabled an ideological discourse based on "paths of least resistance," turning the question of agency into one of alignment with market forces [Berrizbeitia]. Aesthetically, the naturalization of flow and process has negated attention to the putatively top-down methods based on forms, permanence, and legibility, limiting design theory and agency [Snooks].[12]

If so far the role of design has been to aestheticize politics, more than reversing direction into a politicization of aesthetics, an effective counter-ideology of ecology must come from the synthesis of poetics and political economy. Given its amalgamating ability, we propose the island as the heuristic figure to explore how this synthesis might come about.

To frame, critique, and further speculate on this agenda, the 22 contributions forming this volume are divided into two main sections. The first of these leans toward a more general theoretical grounding of island thinking, while the second discusses more explicit implications for design.

Marc Shell and Stefania Staniscia author the first of four pairs of essays included in the first section. The introductory text comes from the first pages of Shell's *Islandology* (2014) and helps open up the figure of the island more generally as a matter of definition. Staniscia thereafter discusses the ambivalence of the island as geographic feature and as metaphor, and proposes the "island *effect*" as a means to mediate between the two. The next pair of essays positions the notion of the island along broad temporal and spatial scales, through a timeline and an atlas. Robin MacKay constructs a lineage of islands as both objects and subjects of thought experiments suggesting an earthbound "geophilosophy," while MAP Office offers an atlas based on an alternative postcolonial taxonomy of the world archipelago. Next, Cary Wolfe and Timothy Morton address the ontological dimension of the island, one discussing the idea of a global biopolitical "community" and

the other elaborating on "molten boundaries" as a solution to the problem of "the excluded middle." Finally, Nina Samuels and Stefan Helmreich discuss the implications of rendering islands visible, as in the case of Mandelbrot's early explorations of fractals, or invisible, as in the case of new technologies aimed at cloaking bodies from waves.

The second section of the volume consists of four groups of three essays each. The first group discusses the implications and limits of process-oriented, in contrast to object-oriented, design strategies. In conversation, Stan Allen reflects on his "stroll" between fields and objects, contrasting his writings on fields, dating from the mid-1990s, with his more recent interest in boundaries. Anita Berrizbeitia critiques design methodologies that use process to privilege indeterminacy in landscape architecture and calls, instead, for design "precision." Lastly, Douglas Spencer elaborates a comparative critique of the performative economies of Landscape Urbanism's "ocean" vis-à-vis the agonistic politics of absolute architecture's "archipelago."

The next group of essays reconsiders object-oriented design approaches. Roland Snooks explains the development of design techniques that are driven as much by top-down formal mechanisms as they are by bottom-up ones, resulting in a dialectic that does not privilege one approach over the other. Garrett Ricciardi and Julian Rose of Formlessfinder illustrate what could be considered an anti-anti-formalism, driven not by ecological metaphors but by immanent material properties. Similarly, Neyran Turan addresses the Anthropocene in design, not through the lens of ecology but rather through geology, shifting focus from flows to matter.

The next three essays explore the island as a design tool, in scales ranging from gardens to cities to regions. Kees Lokman and Susan Herrington explore gardens as enclosed spaces in connection to their surrounding open landscapes. Alexander Felson takes a similar approach with mid-scale ecological experiments—"mesocosmos"—within the context of urban ecology, and Milica Topalovic studies the relationship between Singapore, an island city-state, and its (planetary) hinterland.

The last group of essays expands the definition of the island to encompass the whole planet and beyond. Hashim Sarkis shares research in progress on *The World According to Architecture*, while Roi Salgueiro Barrio follows by suggesting ways in which architecture can be a vehicle to apprehend the earth as a whole and to conceive a new universalism. Joyce Hsiang and Bimal Mendis shine light on the spheres of the unknown, revealing the true scale of urbanization processes that extend not only horizontally but vertically, from sites of underground extraction and the ocean floor to the ionosphere.

008

Lastly, as a coda, Rania Ghosn and El Hadi Jazairy of Design Earth speculate on the post-planetary scale and a new cosmist design imaginary.

***

The collapse of dichotomies characteristic of the Age of Entanglement results from the disappearance of a "constitutive outside" [Hsiang and Mendis]. Old binaries—natural/artificial, city/hinterland—become dated, misleading, or counterproductive. The metabolisms of human civilization and the biosphere are inseparable. And yet, against this all-encompassing, totalizing phenomenon, there is a resistance to conceptualizing totality. Instead, the world seems to retrench into conservative/agonistic forms of isolationism—ignoring that, after all, beneath the water surface all landmasses are connected.[13] To overcome this impasse, it is necessary to consider a reinvigorated cosmopolitical universalism [Ghosn and Jazairy].[14]

The fundamental finitude of the island should not be understood as a secluding boundary condition that creates a dichotomy between itself and the constitutive other. Instead, the island might better be seen through the dialectics established by the word's etymological roots: island as simultaneously "land surrounded and isolated by water" (from the Latin *insula*) and "the moment where land and water blend" (from the Norse for "water-land").[15] It is this dialectical tension that makes the island an epistemological and speculative device. And its framed specificity allows us to better understand the interactions between things and the world [Lokman and Herrington] and also to construct new forms of thought that help reveal the world and render it legible [Sarkis and Salgueiro Barrio]. Precisely by transcending the dichotomy between interior and exterior the island avoids slipping into particularism, and becomes instead the figure through which a new form of universalism can be conceived. In this way, the island bolsters the ecological imaginary, helping design face an entangled world.

01. Jacques Derrida, *The Beast and the Sovereign*, vol. 2, trans. Geoffrey Bennington (Chicago: University of Chicago Press, 2011), 8–9.

02. Alexander von Humboldt, *Reise Auf Dem Rio Magdalena, Durch Die Anden und Mexico*, vol. 1, ed. and trans. Margot Faak (Berlin: Akademie Verlag, 1986), 358. Originally published in von Humboldt's Travel Diary of August 1803, while at the Valley of Mexico.

03. Barry Commoner, *The Closing Circle: Nature, Man, and Technology* (New York: Knopf, 1971).

04. Gilles Deleuze and Felix Guattari, "Introduction: Rhizome," in *A Thousand Plateaus*, trans. Brian Massumi (Minneapolis: University of Minnesota Press, 1987), 7.

05. Ibid., 21.

06. Neri Oxman, "Age of Entanglement," *Journal of Design and Science*, February 22, 2016, http://jods.mitpress.mit.edu.

07. See Zygmunt Bauman, *Liquid Life* (Cambridge, UK: Polity Press, 2005).

08. Michel Serres, *Genesis*, trans. Geneviève James and James Nielson (Ann Arbor: University of Michigan Press, 1995).

"Classes, genera, families or kingdoms," Serres explains, "are still useful. One need only think of them as fuzzy in order to remain sensible." [86]

09. See Immanuel Kant, "Of the Ground of the Division of All Objects into Phenomena and Noumena," in *Critique of Pure Reason*, trans. F. Max Müller (London: Macmillan, 1881), A235/B294; and Friedrich Nietzsche, *The Gay Science*, ed. Bernard Williams, trans. Josefine Nauckhoff and Adrian Del Caro (Cambridge: Cambridge University Press, 2001), sec. 343.

10. See Deleuze, "Causes and Reasons of Desert Islands," in *Desert Islands and Other Texts, 1953–1974*, ed. David Lapoujade, trans. Michael Taormina (Los Angeles: Semiotext(e), 2004), 9.

11. Stéphane Mallarmé, *La musique et les lettres* (Paris: Perrin et cie, 1895).

12. Andrea Branzi, "Fuzzy Thinking," in *Weak and Diffuse Modernity: The World of Projects at the Beginning of the 21st Century* (Milan: Skira, 2006), 29; and Timothy Morton, *Ecology without Nature: Rethinking Environmental Aesthetics*

(Cambridge, MA: Harvard University Press, 2007), 189.

13. A point made eloquently by Martin W. Lewis and Kären Wigen in *The Myth of Continents: A Critique of Metageography* (Berkeley: University of California Press, 1997).

14. From a postmodern perspective, universalism should be qualified as cosmopolitical to avoid a regression to modernism. See Isabelle Stengers, *Cosmopolitics* (Minneapolis: University of Minnesota Press, 2010); and also Albena Yaneva and Alejandro Zaera-Polo, ed., *What Is Cosmopolitical Design? Design, Nature and the Built Environment* (Burlington, VT: Ashgate, 2015).

15. Marc Shell refers to these two meanings of *island*—one boundary-oriented and the other closer to the idea of an interface, of two worlds happening at once—in his book *Islandology* (Stanford, CA: Stanford University Press, 2014). See the chapter "Defining Islands and Isolating Definitions," 13–25.

Daniel Daou & Pablo Pérez-Ramos

The Blue Marble. Captured on December 7, 1972, at 5:39 a.m. EST (10:39 UTC). Earth as seen by Apollo 17 en route to the Moon at a distance of about 29,000 kilometers (18,000 mi), taken by either Harrison Schmitt or Ron Evans.

Rem Koolhaas and Madelon Vriesendorp, *The City of the Captive Globe* Project, 1972.

Keith Tyson, *Large Field Array*, 2006–07.
© Keith Tyson. Previous spread: *Large
Field Array* installation view at Sarvisalo,
Finland, 2016. Photo © Tim Bowditch,
courtesy of the Zabludowicz Collection.

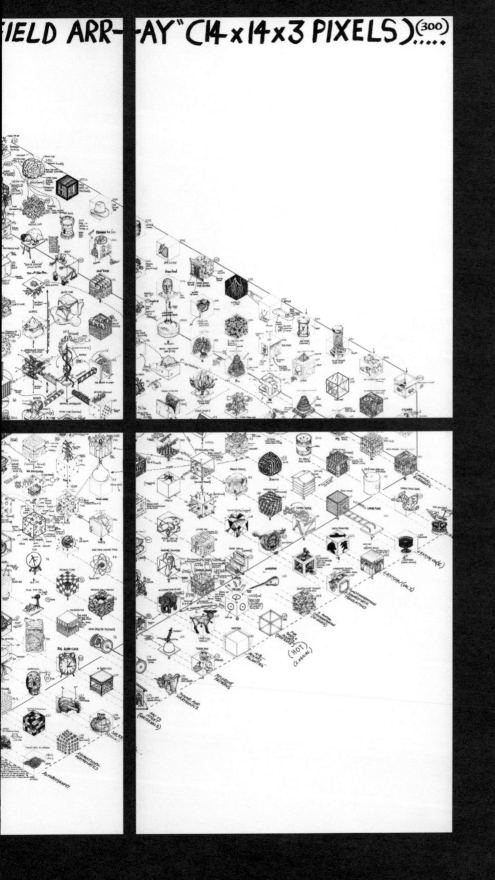

Jamie Mills, "Forest," 2013. © Jamie Mills.

John Stephens, "Games of Chance & Levels
of Meaning," 2010. © John Stephens.

ME-TER	Horizontale STRAHLENBRECHUNG	ENTFERNUNG in welcher Berge gesehen (Meereshöhe einst. reduciert)	HÖHEN-MESSUNGEN in verschiedenen Welttheilen	ELECTRISCHE ERSCHEINUNGEN nach Höhe der Luftschichten	CULTUR DES BODENS nach Verschiedenheit der Höhe	ABNAHME DER SCHWERE durch die Schwingung des Pendels im leeren Raume ausgedrückt	LUFTBLÄU in Graden des Kyanometers	ABNAHME DER FEUCHTIGKEIT in Graden des Saussureschen Hygrometers ausgedrückt	DRUCK DER LUFT in Barometer-Höhen	TOI-SEN

Geographie der Pfla...

...ein Naturge...

gegründet auf Beobachtungen und Messungen, welche vom 10ten Grade nörd...

von ALEXANDER VON

ME-TER	LUFTWÄRME NACH HÖHE DER SCHICHTEN durch den höchsten und niedrigsten Stand des Thermometers ausgedrückt	CHEMISCHE NATUR des LUFTKREISES	HÖHE DER UNTERN GRENZE DES EWIGEN SCHNEES, nach Verschiedenheit der Geographischen Breite.	THIERE, geordnet nach der HÖHE IHRES WOHNORTS	SIEDHITZE DES WASSERS nach Verschiedenheit der Höhen	GEOGNOSTISCHE ANSICHT der Tropen-Welt	SCHWÄCHUNG des LICHTSTRAHLEN beim Durchgange der Luftschichten	TOI-SEN
								4000
6500					Siedhitze zu 71°,0. (67;°6.R.) Bar. 0,320″		0,9164	3500
6000				Kein organischer Stoff an den Erdboden gehefted.	Siedhitze zu 81°,0. (64?8.R.) Bar. 0,390″		0,9047	3000
5500				Der Condor der Anden.				
5000					Siedhitze zu 88°. (67,°7.R.) Bar. 0,448″		0,8922	2500
4500								
4000					Siedhitze zu 88°,2. (70;°5.R.) Bar. 0,574″		0,8787	2000
3500								
3000					Siedhitze zu 91°,8. (73°,0.R.) Bar. 0,638″		0,8640	1500
2500								
2000					Siedhitze zu 94°,5. (75,°5.R.) Bar. 0,603″		0,8478	1000
1500								
1000					Siedhitze zu 97°,1. (77,°7.R.) Bar. 0,757″		0,8309	500
500								
0					Siedhitze zu 100° (80?R.) Bar. 0,762″		0,8223	0

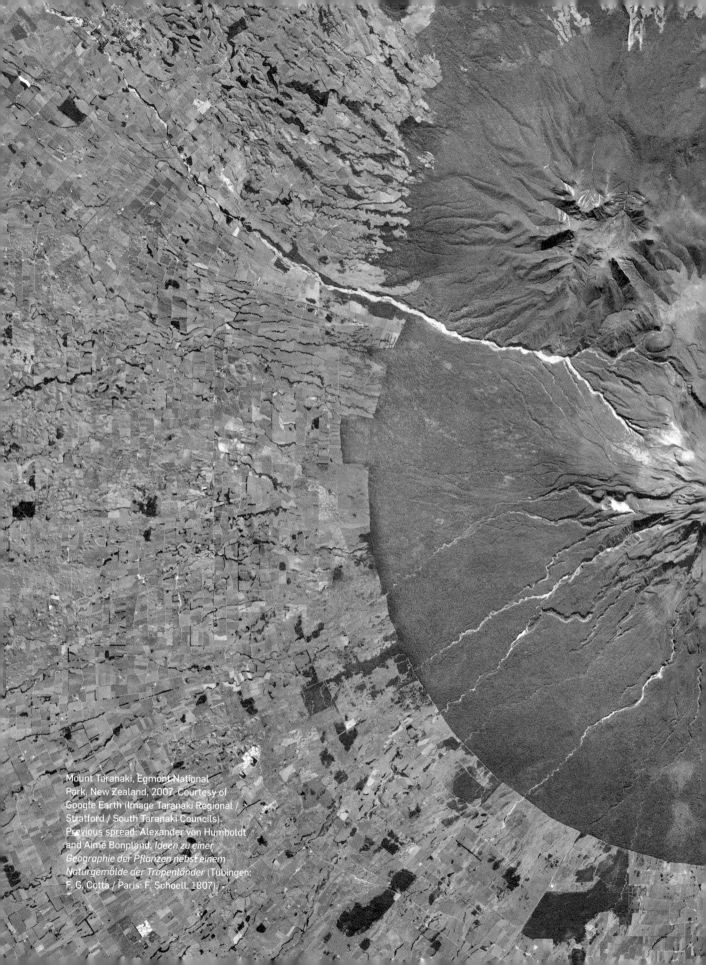

Mount Taranaki, Egmont National
Park, New Zealand, 2007. Courtesy of
Google Earth (Image Taranaki Regional /
Stratford / South Taranaki Councils).
Previous spread: Alexander von Humboldt
and Aimé Bonpland, *Ideen zu einer
Geographie der Pflanzen nebst einem
Naturgemälde der Tropenländer* (Tübingen:
F. G. Cotta / Paris: F. Schoell, 1807).

Israel López Balán, Project for a Church without a God, 2014. © Israel López Balán.

Stephen Petegorsky, *Clump of Trees,*
Tuscany, Italy, 1993. Pigment inkjet print,
17 × 22". © Stephen Petegorsky.

Edward Burtynsky, Canola Fields, Luoping,
Yunnan Province, China, 2011. © Edward
Burtynsky, courtesy Nicholas Metivier
Gallery, Toronto.

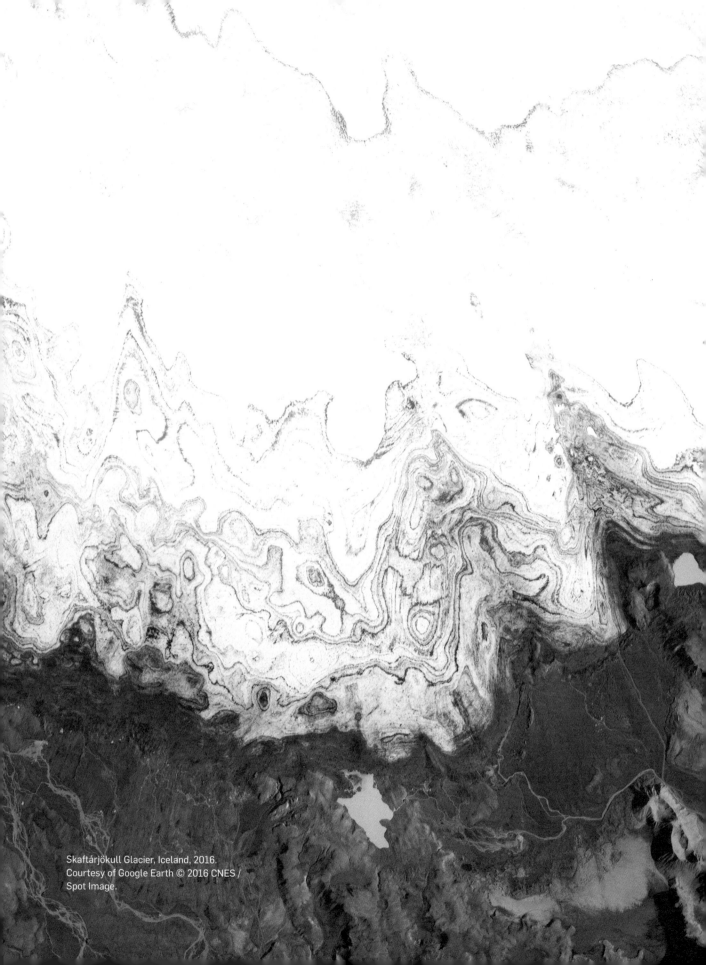

Skaftárjökull Glacier, Iceland, 2016.
Courtesy of Google Earth © 2016 CNES /
Spot Image.

Adjder Oasis, some 100 km northwest of
Timimoun, north of Charouine, Algeria.
© George Steinmetz. Previous spread: Rudi
Sebastian, *Lençois-VI*, 2016. © Rudi Sebastian.

Ouagadougu (Upper Volta, now Burkina Faso),
late December 1930 or early January 1931.
Photo by Walter Mittelholzer (modified).

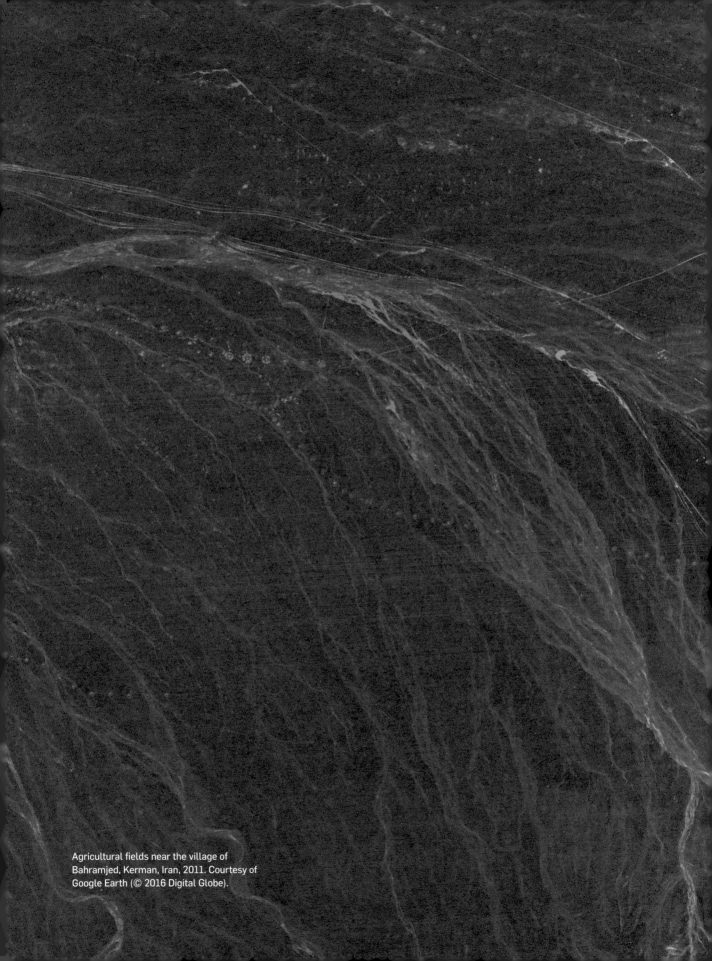

Agricultural fields near the village of
Bahramjed, Kerman, Iran, 2011. Courtesy of
Google Earth (© 2016 Digital Globe).

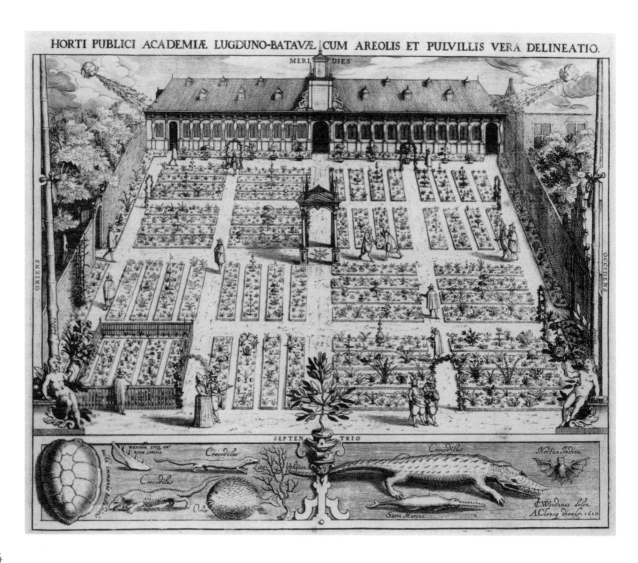

Hortus Botanicus in Leiden, 1610. Engraving
by Jan Cornelisz Woudanus.

Peter Zumthor and Piet Oudolf, Serpentine
Gallery Pavilion, 2011. Photo © Walter Herfst.

Élisée Reclus and Louis Bonnier, *Projet
de globe terrestre au 100 000e*, Universal
Exhibition, 1900.

Oscar Newman, Nuke-proof Manhattan
below New York, 1969.

John Claudius Loudon, Greenhouse for the
Royal Horticultural Society, 1818.

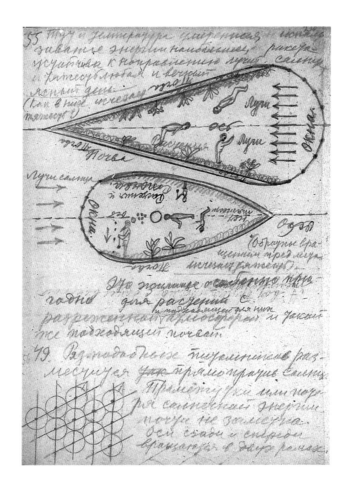

Konstantinos Tsiolkovsky, Sketches for a
Green House in a Space Capsule, 1932.

040

Charles Ross, *Star Axis*, 1971–present.
(www.staraxis.org) Composite photo: Kerry
Loewen and Charles Ross.

The Mir Space Station, photographed by
Atlantis (STS-71), July 1995.

BOUNDARIES

There is a place where the town ends,
        and the fields begin.
It's not marked but the feet know it,
also the heart that is longing for refreshment
        and, equally, for repose.

Someday we'll live in the sky.
Meanwhile, the house of our lives is this green world.
The fields, the ponds, the birds.
The thick black oaks—surely they are
        the invention of something wonderful.
And the tiger lilies.
And the runaway honeysuckle that no one
        will ever trim again.

Where is it? I ask, and then
my feet know it.

One jump, and I'm home.

                                        —*Mary Oliver*

Islandology

Marc Shell

"Islands have always fascinated the human mind," perhaps because fascination "is the instinctive response of man, the land animal, welcoming a brief intrusion of earth in the vast overwhelming expanse of sea." So wrote Rachel Carson in her best-selling book *The Sea around Us* (1951).[01] Islandology argues that there is more to it than that.

We begin this argument by defining islands and isolating certain definitions, including the definition of definition. After pinpointing the meaning of what logician John Venn calls an "island of meaning," we explore ways of speaking about actual islands and consider how human imagination of islandness has variably informed cultures. Islandness, we discover, resides in a shifting tension between the definition of island as "land as opposed to water" and the countervailing definition as "land as identical with water."

[...]

The "critical topography" or "philosophical topography" of place (*locus*) involves more than just the real estate slogan "Location, location, location."[02] The leading modern geographer, Immanuel Kant, in *Physical Geography*, defines *geography* in terms of nature and politics, distinguishing among the physical objects of study: geography (the entire world), topography (single places), and chorography (regions), as well as orography (mountains) and hydrography (water areas).[03] Spatiality influenced Kant's thinking in general,[04] including his epistemology, his topography of mental faculties,[05] and his notion of worldly unity and ownership, as discussed in the *Metaphysics of Morals* (1785).[06]

Said the Sicilian islander and mathematician Archimedes, in the third century BC, "Give me a place to stand on and I can move the earth."[07] Understanding islandness requires that place to stand (*pou stō*). Pappus of Alexandria, who reported this statement of Archimedes, was a specialist in projective geometry with a focus on points at infinity on horizons. The limiting beach, which everywhere surrounds dry land on Earth, likewise defines the sea's coasts.

Suppose oneself, then, at a beach. The coastline marks the cutoff where land ends and water begins. If one believes that one can walk or sail around the land perimeter and end up where one began, then one is probably on an island. (In this sense, an island is an *insula*: "solid earth [*terra firma*] surrounded on the horizontal plane by water [*aqua liquida*].") If one believes one cannot go all around, or circumambulate, that land, then one probably does not call it "island." One does not always know, of course, whether one is on an island or on something else, maybe a peninsula or mainland. That uncertainty was especially common before the exploration of the world was complete. On the Europeans' first sighting of Guanahani (modern Bahamas) or Maracaibo (modern Venezuela), who really knew for sure whether or not the "terra firma" where they might land would be circumnavigable? Floating? Animate? The world, as we will see, remains much unexplored. Just so, we will see how naming a place like Guanahani—or, indeed any land or water place on Earth—remains much vexed.[08]

From the viewpoint presented in the last paragraph, an island is "land on which, when one walks along its coastline in one direction, one eventually gets back to where one started." This perambulatory viewpoint distinguishes sharply the "edge" or "coast" between land and sea, but usually ignores how the difference between earth and water already implies their identity and, in fact, how the word *island* already also means "sea-land" (*is-land*), or the place, no matter how small or large, where water and earth are one and the same.

Islandness, in this sense of identity confronting difference, informs primordial issues of philosophy: how, conceptually, we connect and disconnect parts and wholes, for example, and how we connect and disconnect one thing and another. Whether islandness, and hence geography, is fundamental to philosophy and its history or is merely contingent or exemplary is a question we pursue in *Islandology*. If there were not islands already, it would be necessary for human beings—the logical and political creatures that we are (or strive to be)—to invent them. This book thus names "islandology" the discourse that marks off human beings not only as children of the main, understood as both "land" and "sea," but also as creatures of the natural shore who inhabit, at once, both positive and negative space.

In the previous discussion, we considered a patch of land when we are standing on it, so that it seems possible to begin immediately its attempted circumambulation. Consider now a patch of land, seen at a distance from across the waters, as if we were on another patch of land, or imagine a ship (or a "floating island"), or picture a peninsula that, without our knowing, is connected horizontally with the land whereon we stand. For all we know, we cannot get there without going underwater (like seals, submarines, or passengers in underwater tunnels) or without traveling on the surface of the water (like water striders, surface ships, or pedestrians on pontoon bridges) or without flying above that surface (like birds, airships, or passengers on airships). We dream of swimming now instead of walking.

Swimming is understood here as natation, an English language term that is cognate with the Greek *nēsos* (usually translated as "island").[09] The term emphasizes the sense in which main and mainland are one and how all stations, including Earth and the place where the little boy sits in *A Child Geography's of the World* (1951), are equally insular and mainland. To understand islandology after the first scientific Age of Exploration means not only looking out to sea from the viewpoint of land but also looking out to land

from the viewpoint of sea. It means wondering whether there is any safely stable harbor, *pou stō*, wherefrom even to look out.

The study of islands, as isolates known and unknown is not new. There have been dozens of approaches to the topic. Some focus on particular colonial and postcolonial settings—as does Rebecca Weaver-Hightower in *Empire Islands* (2007).[10] Others speculate on how thinking about islands encourages scientific hypothesis and literary fictions—as does Jill Franks in *Islands and the Modernists* (2006).[11] A few provide psychological examinations of persons who suffer from island mania—as does Jill Franks in "Men Who Loved Islands" (2008).[12]

Professional geographers study the smallness of islands in relation to the largeness of mainlands,[13] examine the effect of bridging islands with mainlands,[14] scrutinize the sociology of modern tourism,[15] investigate specific environmental issues and study the characteristics of insular cartography.[16] Richard Grove, in *Green Imperialism* (1991), shows how global politics exacerbates islandic environmental issues.[17] The anthropological historian Marshall Sahlins, in *Islands of History* (1985), stresses the intellectual advantages of an island centered historiography of mobility.[18] Fernand Braudel argues in *The Mediterranean* (1949) that "the events of history often lead to islands."[19] And John R. Gillis, in *Islands of the Mind: How the Human Imagination Created the Atlantic World* (2004),[20] discusses how conceiving islands in terms of long distance helps explain the historical process of continental discovery. Islandology, in its study of how we speak about islands, recognizes these approaches [. . .] and, at the same time, builds on them.

[. . .]

Islandology engages problems of political import: the modern tendency to confuse circumferential natural borders with political ones and the ancient inclination to except circumferential seas from imperial sovereignty. Both problems focus on issues of pressing environmental concern. A reexamination of the Darwinian theory of coral island reefs and volcanic islands in relation to insular plate tectonics conceives anew the pressures of "global warming," for example. Likewise, contextualized interpretations of movies, among them the Danish *Smilla's Sense of Snow* (1997) and the German-American *S.O.S. Eisberg* (1933), rethink the melting of the polar ice caps in terms of both different states of matter and different material substances.

Nineteenth-century thinkers, both American and German, often relied on tendentious and needless theories of climatic and geographic determinism; this reliance, no

matter how productive in its way, brought with it needless and unhappy political consequences. Most likely, the extensive closings of departments of geography worldwide—especially in the United States—during the latter part of the 20th century had some of the "value-neutral purposes"—beneficent at least in the short term—that backers of the then-competitive disciplines (international politics, comparative literature, earth and planetary sciences, linguistics, and environmental studies) often articulated. Yet none of these disciplines has recovered the global and philosophical vision of geography, now so much required, that sees all lands and seas on Earth as participants in a single archipelago.

The word *islandology* provides this volume with its title. It refers both to the *rhetoric* of speaking about islands and to the *science* of islands. (The suffix -logy indicates no less a way of speaking, as for *brachyology* [a condensed expression][21] and *tautology* [a proposition which is unconditionally true . . . by virtue of its logical form], as a field of study *theology* [the study of God].)[22] Where the subject matter is the definition of definition, the rhetoric and the science verge on the same. How the logical definition of definition merges with the geographic definition of island is part of the science of rhetoric. *Islandology*, in this context, is one of those neologisms that, no matter how awkward, has its place in the language. In Thomas Hardy's *Tess of the d'Urbervilles* (1891), Angel Clare comments on Tess's imaginings this way: "What are called advanced ideas are really in great part but . . . a more accurate expression, by words of logy . . . of sensations which men and women have vaguely grasped for centuries."[23]

The introduction of the word *islandology* combined institutional aspects with a geopolitical impetus. In 1945, Raine Edward Bennett founded the American Institute of Islandology (Washington, DC), partly in response to his island experiences during the two world wars. The institute's first purpose was determining whether Australia was an island or a continent. While Bennett said that Australia was "the world's largest island," an Australian newspaper reporter probably had it right when he said, "We [Australians] will want [the nomenclature] both ways . . . as the smallest of the large [continents] and the largest of the small [islands]."[24] This droll impasse caused the institute's founders to stumble out of the starting gate, which explains why the institute's second goal was never accomplished: assembling and publishing a fifteen-volume encyclopedia of islands with a worldwide focus.

Half a century later, other scholars published an *Encyclopedia of Islands*,[25] which presented no general "islandology" of a philosophical and historical nature. The editors of this modern encyclopedia use island loosely to mean "any discrete habitat isolated from other habitats by inhospitable surroundings." For them, it seems to mean *biosphere*. Yet the

Opposite page: Jamie Mills, "Islands," 2016. Next spread: Emma McNally, "BH1," 2009.

Marc Shell

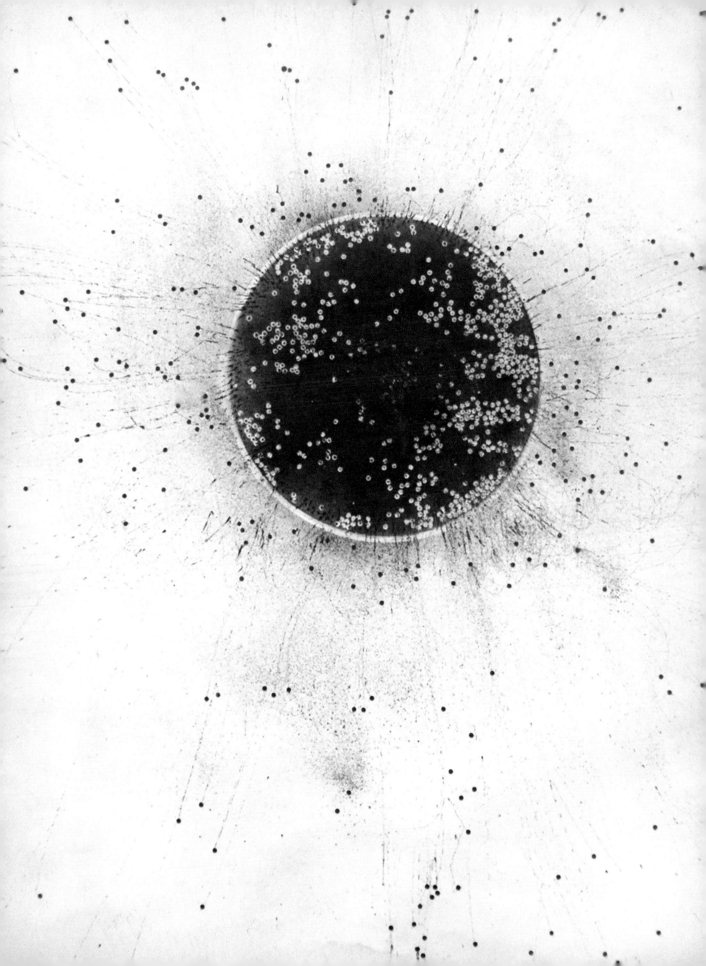

word *island* has cross-cultural political, geographic, and cultural baggage, in a different sense from that of the presumably value-neutral word *biosphere*, whose inventor, the geologist Eduard Suess, defined in his study of the Alps (1857) as "the place on Earth's surface where life dwells."[26] (Vladimir Vernadsky in his 1926 *Biosphere*, teased out of Suess's notion the idea that the *geosphere* is where there is only inanimate matter.[27]) Such ways of defining *island* have no determinate reference either to the interaction of land with water (geology) or to the different ways of understanding that interaction among cultures and logical systems. In that sense, these scholars avowedly apply an island "metaphor" to a palpably insular setting, whether biospherical or otherwise characterized.

Edmund Burke, in *A Philosophical Inquiry* (1759), says, "When we define, we seem in danger of circumscribing nature within the bounds of our own notions."[28] The logical definition of island is linked with the logical circumscription of definition in a way that cannot avoid the linguistics and natural history of islands.

Editors' note: This essay is an excerpt from the preface to Marc Shell's *Islandology: Geography, Rhetoric, Politics* (Stanford: Stanford University Press, 2014).

01. Rachel Carson, *The Sea around Us: An Illustrated Commemorative Edition* (1951; New York: Oxford University Press, 2003), 110.

02. "Attention Salesmen, Sales Managers: Location, Location, Location, Close to Rogers Park," 1926 classified advertisement in the Chicago Tribune; cited in William Safire, "On Language: Location, Location, Location," *New York Times*, June 26, 2009.

03. Friedrich Theodor Rink, ed., *Kant's Gesammelte Schriften,* Königlich Preussische Akademie der Wissenschaften (Berlin: G. Reimer, 1902), 9:159–162.

04. On this, see Onora O'Neil, "Orientation in Thinking: Geographical Problems, Political Solutions," in *Reading Kant's Geography*, ed. Stuart Elden and Eduardo Mendieta (Albany: State University of New York Press, 2011.)

05. See Paul Richards, "Kant's Geography and Mental Maps," *Transactions of the Institute of British Geographers* 61, no. 1 (1974): 1–16.

06. See Marc Shell, *Islandology*, 81–92.

07. The Greek text, *Dos moi (phēsi) pou stō kai kinō*, is from *Pappi Alexandrini Collectionis*, ed. Friedrich Otto Hultsch (Berlin: Apud Weidmannos, 1878), 1060. This translation is taken from T. L. Heath, ed., *The Works of Archimedes with the Method of Archimedes* (New York: Dover, 1953), xix.

08. See Shell, *Islandology*, 81–92.

09. Compare the Celtic-French word *nadio*.

10. Rebecca Weaver-Hightower, *Empire Islands: Castaways, Cannibals, and Fantasies of Conquest* (Minneapolis: University of Minnesota Press, 2007); and Diana Loxley, *Problematic Shores: The Literature of Islands* (Houndmills, UK: Palgrave Macmillan, 1991).

11. Jill Franks, *Islands and the Modernists: The Allure of Isolation in Art, Literature and Science* (Jefferson, NC: McFarland, 2006.)

12. Jill Franks, "Men Who Loved Islands: D. H. Lawrence and J. M. Synge in Sardinia and Aran," *Études Lawrenciennes* 28 (2003): 133–147.

13. Godfrey Baldacchino and David Milne, eds., *Lessons from the Political Economy of Small Islands: The Resourcefulness of Jurisdiction* (London: Macmillan / Institute of Island Studies, 2000); and Stephen A. Royle, *A Geography of Islands: Small Island Insularity* (London: Routledge, 2001.)

14. Stephen A. Royle, "Inseltourismus: Inseln der Träume" in *Trauminlsen? Tourismus und Alltag in "Urlaubsparadiesen,"* ed. Heidi Weinhäupl and Margit Wolfsberger (Vienna: Lit Verlag, 2006), 13–36.

15. Janis Frawley-Holler, *Island Wise: Lessons on Living from Islands of the World* (Louisville, KY: Broadway, 2003).

16. Tom Conley, *The Self-Made Map: Cartographic Writing in Early Modern France* (Minneapolis: University of Minnesota Press, 1996), esp. 178–182.

17. Islands were "in practical environmental as well as in mental terms, an easily conceived allegory of a whole world." Richard Grove, *Green Imperialism: Colonial Expansion, Tropical Island Edens, and the Origins of Environmentalism, 1600–1800* (Cambridge: Cambridge University Press, 1991), 32.

18. Marshall Sahlins, *Islands of History* (Chicago: University of Chicago Press, 1985.)

19. Fernand Braudel, *The Mediterranean and the Mediterranean World in the Age of Philip II* (New York: Harper & Row, 1972), 2:154.

20. Relevant here is Gillis's anthropologically directed *Back to the Sea: Coasts in Human History* (Chicago: University of Chicago Press, 2012) and his contribution to *Seascapes, Littoral Cultures, and Trans-Oceanic Exchanges*, Library of Congress Conference, Washington, DC, February 12–15, 2003.

21. For example, *O*.

22. *Oxford English Dictionary* (hereafter, *OED*), s.vv. "brachyology," "tautology," n.f. Other examples include: *acrylogia, aetiologia, analogy, battology, bomphilologia, dialogismus, dicaeologia, dissoi logoi, homiologia, hysterologia, ideology, leptologia, neologism, paliologia, paromologia*, and *syllogism*.

23. Thomas Hardy, *Tess of d'Urbervilles* (London, 1891), 1:249.

24. "Continent vs. Island," *Spokane Daily News,* August 21, 1945. See also *Far Eastern Review* 14, no. 17 (1945): 246.

25. Rosemary G. Gillespie and David A. Clague, eds. *Encyclopedia of Islands* (Berkeley: University of California Press, 2009).

26. Eduard Suess, *Die Entstehung der Alpencow* (Vienna: W. Braunmüller, 1875).

27. Vladimir Vernadsky, *Biosphere*, ed. Mark A. S. McMenamin, trans. David B. Langmuir (New York: Copernicus, 1998).

28. See Shell, *Islandology*, 231–248.

Image Credits

The "Island Effect": Reality or Metaphor?

Stefania Staniscia

In spite of its clear and well-defined boundaries, the island is a very fuzzy entity.

The island is a geographical reality and, at the same time, a concept that has been extensively used as a metaphor—"*the* central metaphor within western discourse"[01]—and signifier for very diverse and often opposite meanings. Literature presents us with an infinity of fictional islands, the most representative of which have repeatedly been addressed by scholars of islands studies. "Islands are sites of innovative conceptualizations, whether of nature or human enterprise, whether virtual or real,"[02] sociologist and island studies scholar Godfrey Baldacchino asserts, able to embody a variety of dichotomies without resolving them. Islands can be defined through almost oppositional categories: paradise and prison, utopia and dystopia, insularity and connectedness, hard-edge and permeable boundaries, roots and routes, vulnerability and resilience, irrelevant backwaters and cutting-edge laboratories, just to list a few.

The amplitude and ambiguity of the concept of island is, indeed, the reason why many scholars of island studies still question the very possibility of developing a coherent theory of islandness.[03] The viewpoints of scholars from the many different disciplines who deal with islands and islandness—geographers, geologists, geomorphologists, naturalists, island biogeographers, social scientists, and others—are so diverse that it is impossible to agree on one definition. According to cultural geographer Pete Hay, "Even the question of what constitutes an island is not conclusively settled."[04] Nevertheless, one of the most debated issues is the ambivalence between the island as a physical reality or geographical entity and the island as metaphor. "Is 'islandness' to do with a generalizable condition of physical isolation or a state of personal disconnection (a robust and tenaciously familiar metaphor and literary trope)? Or is it to do with the stuff of *real* geographical entities that more or less accord with one of those contested definitions of an island as a physical reality?" Hay wonders.[05] Although the use of the island as a conceptual device may be of great intellectual interest, a perspective that does not completely dismiss the reality of islands seems to be more fecund from the perspective of the design disciplines.

The metaphors of the island and the archipelago have been used widely within urban studies, architecture, and planning disciplines as literal and figurative (rather than ideal and abstract) references to material forms, as well as to models of urban and land occupation, use, and transformation.[06] At times, the two have been used metaphorically to clarify the functioning of single parts. For example, architect Alessandro Petti, director of the program Campus in Camps at Al Quds University, Palestine, casts them as physical and spatial devices for territorial modification and construction "derived from a security and control paradigm" (as in gated communities,

occupied Palestinian territories, or residential offshore islands), based on separation, isolation, and fragmentation dynamics.[07] Alternatively, islands and archipelagos have proved helpful in representing the functional relations between parts. This is the case in relation to the spatial organization of the city and the territory, which evermore often organize themselves through functionally specialized units. These units, although necessarily interconnected, present autonomous spatial configurations with very well-defined boundaries.[08]

Island references may also be more concrete than metaphoric.[09] More than just analogue models, islands bear witness to large-scale phenomena that affect vaster contexts. Thus they become physical places where these phenomena can be better observed. Migratory flows that are currently traversing the Mediterranean region and leaving deep marks on islands such as Lampedusa, Malta, Lesbos, and Samos provide just one compelling example. As Baldacchino notes, "most scholars . . . enter into the study of small islands precisely in order to test and explore conceptual schemes and specific hypotheses emerging from academic and policy debates at a mainland, regional or global level."[10]

These examples show that the island has been used to read and interpret reality, as if it were a lens through which the physical world can be explained and described. From this point of view, the island seems to be a very powerful cognitive device. It is not, however, exclusively that. Very often, it is regarded as a "potential laborator[y] for any conceivable human project, in thought or in action."[11] Any design intervention on islands is perceived as potentially whole, as well as more easily organizable, controllable, and measurable in its effects, possibly becoming an exemplary practice. Small islands are particularly suitable for design experimentation. The island's spatiality allows designers to sidestep one of the thorniest problems connected to design—or at least, of the design of landscapes and territories. Namely, it allows the designer to surmount the issue of defining the limits of the area of intervention, which—given the boundlessness of natural systems—are notoriously not clear-cut. In the case of islands, however, where geographical limits usually correspond to biological limits, this is not completely true.[12] At the same time, working on fragile, vulnerable, limited spaces with limited resources offers the ideal conditions for projects that aspire to confront current challenges such as climate change, sea level rise, population decline and diaspora, globalization, environmental disasters, and the like. For these reasons, islands provide an attractive laboratory for experimentation. As Ilan Kelman, from the Center for International Climate and Environmental Research in Oslo, Norway, observes, "islands face immense challenges while providing important opportunities for better understanding how to resolve the challenges."[13]

If we expand our scope of research from the consideration of the spatial attributes of islandness itself to include the aspects that allow islands to be regarded as places and not just as mere spaces, islands would emerge as even more attractive from the point of view of designing. These places, in fact, perfectly embody the notion of *territorialization*, a concept that "fram[es] the whole manifestations of the interaction between human communities and nature—including those that usually are not considered as culturally relevant—into a comprehensive, culture-rooted, discourse."[14] Islands are physical entities in which the relations between space and the human communities that inhabit it are stronger, more noticeable, and easily detectable. Islands are an excellent example of what has been termed a "cultural landscape," one that is "illustrative of the evolution of human society and settlement over time, under the influence of the physical constraints and/or opportunities presented by their natural environment and of successive social, economic and cultural forces, both external and internal."[15] One might suggest that the island's spatiality and its specific physical features are able to elicit affection and identification that lead to the production of place.

Not only do islands emerge as suitable places for designing, they also serve at times as potent design tools. Within urban studies, O. M. Ungers's 1977 manifesto *The City in the City: Berlin, the Green Urban Archipelago* remains one of the seminal texts regarding the figure of the archipelago. Ungers, a German architect and architectural theorist, employs the image to reinterpret Berlin's urban structure at a moment when the city's population was expected to drop by more than 10 percent. The projected scenario in which densely populated neighborhoods would coexist alongside sparsely inhabited ones ran the risk of "jeopardiz[ing] the general quality of the urban environment"[16] in the architect's view. The archipelago model embodied for Ungers a design possibility for a city that would not require "the invention of a new urban system, but the improvement of what is already there; not the discovery of a new order, but the rediscovery of proven principles, not the construction of new cities, but the restructuring of the old ones."[17]

Above: Oswald Mathias Ungers, Rem Koolhaas, Hans Kollhoff, Arthur Ovaska, and Peter Riemann, The City within the City—Berlin as a Green Archipelago, 1977. Graphic identification and extraction of the islands from the urban fabric. Opposite page: Plan.

052

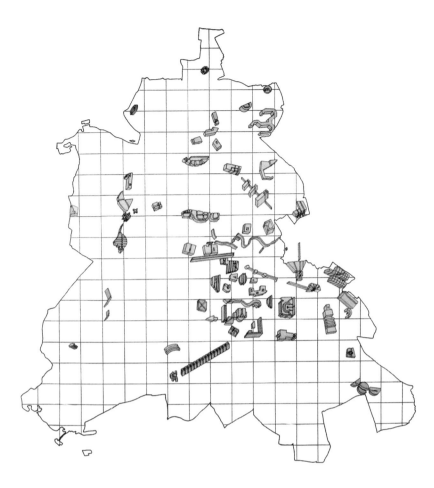

Ungers based his city archipelago construct on the assumption that a structure—whether economic, urban, or natural—loses its functional capacity as its size increases.[18] Ungers asserts that there is a size threshold beyond which a city cannot function well. Exceeding this threshold causes technical and organizational problems that affect the quality of life and of the human environment. He maintains, "Reality has instead shown that reduction and diminution also make for better quality, and not least in the quality of life itself. For this reason small and legible units ought to be created. This applies to production, the way of life, and any other component of our environment."[19] The idea of a "city in the city" and of "Berlin as a city archipelago" originates here.

The different urban entities—the islands—of the city archipelago are characterized by "an identity in keeping with their history, social structure and environmental characteristics."[20] "The space in between," Ungers notes, would consist of "natural zones and pastures. . . . Hence, the urban islands would be divided from each other by strips of nature and green, thus defining the framework of the city in the city and thereby explaining the metaphor of the city as a green archipelago."[21] In the 1970s the figure of the archipelago emerged

as a response to many pressing issues regarding the city, especially its decline in population. Island metaphors stressed the importance of small sizes in maintaining the quality of living spaces, the strengthening of identity, and the intensifying of a sense of place.

If in the work of Ungers the organizational model of the archipelago enables "the existing condition of the as-found city" to become a "projective model for Berlin's future,"[22] in the design experimentation of LCLA Office—an architecture studio founded in 2011 by architect Luis Callejas—the figure of the island serves as a literal reference in the designing praxis. In other words, the island no longer functions as a metaphor but serves instead as the project's very subject. Unger's "reduction and diminution" theory recurs, however, as a way to approach the complexity of projects that work at the scale of landscape and territory. Here, the large scale is controlled through "very small-scale interventions that replicate and connect with infrastructural operations."[23] Typically these are water elements, which provide new forms of transportation. A separate, fractal entity characterized by well-defined boundaries, the island here constitutes the elementary unit of territory and landscape projects. The fascination for

053

Stefania Staniscia

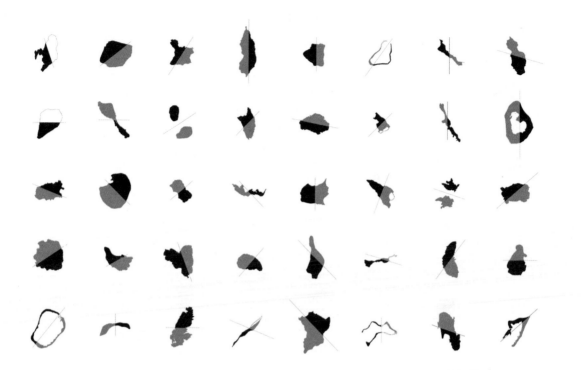

Luis Callejas and Charlotte Hansson, "Pelagic Alphabet," 2016.

the islanding medium goes hand in hand with the fascination for the boundedness and the limitedness—for the possibility to "have a high control over the limits of interventions"[24]—for contained territories, and for isolated ecologies "as a means to trigger unexpected reactions."[25] In fact, as Callejas argues, the "future is not as much about the territory within the boundaries of the islands . . . as it is about really engaging with the systems in which the islands float. . . . You can employ relatively small-scale platforms to transform vast territories, as opposed to actually design[ing] vastness."[26]

The approaches represented by Ungers and Callejas make a strong case for the potential of the island and the archipelago as generative models for design. The spatial attributes of islandness—smallness, boundedness, oneness, limitedness, separateness, distinctiveness—allow for the implementation of design strategies of control, containment, determinacy, repeatability, and cross-scaling, which seem to be ways to manage complexity. If we agree, coming back to the two alternatives offered in the title of the essay, that speaking of the island as a *reality* means referring to its physical and spatial conditions (that is, as an isolated entity surrounded by a medium different from itself), whereas speaking of the island as a *metaphor* means referring to a process of symbolic transposition through which the island is used figuratively, as signifier of a different concept, then we might also agree that, as shown by the examples described above, it is the island's very consistence—its being a reality and not a metaphor—that produces the island *effect* and makes the island both a powerful cognitive device for interpreting reality and a generative design tool for intervening on it. And this resonates very well with Hay's own definition of the 'island effect:' "An 'island effect' differs from the mother concept, 'island,' in this: its real-world referent is *not* 'girt by sea' but is 'islanded' by some other enveloping medium. 'Island effect' sites are, however, hard- and distinctly-edged, their borders constituting barriers that are not easily crossed, and island signifiers such as 'isolated,' 'vulnerable,' 'contained,' and 'disconnected' are deemed applicable."[27] Nevertheless, if we asked whether the island's spatiality affects the way people settle and transform their environment, the answer would be that it does so in the same way as do mountains, deltas, deserts, and the like. These are all places in which geographical attributes are extremely powerful design tools.

Hand models by Luis Callejas and Charlotte Hansson; fire, advice, and obscure formulas by Rodrigo Callejas and Juliana Velez.

01. Pete Hay, "A Phenomenology of Islands," *Island Studies Journal* 1, no. 1 (2006): 26.

02. Godfrey Baldacchino, "Islands, Islands Studies," *Island Studies Journal* 1, no. 1 (2006): 6.

03. Ibid., 20.

04. Ibid., 21. *Italics* in the original.

05. See Adam Grydehøj et al., "Returning from the Horizon: Introducing *Urban Island Studies*," *Urban Island Studies* 1, no.1 (2015): 1–19. See also Wolfgang Andexlinger, "Suburban Processes of Islandisation in Austria: The Cases of Vienna and Tyrol," *Urban Island Studies* 1 (2015): 118–33; and Stefania Staniscia, "The Island Paradigm and the Mediterranean," *New Geographies* 5, *The Mediterranean* (2013): 255–62.

06. Alessandro Petti, *Arcipelaghi e Enclave: Architettura dell'Ordinamento Spaziale Contemporaneo* (Milan: B. Mondadori, 2007), 11.

07. See Andexlinger, "Suburban Processes of Islandisation in Austria"; and Francesco Indovina et al., *Dalla Città Diffusa all'Arcipelago Metropolitano* (Milano:

Franco Angeli, 2009).

08. See Stefania Staniscia, *Islands* (Barcelona: ListLab, 2011).

09. Baldacchino, "Islands, Islands Studies," 9.

10. Baldacchino, "Islands, Islands Studies," 5.

11. Alfred Russel Wallace, *Island Life; or, the Phenomena and Causes of Insular Faunas and Floras. Including a Revision and Attempted Solution of the Problem of Geological Climates* (New York: Harper & Bros., 1881).

12. Ilan Kelman, Foreword to Sonya Graci and Rachel Dodds, *Sustainable Tourism in Island Destinations* (London: Earthscan, 2010), xiii.

13. Adalberto Vallega, "The Role of Culture in Island Sustainable Development," *Ocean and Coastal Management* 50, nos. 5–6 (2007): 281.

14. UNESCO World Heritage Centre, "Operational Guidelines for the Implementation of the World Heritage Convention," July 2008, 167, http://whc.unesco.org/archive/opguide08-en.pdf.

15. Oswald M. Ungers et al., *The City in the City: Berlin, A Green Archipelago* (1977;

rprt. in Zürich: Lars Müller, 2013), 87.

16. Ibid., 126.

17. Ibid.

18. Ibid., 92.

19. Ibid., 94.

20. Ibid., 106.

21. Mark Lee, "Two Deserted Islands," *San Rocco* 1, *Islands* (2011): 7.

22. "Interview with Luis Callejas," *Harvard Design Magazine* 36 (2013): 71.

23. Luis Callejas, *Islands & Atolls* (New York: Princeton Architectural Press, 2013), 50.

24. Ibid.

25. Ibid., 51.

26. Pete Hay, "What the Sea Portends: A Reconsideration of Contested Island Tropes," *Island Studies Journal* 8, no. 2 (2013): 215.

Image Credits

052, 053: Courtesy of the Ungers Archive for Architectural Research UAA.

054, 055: Courtesy of Luis Callejas and Charlotte Hansson.

Philosophers' Islands

Robin Mackay

During the last half-century, theoretical physics and cosmology have provided us with a new context within which to pose some of the most fundamental questions of philosophy, lending these new life and a new sense. Within this new context, we find the recurrence of an image as old as Western philosophy itself: the image of the island.

If we think of the fundamental parameters that govern the laws of physics as the axes of a topographical space—a landscape of possible universes—then to our best knowledge, only a very small area of that space is habitable by life. We live on an island—or rather, life as we know it is itself an island. Of course, this does not mean that the universe was purposefully designed for us; rather, it opens up the question of whether there might be other, neighboring islands— other possible universes—within which could emerge radically different forms of life. Astronomist and SETI researcher Milan Ćirković, posing this question of astrobiology, insists that we ought not to let the confined shores of our island existence mislead us into thinking that this is the only habitable zone in the sea of possibilities. Instead, he hypothesizes, there may be an "archipelago of habitability"—a system of possible islands of life, the pattern of which might even be mathematically discoverable.[01]

This notion of the tiny, habitable island set within a vast sea of possible universes belongs to this novel, emergent philosophical discourse, subtended by contemporary physical and mathematical concepts; but at the same time it attests to the fact that certain enduring images continue to constitute something like pieces of a reusable theatrical stage-set for philosophical thinking. What follows is a historical tour (inevitably very selective) of the philosophical island throughout various ages, from its ancient origins to its contemporary incantations/incarnation. This tour is particularly rich in light of the fact that philosophy shares the geophilosophical concept of the island with literature. Indeed, the island has always defined an important relationship between philosophy and literature. The island serves as a kind of conceptual laboratory for transplanting stories into ideas, for imbuing narratives with concepts, and for bringing ideas alive through myths.

The island makes its first appearance when Western philosophy, at its birth, is still negotiating the separation from its other: namely, myth. In Plato's *Timaeus* (about 360 BCE) the fable of the island of Atlantis occurs within a discussion concerning the rational principles of a perfect society. Socrates complains that, although he understands the conclusions arrived at, he would "compare [him]self to a person who, on beholding beautiful animals either created by the painter's art, or, better still, alive but at rest, is seized with a desire of seeing them in motion or engaged in some struggle or conflict to which their forms are suited."[02] This demand

of Socrates sets in motion the history of the philosophers' island. The demand for something to bring alive ideas, to quicken the still body of rational discussion, finds satisfaction in the story of Atlantis, the lost island.

As we know, Plato's dialogues often comprise secondhand reports, but the *Timaeus* ramifies further this strategy of framing, as the story of Atlantis is reported by Socrates' friends as an ancient story heard from a grandfather, who in turn heard it from a friend of his great-grandfather, Solon, who received it from an Egyptian priest. Through this relay of memory, Plato establishes Atlantis at an immemorial distance from his audience, endowing it with properly mythical status.

The priest's story is one of war waged by the island kingdom of Atlantis against the city of Athens. This is an Athens separated from Plato's contemporary Athens, however, by an impassable gulf of forgetting. As the priest tells Solon, the flooding of the Nile has on many occasions saved the Egyptians, and their knowledge, from great catastrophes that have been periodically visited upon the Earth and which have wiped out many other peoples, including the Greeks. In this way, Plato gives his audience to understand that they belong to a shallow memory, cut off from the deep past in which the story takes place. Hence the priest's gnomic declaration, "You Hellenes will never be anything but children."[03]

At the climax of the war, both Athens and Atlantis are inundated by a great flood, their people "disappear[ing] in the depths of the sea." Although Atlantis never reappears, Athens rises again from the waters, reborn in an immature state stripped of its former glory: it would have to learn once again how to be the perfect republic.

This unveils the original function of the philosophers' island as connected to a mythical conception of time—that is, with memory and forgetting, founding and rebeginning. The story sets up the theme of utter oblivion and forgetting, only so as to pose the question of a new foundation: no island, therefore, without the flood.

How does this myth transform the philosophical discussion of Socrates and his friends? "The city and citizens, which you yesterday described to us in fiction, we . . . now transfer to the world of reality."[04] Paradoxically, fiction imparts reality to the philosophical discussion, for the ideal city they had discussed now becomes the city of their own lost ancestors. Where there was the mere idea of a city governed on rational grounds, now there is the prospect of a repetition—the fulfillment of a cycle. The island myth, of course, dramatizes the notion of anamnesis, or unforgetting. Rational insight comes not from our experience of this world but from a remembering of another world, the recovery of a pure knowledge that was lost when we were incarnated.

Plato's Atlantean myth rises again as the perfect narrative form for the ideals of the humanist Renaissance—naturally,

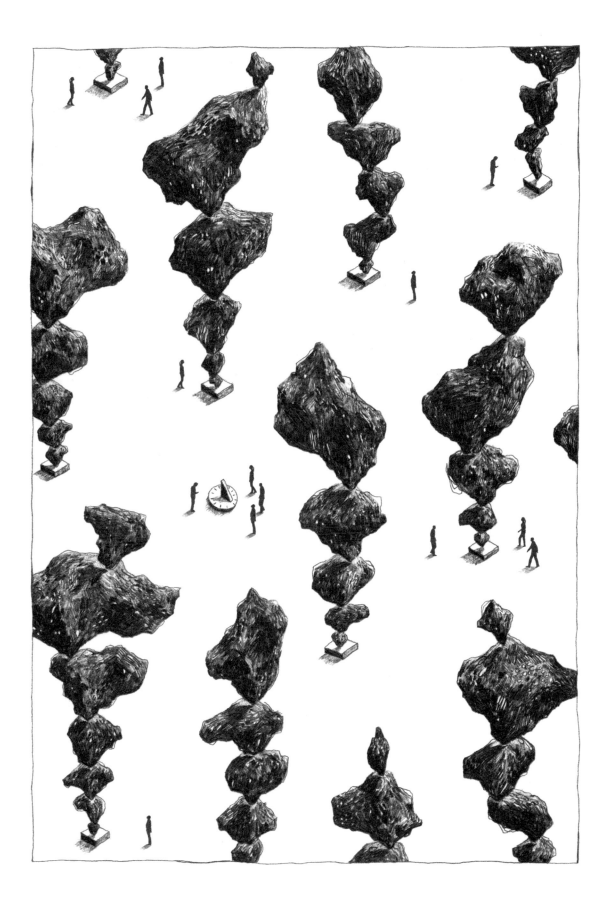

considering that it precisely concerns a "rebirth." In Francis Bacon's 1623 *New Atlantis*, for example, all the important elements are reworked. A crew lost in a "part of the South Sea…utterly unknown," cut adrift "in the midst of the greatest wilderness of waters in the world," discover the island of Bensalem, the perfectly calibrated civilization of which, with its gentle, humanistic, scientifically advanced government, embodies all of Bacon's aspirations for the improvement of human society.[05] Whilst their existence is perfectly unknown to the rest of the world, the people of Bensalem have an astonishingly complete knowledge of the whole globe. Their civilization has endured from time immemorial, from before the "universal flood." Of the people of this island too, one could well say, "you Europeans will never be anything but children." Again, Bacon's advanced ideas on society and science, in the mouths of these fictional, antediluvian islanders, become an invitation to repeat: not only does his "New Atlantis" repeat Plato's, it also calls his contemporaries to follow the example of the people of Bensalem.

But we are getting ahead of ourselves, for we should remember the extent to which, before the Renaissance, it was Arabic philosophers and commentators who nurtured and developed philosophical thought. The concept of the philosophical island is no exception. One remarkable text by a Spanish Muslim philosopher could, without much exaggeration, be described as midway between Aristotle and *Robinson Crusoe* (1719). This is Ibn Tufayl's book *Hayy ibn Yaqzān*, a 12th-century Arabic text known in Latin as *Philosophus Autodidactus* (The Self-Taught Philosopher). The 1708 English translation of this text, titled *The Improvement of Human Reason*, influenced some of our most enduring modern myths, including *Crusoe* but also *The Jungle Book* and *Tarzan*, to name but a few. Tufayl's narrative tells the story of a child named Hayy ibn Yaqzān who is cast away on an unpopulated island and raised by gazelles. The narrative follows the development of this castaway's philosophical meditations as he grows up and discovers the world, isolated from all human contact.[06]

Tufayl's book is essentially a philosophical treatise, speaking of all things from biology to planetary motions. But its form is that of a progressive narrative, recounting how these philosophical reflections emerge spontaneously in a man reduced to his natural state, removed from all cultural influence. We see Yaqzān growing up among animals, first lamenting his own weakness and vulnerability relative to them and then, having realized the uses of his hands, making clothes and devising tools and weapons. He discovers fire and cooked food, thus awakening his human difference from the animals. His philosophical development really

begins in earnest, however, when his gazelle foster-mother dies. This precipitates a reflection upon what is alive in an animal being, with Yaqzān concluding that the body is a "very inconsiderable thing" and beginning to cultivate a conception of the soul. Thence to the questions of how the soul is conjoined with the body, with the conclusion that the soul is akin to fire, a kind of warm vapor. The individuality of each being must then consist in this vapor, and Yaqzān conceives an analogy between his own use of various tools and this vaporous spirit's use of the various animal bodies for different purposes. With lengthy meditations on unity and plurality, individuals and species, the self-taught philosopher rediscovers the principles of Aristotelian taxonomy and proceeds to classify the entire animal and vegetable kingdom, finally considering inanimate objects, and coming to the conclusion that "all these things [are] in reality one, though multiplied and diversified accidentally as [are] the plants and animals."[07] But what then is the nature of this unified substance that underlies all these various things in the world? With further meditations reaching evermore abstract questions and lofty conclusions, the feral child Yaqzān achieves philosophical enlightenment as an adult.

In fact, Yaqzān does make contact with civilization again, through the medium of a holy man who comes to the island to meditate; however, after having returned to his fellow humans, he finds them so unwilling to consider the way of wisdom that he returns to his island.

This remarkable story is the first fully philosophical use of the island. Recounting the genesis of philosophical thought as a natural development, it serves to ratify a body of doctrine as belonging to the natural progression of reason, untainted by outside influences. The function of philosophical islands continues to be involved with this desire for purity—with philosophy's impatience with dogmatism or received wisdom, its compulsion to begin from nothing, to rebegin with no presuppositions, to found itself. For the philosopher, the island is a chance to begin over again, giving us the possibility of refounding our knowledge on the basis of an imaginary innocence.

Returning to the Renaissance and to its utopias—those New Atlantises reflecting the optimistic spirit of the age—the most important is probably Thomas More's 1516 fictional, crescent-shaped Atlantic island *Utopia*, this name itself harboring an etymological ambiguity: "no-place" and "good-place." *Utopia* is precisely an ideal that cannot be fully realized but that might serve as an orientation, a navigation point. More's discussion of the ills of society, the vanity of people, the belligerence of leaders, gives us an enduring model of sociological and philosophical reflection that is very much alive two hundred years later—in more satirical form—in *Gulliver's Travels* (1726), which teaches, however,

Opposite page: Jamie Mills, "Yellow," 2015.

Robin Mackay

not by example but through a mocking *reductio ad absurdum*, and is all the more entertaining for it.

Whereas Ibn Tufayl's account of the gazelle-child Hayy ibn Yaqzān contained both a treatise of philosophy and a philosophical thesis on the genesis of thought in one isolated individual, these political fables use the island as a controlled setting for thought-experiments concerning the foundations of the social enterprise. A great seminal moment in philosophical island literature occurs, however, when these two aspects—the innocent individual, finding enlightenment in the seclusion of an island, and the ideal island society, prompting reflection on our own—are brought together. This is Daniel Defoe's *Robinson Crusoe*.

In *Robinson Crusoe* all the essential problems of the philosophical island are brought together beautifully. We have Crusoe as Christian autodidact, discovering true faith through his own solitary meditations. And not only does Crusoe discover God, he also enacts the origins of sedentary human society. The need to settle and defend, the planting of crops and building up of stores, the need to domesticate wild animals, even the development of hierarchy and the legitimacy of servitude: all of these are taken up in the text. But *Crusoe* also represents the point at which the philosophical island comes into disrepute, when we begin to harbor suspicions about the supposed innocence of the protagonist. Readers excited by the idea of the shipwrecked mariner exploring the virgin isle and surviving on his wits cannot but be somewhat disappointed when Crusoe spends his first two weeks rowing back and forth to the shipwreck to bring out everything he needs to set up home, from gunpowder to tunics, oatcakes to a complete set of carpentry tools. Readers cannot help feeling a little cheated when he takes his smug walks to his "country house," with his four guns slung around him, or when by "chance" he discovers some ears of wheat and prudently sews and stores his harvests for three years.

From a century's distance, Karl Marx sums it up drily in the first volume of *Das Kapital* (1867): "having saved a watch, ledger, ink and pen from the shipwreck, he soon begins, like a good Englishman, to keep a set of books."[08] For Marx, Crusoe represented "a totally illusory foundation for economics, that of the independent, non-social being." The story was an ideological sham, serving to naturalize the system of bourgeois capitalism. Its function was to justify a system through a bogus mythical "proof" of its spontaneous nature. In short, the island is "a false 'origin.'"

In his 1946 essay "Causes and Reasons of Desert Islands," Gilles Deleuze, whilst affirming the philosophical power of the island myth, seconds Marx's suspicions. The problem with *Robinson Crusoe*, he writes, is that Defoe's narrative fails to create the profound sense of the reinvention of mythology that characterizes the philosophical island: in *Crusoe*, "The mythical recreation of the world from the deserted island gives way to the reconstitution of everyday bourgeois life from a reserve of capital. . . . Robinson's vision of the world resides exclusively in property. Nothing is invented." Deleuze continues, somewhat harshly, "One can hardly imagine a more boring novel, and it is sad to see children still reading it today . . . Any healthy reader would dream of seeing [Friday] eat Robinson."[09]

Despite these cavils, the structure of *Robinson Crusoe* seems to so perfectly distil the island concept that it has proved robust enough to be critically rewritten, not only in countless inferior and derivative novels but also in many inventive and subversive works; for example, in the philosophically rich 1972 novel *Friday, or the Limbo of the Pacific* by Deleuze's friend Michel Tournier. Tournier's Robinson, on the island he names Speranza, is depicted in the light of a philosophical and psychoanalytical mélange combining Sigmund Freud, Karl Jung, Jean Paul Sartre, and Claude Lévi-Strauss. For Tournier, the story becomes that of Robinson discovering that what made him human was his interaction with others. Alone on the island, he begins to succumb to dehumanization, alternately trying to make the lineaments of a civilization and sinking into various modes of delirium in which he enters into strange relation with the island and the elements. The very delirium against which Defoe's Crusoe had defended himself implacably with all the salvaged accouterments of civilization becomes, for Tournier, the truth of the island adventure as philosophically charged psychotropic and spiritual journey. As he struggles to "humanize" the island, Robinson becomes dehumanized: he becomes the island.

The influence of Tournier's novel can be read in the brief *Concrete Island* (1973), written (with typical mordant wit) by J. G. Ballard, in which a businessman finds himself carwrecked on a traffic island.[10] Unable to escape, the hapless protagonist also undergoes a kind of psychogeographical ordeal, repeating at its height the declaration of Tournier's Robinson, "I am the island."

Between *Crusoe*'s island and *Concrete Island*, we must also note a great efflorescence of what can only be called island narratives without islands. The thought-experiments of Thomas Hobbes, John Locke, and Jean-Jacques Rousseau imagining how society might develop from a "state of nature" are the great speculative works of modern political philosophy. These social contract theorists rightly saw that the island-principle corresponded to an important truth: the real—even the reality of society—can be profoundly explored only through an ideal scenario, a controlled experiment, that steps beyond the bounds of that reality. In the twentieth century, John Rawls reimagines the social contract experiment using imagery that corresponds to that of isolated islands such as Bensalem, with the "veil of ignorance" an impenetrable bank of fog around the philosophical island.[11] To make his argument, however, Rawls for the first time posits the "original position" of the philosopher *outside* the island, meditating on the possibilities of what it might hold and planning his disembarkation.

Even if social contract theory represented in certain respects the consummation of the political employment of the philosophical island, in a new modern conception of the grounding or refoundation of the social on the model of a civil contract, from the 19th century onward its works were liable to come under suspicion and to be dismissed as "robinsonades": post–*Robinson Crusoe*, any supposedly innocent deployment of the island as a speculative device would be subject to great critical scrutiny.

In marking out Reason's legitimate uses from its illegitimate ones, Immanuel Kant's *Critique of Pure Reason* (1781) aims to provide the map for a domain of well-founded, systematic knowledge and to secure it against the flights of fancy and speculative excesses to which Kant considered earlier philosophers had all-too-easily abandoned themselves. And yet, to promote this somewhat grueling task Kant employs the image of the island of truth:

> We have now not merely explored the territory of pure understanding, and carefully surveyed every part of it, but have also measured its extent, and assigned to everything its rightful place. This domain is an island, enclosed by nature itself within unalterable limits. It is the land of truth—seductive name!— surrounded by a wide and stormy ocean, the native home of illusion, where many a fog bank and many a swiftly melting iceberg give the deceptive appearance of farther shores, deluding the adventurous seafarer ever anew with empty hopes, and engaging him in enterprises which he can never abandon and yet is unable to carry to completion. Before we venture on this sea, to explore it in all directions . . . it will be as well to begin by casting a glance on the map of the island which we are about to leave, and to enquire, first, whether we cannot in any case be satisfied with what it contains—are not, indeed, under compulsion to be satisfied, inasmuch as there may be no other territory upon which we can settle; and, secondly, by what title we possess even this domain, and can consider ourselves as secured against all opposing claims.[12]

As Michèle le Doeuff remarks in *The Philosophical Imaginary*, Kant uses the image of the island in this famous passage to defend his sober, critical philosophy against the more colorful and grandiose promises of speculative metaphysics: the "critical" island is certainly not a paradise, but it is infinitely preferable to the frustrations and dangers of the boundless ocean, upon which metaphysical speculation recklessly sets out. If he claims to re-place our knowledge on its proper ground, Kant is most circumspect about what sort of territory philosophy can promise to secure for us.

Le Doeuff notes that elsewhere Kant warns against another island: the paradisiac island of the South Seas. The yearning for its easier climes and its innocence is a snare, Kant suggests: these islands represent a pernicious, imaginary utopia. Thus Kant sets the seduction of the southern isle against the foggy northern isle, which, while somewhat bleak, is true and solid. As Deleuze says in his book on Kant, this is the element in which Kant's thought is at home: "the fog of the North." When Kant trills "the island of truth— seductive name!" this is nothing but sarcasm. The serious philosopher has no business with seductive, pretty islands, where he can lounge about all day under palm trees.

So Kant reinvents the philosophical island as a duality. There is the southern isle, with its dangerously desirable holiday-brochure illusion of luxury and leisure, and the northern isle—safe, secured, and systematic, if a bit grey. In short, the island of truth is a *dreich* isle, but it is all we've got.

Even Kant's carefully delimited and hard-won piece of solid territory doesn't last long in the history of the philosopher's island, however, as in 1882 Friedrich Nietzsche announces the crisis of late modernity in *The Gay Science*. Not only have we left Kant's island of stability, but our own critical self-consciousness has destroyed it:

> In the horizon of the infinite.—We have left the land and have embarked! We have burned our bridges behind us—indeed, we have gone further and destroyed the land behind us! Now, little ship, look out! Beside you is the ocean: to be sure, it does not always roar, and at times it lies spread out like silk and gold and reveries of graciousness. But hours will come when you will realize that it is infinite and that there is nothing more awesome than infinity. Oh, the poor bird that felt free and now strikes the walls of this cage! Woe, when you feel homesick for the land as if it had offered more freedom—and there is no longer any 'land'![13]

In the epoch announced by this declaration, the problem is no longer that of founding or refounding. Instead, it is the crisis of the fruits of enlightenment turning bad, of science and critical thought having gnawed away the very foundations of human existence. But even Nietzsche's declaration that there is "no longer any 'land'" cannot prevent literature from reengineering the island for this age, and according to its dreams and fears. From the end of the 19th century, the philosophical island becomes a dystopia where the most extreme possibilities, doubts, and horrors of Western civilization are given free (if safely sequestered) rein. This tradition begins with H. G. Wells's *Island of Doctor Moreau* (1896).[14]

Robin Mackay

Here, rather than the island being a metaphorical setting for a philosophical thought-experiment, we find ourselves on an island where actual (scientific) experiments are underway and running out of control. The island becomes a warning, concentrating the most threatening aspects of contemporary reality into its confined laboratory space.

Instead of accommodating an ideal society whose principles instruct our own, then, the 20th-century island—in which we can include, of course, many of science-fiction's alien planets and stranded space-stations—is more likely to amplify developments of real society, concentrating them into an imagined future that is all too near. Rather than being owned and judiciously employed by philosophy, the power of ideas is now a power effectively at work in the world, embodied in technology, uncontrolled or controlled by megalomaniacs and evil geniuses, perplexing and injuring humanity. This, in short, is the philosopher's island resounding with the aftershock of world wars: the island *after* Marx, *after* Freud, *after* Darwin.[15] And after the 20th-century revolution in physics, it is the island of the fateful experiment—the Bikini Atoll—and its aftermath (*Lord of the Flies* and countless other postapocalyptic fantasies). The caesura of the flood visited on humanity from above has been replaced by anthropogenic disaster.

In his last novel, entitled simply *Island* (1962), Aldous Huxley seems to reverse the trend.[16] He turns the island once more into a utopia contrasting with the dystopia of reality. Imagining science as being harnessed only for the use of man, rather than overpowering man, Huxley's Pala is an imaginary island of sanity in a mad world, where Eastern wisdom and Western science come together in the persons of a shipwrecked scientist and an indigenous quasi-Buddhist order, giving birth to a society stable and free from madness and venality. Like the autodidact Yaqzān, everyone on the island is in a state of enlightenment, nirvana even. Through the great slogan of this modern utopia still echoes the voice of Platonic *anamnesis*: "Nobody needs to go anywhere else. We are all, if we only knew it, already there." If only we knew it, we could repeat, return to where we really are. Ultimately, however, the final twist in Huxley's tale shows that he was himself no longer convinced of the possibility of such a "sane society," such a return to the source.[17]

* * *

Can we make out the shape of a new, 21st-century philosophical island? Previous models still haunt us, just as they did in the 1960s, when the television series *Lost in Space* reworked *The Swiss Family Robinson* for the space age, and more recently, when Koushun Takami's 1999 comic book *Battle Royale* and its 2001 and 2003 film adaptations revisited *Lord of the Flies* (1954) in an ultraviolent unfolding. The

television series *Lost* (2004–2005), with its plane-crash survivors Locke and Rousseau, remixes a bygone era of island thinking. At the end of the second episode, entitled "Tabula Rasa," one of the characters declares, "This is a chance for everyone to start again, regardless of what they were before the crash." Utopia endures in Hollywood, even if the tale of *Lost* becomes darker and more twisted (fatiguingly so) as the episodes progress.

Perhaps ours is more properly the age of the house-island, isolated but visible by millions and manipulated by an unseen controller. Although they harbor no illusions of a *tabula rasa* or of a complete new beginning, *Big Brother* (2000–2014) and its various reality-television imitators (several of which take up the island theme very literally, with woeful results) are perhaps still rather tied to antiquated forms. Their social engineering is redolent of *The Tempest* (1611), where the audience delights in Prospero's behind-the-scenes manipulation of the hapless groups shipwrecked on his enchanted isle. But ours is also the age of real-life island-building: the geoplastic megalomania of Dubai's man-made archipelagos, where millions of tons of sand dredged from the bottom of the sea create new islands full of luxury villas. Since every modern convenience has already been imported, however, the rich man's island is never interesting: it is never a desert island. A more recent addition to the canon is the promotion, in well-heeled Silicon Valley circles, of "seasteading," in which millionaires dream of exiting established polities and founding their own floating city-states. Rather than claiming to embody rational principles or to enact a pure beginning, according to their champions, these artificial utopias seek to extend the Darwinian principles of neoliberal economics to the state itself: their vision is that of an archipelago of island micro-societies in competition with existing, obsolescent models of the state.[18] If any of these can be said to constitute a philosophers' island for today, it is only in the sense that it transforms the figure of the desert island through modern narratives that are no longer literary or mythical but instead economic and ideological.

As we have seen, the history of philosophers' islands is a moving image of the eternal hope that one can begin again, if not in practice then at least in thought. In engaging in this repetition through narrative and dramatization, philosophy also rediscovers a common bond with myth and ritual, in an appeal to the immemorial and in the reenactment of a kind of *initiation*: the trial of the desert island. Yet, as Deleuze has demonstrated in his critique of the "image of thought,"[19] philosophy's dream of starting again from nothing is rarely innocent; and as anticipated by Marx's critique of *Robinson Crusoe*, many "robinsonades" have been guilty of surreptitiously smuggling artifacts onto their islands so as to ensure the reproduction of the social order. In these tales, the island serves to legitimate the return of the same kind of repetition that, in returning to the immemorial by endowing it with the imprimatur of necessity or inevitability; starting again becomes a mere pretext for asserting "natural" authority. Yet, as seen most clearly, for example, in the psychic reshaping of Robinson in Tournier's *Friday*, the desert island also holds open the possibility of another kind of repetition that, in returning to the immemorial or in imagining the future, finds in the effects of isolation resources with which to differentiate from the present, to question the "natural" order of things, and to imagine humans stripped of their conventional social nature and receptive to new becomings.

01. See Milan Ćirković, "Sailing the Archipelago," *Collapse V* (Falmouth, UK: Urbanomic, 2009), 292–329.

02. Plato, *Timaeus*, 19b, in *Plato: Collected Dialogues*, ed. Edith Hamilton and Huntington Cairns (Princeton, NJ: Princeton University Press, 2002), 1154–1155. A full open-source text can be found at http://classics.mit.edu/Plato/timaeus.html.

03. Plato, *Timaeus*, 22b.

04. Ibid.

05. Francis Bacon, "New Atlantis" (1626), repr. in Susan Bruce, ed., *Three Early Modern Utopias* (Oxford: Oxford University Press, 1999).

06. Ibn Tufayl, *The Improvement of Human Reason, Exhibited in the Life of Hai Ebn Yokdhan: Written in Arabick above 500 Years ago, by Abu Jaafar Ebn Tophail . . .*, trans. Simon Ockley (London: Edm. Powell, 1708).

07. Ibid., part 38, http://www.erbzine.com/mag18/yaqzan.htm.

08. Karl Marx, *Capital*, vol. 1 (1867), trans. Ben Fowkes (London: Penguin, 1992), 170.

09. Gilles Deleuze, "Causes and Reasons of Desert Islands" (1946), repr. in *Desert Islands and Other Texts*, ed. David Lapoujade, trans. Michael Taormina (Cambridge, MA: MIT Press, 2003), 12.

10. J. G. Ballard, *Concrete Island* (New York: Farrar, Straus, and Giroux, 1973).

11. John Rawls, *A Theory of Justice* (Cambridge, MA: Belknap Press, 1971).

12. Immanuel Kant, *Critique of Pure Reason* (1781), trans. Norman Kemp Smith (London: Macmillan, 1964), 257, A235–6 and B294–5.

13. Friedrich Nietzsche, *The Gay Science* (1882), trans. Walter Kaufmann (New York: Vintage, 1974), 180–81, sect. 124.

14. H. G. Wells, *The Island of Doctor Moreau* (New York: Duffield, 1896).

15. Incidentally, we should remark that we owe the whole elaboration of evolutionary theory from Darwin onward to an island voyage—Darwin's journey, onboard the HMS *Beagle*, to the Galápagos, islands whose slow geological drift apart had effectively isolated the different species of finches, which thus provided a living stop-motion image of the process of natural selection. Note, however, that in his new book, biologist Steve Jones argues that despite the mythic importance of the Galápagos in the popular imagination, the most important island for Darwin's work was, in actual fact, England. Steve Jones, *Darwin's Island: The Galápagos in the Garden of England* (London: Little, Brown, 2009).

16. Aldous Huxley, *Island* (1962: repr. London: Flamingo, 1994).

17. In a typically cynical reappropriation of Huxley's combination of science and religion, Michel Houellebecq's *The Possibility of an Island*, trans. Gavin Bowd (London: Weidenfeld & Nicolson, 2005) brings it down to earth with a resounding thump. Houellebecq envisions an island run by a cloning cult who alone can expect to survive the "flood" of the anthropogenic apocalypse. The author bases his fictional sect on the actual UFO religion Raëlism, a real-world example of the terrifying combination of genetic engineering, nanotechnology, and religious messianism.

18. See the Seasteading Institute's website, http://www.seasteading.org, for details about how this think-tank seeks, through the use of technologically enabled "floating cities," to "provide a machinery of freedom to choose new societies."

19. Gilles Deleuze, *Difference and Repetition* (1968), trans. Paul Patton (New York: Columbia University Press, 1994), chapter 3.

Image Credits

Robin Mackay

Desert Island:
An Atlas of
Archipelagic
Laboratories

MAP Office
(Laurent Gutierrez
& Valérie Portefaix)

In the Anthropocene, the history of the 21st century will be written on water. With sea level on the rise, the ocean has become both the new frontier and the last space, to be either uncovered for the benefit of humankind or condemned as the locus of its final demise. Islands offer possibilities for expansion and opportunities to start anew. They have long played a major role in nourishing the imagination and establishing new points of reference in defining the world. The Desert Island map presents the ocean as island, as an imaginary world of islands, each informed by literary tales, narratives, and statistics.[01]

The map serves as an artistic atlas or inventory of islands that have been extensively manipulated by man or used by global networks of corporations and nations. It charts human action and experimentation in the form of utopian communities, fiscal paradises, ecosystems, military regimes, and occupied domains, characterized at turns by clandestine or forced migration, exclusive leisure, private extravagance, and imposed landscape formations. From the 100,000 landmasses surrounded by water on Earth, 101 have been selected with an eye toward lending insights into multiple periods and locations across the globe. Our selection was informed by the work of two great anthropologists: Epeli Hau'ofa, who writes on the Pacific Ocean, and Edouard Glissant, who focuses on the Caribbean. Engaging their discourse allowed us to construct a postcolonial perspective on insularity, opening up new sets of interconnected relations and flux outside the continental landmasses.

In thinking of islands, Hau'ofa puts in perspective a unique geography of the Pacific. He proposes a "sea of islands" interconnected by multiple histories of culture, trade, and migration. His collection of essays *We Are the Ocean* (2015) evokes the extraordinary mobility of the population around Oceania and the absurdity of all national and economic borders that have recently carved up the sea. Against political boundaries, Hau'ofa advocates for modes of living at sea, navigating or interacting with water, and letting the cultures move and mingle—a process, or what he identifies as a "world enlargement."[02]

From our consideration of Glissant's work emerged an outline of a metaphorical map of the world based on a selection of islands working as a collection of human issues.[03] This research corresponds to a desire to open up another form of narration through the classification and connection of these islands. Organized into twelve groups, they create different discrete archipelagos of conceptually related territories functioning in a composed yet diffuse geography. Starting from a set of keywords or phrases, each island embodies a unique story in connection to the other islands of the same group.

This collection of islands is conceived as a tool for further exploration. Its speculative system of classification is borrowed from the Chinese Encyclopedia *Celestial Emporium of Benevolent Knowledge*, famously imagined by Jorge Luis Borges in 1942.[04] Breaking the familiar conventions of territorial classification, this new order supports differences and heterogeneities, and defines a new *étendue* or extended platform of possibilities and principles by moving toward a common yet improbable geography.

Following Borges's methodology, we established new categories in which to classify islands: original ones, resemblance to a moored ship, isolated ones, those full of resources, those that have constructed alternatives, site of possible abomination, those of immoral values, deregulated ones, those that are intensely inhabited, those that have (de)constructed landscape, disappearing ones, and other heterotopias. These categories go well beyond the traditional means of defining islands by geographic borders and national interests, to propose a different taxonomy in which islands are defined by their narrative potential and the manipulation of their original land. Like a jigsaw puzzle, no island can exist without those surrounding it; they form a network connected by the complex system of *portolan*, a navigational measure using triangulation. Each island becomes an entity inviting the viewer to engage in a complex set of histories, both real and fictive. In the archipelagic system, each island presents the opportunity to dream about the next one.

What follows are excerpts from this atlas.

THE FLORIDA KEYS 24°40'01" N - 81°32'26" W	CASTAWAY CAY 26°05'00" N - 77°32'00" W	PARADISE ISLAND 25°05'00" N - 77°20'00" W	MANHATTAN 40°43'42" N - 73°59'28" W	BERMUDA 32°18'00" N - 64°47'00" W	GUANA ISLAND 18°28'30" N - 64°31'55" W	SAINT KITTS AND NEVIS 17°20'00" N - 62°45'00" W	SABLE ISLAND 43°57'00" N - 59°54'57" W	AZORES 37°44'00" N - 25°40'00" W
NECKER ISLAND 23°34'00" N - 164°42'00" W	BIMINI 25°73'00" N - 79°15'00" W	BLUE LAGOON ISLAND 23°43'18" N - 74°53'47" W	TORTUGA 20°04'00" N - 72°49'00" W	NORMAN ISLAND 18°19'00" N - 64°37'00" W	SAINT MARTIN 18°04'00" N - 63°03'00" W	MONTSERRAT 16°45'00" N - 62°12'00" W	GRENADA 12°03'00" N - 61°45'00" W	BARBADOS 13°10'00" N - 59°32'00" W
CAYMAN ISLANDS 19°20'00" N - 81°24'00" W	NAVASSA ISLAND 18°24'10" N - 75°00'45" W	NORMAN'S CAY 24°37'00" N - 76°49'00" W	ABC ISLANDS 12°10'00" N - 69°00'00" W	VIEQUES 18°07'00" N - 65°25'00" W	MARGARITA ISLAND 11°00'00" N - 64°10'00" W	REDONDA 16°56'20" N - 62°20'30" W	TRINIDAD AND TOBAGO 10°40'00" N - 61°31'00" W	SAINT VINCENT AND THE GRENADINES 13°10'00" N - 61°14'00" W
AMBERGRIS CAYE 18°00'50" N - 87°55'52" W	OMETEPE ISLAND 11°37'00" N - 85°21'00" W	COIBA 7°25'59" N - 81°45'58" W	HAT ISLAND 18°13'14" N - 63°04'07" W	TOKELAU 9°10'00" S - 171°48'35" W	TAHITI 17°40'00" S - 149°27'00" W	FERNANDO DE NORONHA 3°51'14" S - 32°25'26" W	SAINT HELENA 15°57'00" S - 05°42'00" W	ANNOBON 1°25'00" S - 5°38'00" E
CLIPPERTON ISLAND 10°18'00" N - 103°12'00" W	SAMOA 13°50'00" S - 171°44'00" W	SWAINS ISLAND 11°03'00" S - 171°04'40" W	TONGA 21°08'00" S - 175°12'00" W	COOK ISLANDS 21°12'00" S - 159°46'00" W	EASTER ISLAND 27°09'00" S - 109°35'00" W	ISLA DE LOS ESTADOS 54°45'13" S - 63°53'19" W	FALKLAND ISLAND 51°42'00" S - 57°51'00" W	TRISTAN DE CUNHA 37°06'44" S - 12°16'56" W

Original Ones

Myths reveal an enduring fascination with islands as literary or philosophical tropes. When sailing in the Mediterranean Sea, it is impossible not to think of Odysseus' navigation across the sea of gods and monsters, from the nymph Calypso in Ogygia to the Phaeacian sea masters of Scheria, known today as Corfu [026]. In addition to playing an important role in the foundational myths of Western morality, islands have also inspired a great number of modern fictions. How many voyagers have gone in search of the curative waters of Bimini's fountain in order to gain eternal youth [011]? Is there a solar-powered laser poised to blow up the world, hidden deep within the core of Ko Tapu [046, labeled "James Bond Island" on tour operators' maps]? Island fantasies span the collective imaginary, as evidenced by hundreds of references in literature and popular culture.

Resembling a Moored Ship

A boat is a mobile territory on a quest for land, or an island in and of itself on which to land. Boats sometimes hide out on the high seas, braving storms to avoid border patrols. Too often they crash on hostile coastlines. Boats often carry the story of refugees, wrecked in collective tragedy witnessed by helpless islanders. From Vietnam to Cuba and from Lesbos to Lampedusa [047], are there any islands that have not become safe havens—or new prisons—for refugees? Are there any oceans that have not witnessed this kind of tragedy? This is the collective memory of a world still in search of a global sanctuary. What if the oceans were transformed into one giant island?

Isolated Ones

Extremely remote islands, often surrounded by shark-infested waters, have been considered the perfect prison environment. Strategically misplaced on navigation or portolan charts so as to conceal their exact location from potential escapees, these islands become isolation points operating outside the coordinate system. On Coiba [023] and Isla de los Estados [041], the sea provides a natural barrier within which to isolate, punish, or banish. Off the coast of South America, Devil's Island houses a notorious penal colony for the French Guiana capital of Cayenne, home to the world's most dangerous criminals. After his defeat at the Battle of Waterloo in 1815, Napoleon Bonaparte was imprisoned on the remote volcanic island of Saint Helena [072], off the coast of southwest Africa. Our imagination of the island castaway is generally associated with the accidental and the voluntary, and yet it must also encompass forced exile from society.

Those Full of Resources

An extension of the Silk Route crossing mountains and deserts, the Spice Route created a new, complex network of trading ports. In 1529 the Moluccas Islands served as a geographic nexus of imperial greed, dividing the world between the Portuguese and Spanish crowns. Later, the Dutch East India Company became the world's first multinational corporation to use

VENICE 45°26'15" N - 12°20'00" E	HELIGOLAND 54°10'00" N - 8°04'00" E	CORFU 39°40'00" N - 19°45'00" E	VOZROZHDENIYA ISLAND 45°30'00" N - 59°19'00" E	YAS ISLAND 24°30'00" N - 54°36'00" E	BHOLA ISLAND 22°47'00" N - 90°25'00" E	CAT BA ISLAND 20°48'00" N - 106°59'59" E	PRATAS ISLANDS 20°42'00" N - 116°42'00" E	JEJU-DO 33°22'00" N - 126°32'00" E
LAMPEDUSA 35°30'00" N - 12°36'00" E	GOTLAND 57°30'00" N - 18°33'00" E	SANTORINI 36°25'2" N - 25°25'9" E	SOCOTRA 12°29'21" N - 53°54'26" E	THE WORLD 25°15'00" N - 55°11'00" E	HONG KONG 22°16'42" N - 114°09'32" E	SURIN ISLANDS 14°30'00" N - 103°30'00" E	SPRATLY ISLANDS 8°38'00" N - 111°55'00" E	OKINAWA 26°30'00" N - 127°56'00" E
COCO ISLANDS 14°07'00" N - 93°22'02" E	SÃO TOMÉ AND PRÍNCIPE 0°20'00" N - 6°44'00" E	FAILAKA ISLAND 29°26'00" N - 48°20'00" E	DAHLAK ARCHIPELAGO 15°50'00" N - 40°12'00" E	MALDIVES 3°20'00" N - 73°22'00" E	ANDAMAN ISLANDS 7°05'00" N - 93°48'00" E	MERGUI ARCHIPELAGO 12°00'00" N - 98°00'00" E	BALI 8°25'23" N - 115°14'55" E	NORTHERN MARIANA ISLANDS 15°91'00" N - 145°04'05" E
DIEGO GARCIA 7°18'48" S - 72°24'40" E	CHRISTMAS ISLAND 10°30'00" S - 105°40'00" E	BANDA ISLANDS 4°35'00" S - 130°55'00" E	BOUGAINVILLE ISLAND 6°00'00" S - 155°00'00" E	NAURU 0°32'00" S - 166°55'00" E	KU TAPU 6°25'43" N - 99°38'41" E	PALAU 7°21'00" N - 134°28'00" E	MARSHALL ISLANDS 7°70'00" N - 171°40'00" E	KIRIBATI 1°28'00" N - 173°02'00" E
COMOROS 11°41'00" S - 43°16'00" E	RODRIGUES 19°43'00" S - 63°25'00" E	COCOS (KEELING) ISLAND 12°07'00" S - 96°54'00" E	THE CORAL SEA ISLANDS 22°11'00" S - 155° 20'00" E	SOLOMON ISLANDS 9°37'00" S - 160°11'00" E	NEW CALEDONIA 21°30'00" S - 165°30'00" E	VANUATU 17°45'00" S - 168°18'00" E	FIJI 18°00'00" S - 178°27'00" E	TUVALU 8°31'00" S - 179°13'00" E

the island circuit to consolidate a monopoly on the spice trade. From Europe to the Indonesian Banda Islands [007], the power of the company was visible through the mercantile logic of its economic enterprise, illustrated by key positions in Malacca and Batavia. Its attempt to exclusively control the sea and its ports resulted in numerous conflicts with local populations, pirates, and mercenaries. As a matter of fact, the Dutch gave the island of Manhattan to Britain in exchange for the Banda Islands in Indonesia, a source of the much-prized nutmeg.

Constructed Alternatives

From the beginning, most island civilizations appear to have been composed of nomadic settlers in search of new opportunities. Failaka Island [030] in the Red Sea, first known as Agarum, was the center of the Dilmun civilization, masters of traditional agriculture. It was later taken over by Mesopotamians, traders, and so on, throughout the centuries. European expansion and the establishment of colonies, essential to the process of imperialism, dramatically altered the definition of the island, giving rise to their contemporary identity as national and private property.

On Guana Island [037], Quaker experimentation encouraged the "fair" treatment of African slaves, who took an active part in constructing the island economy around sugarcane farming. On Swains Islands [085], the Jennings family arrived from the United States in 1856 to claim the coral atoll as its own. Located in the Tokelau chain, it has remained unchanged ever since. Used as a copra plantation, it is today inhabited by 37 Tokelauans who harvest the owner's coconuts. The Gay and Lesbian Kingdom of the Coral Sea Islands [088] was created off the coast of Australia in 2004 to protest against the conservative government that refused to recognize same-sex marriage. The independent kingdom has become an emblem of queer nationalism.

Sites of Invisible Abomination

We remember wars when they happen on land, flattening cities and leaving thousands dead on the battlefield. But the sea and its islands have also been sites of conflict and war. The legendary *Mutiny of the Bounty* recalls the story of a rebellion onboard a ship, resulting in the escape of the crew to the Pitcairn Islands [067]. The first Opium War of 1840 pit the British against the Chinese in a contest for sea power and trade profits and resulted in the devastation of China's coastal defense. Conflict, terror, and disasters often come from—or happen to—people on the water.

Formally a Danish and British property, Germany's Heligoland [039] was a strategic center for smuggling and espionage during the Napoleonic War. An important site of World War II battles as well, the uninhabited island has been used as a testing ground for the British Royal Navy, which has detonated no less than 6,700 tons of explosives there, and partially flattened its sedimentary rock.

One of the most devastating island abominations has to be the atomic bombing of the Bikini Atoll in the Marshall Islands at the end of World War II. Having identified the

MAP Office

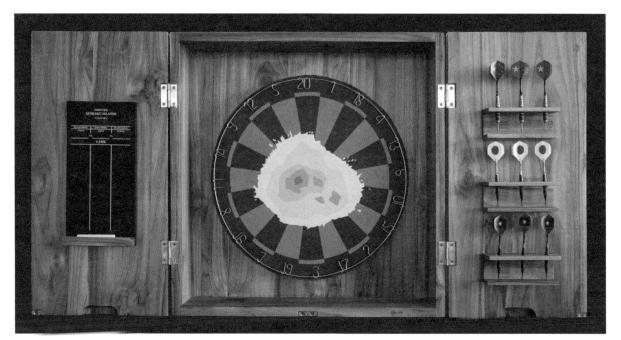

"Disputed: Senkaku Islands," 2014.

inhabited island as the perfect place to experiment with nuclear testing and atomic bombing, the United States forced the islanders to move to another island. France followed soon after, and between 1966 and 1996 the two countries have used the Bikini Atoll, Mururoa, and many other Pacific islands as open laboratories for weapons testing, forever devastating and contaminating their waters and their shores.

Other islands have served as camouflage for other types of military operations and high security procedures. In the Indian Ocean, Diego Garcia [028] saw the relocation of its indigenous population beginning in the late 1960s so that the British territory could be transformed into a United States military base. Today, the high-security Camp Thunder Cove serves the "War on Terror." A "law-free zone" similar to the more visible Guantanamo Bay detention camp, this little atoll provides a landing site for aircraft carriers and nuclear submarines, a violation of its plead to remain a nuclear-weapon-free zone.

Those of Immoral Values

On a global level, fiscal evasion, drug smuggling, enslavement, and prostitution often occur on islands. Islands off the shores of Africa have become the symbol and memory of the slave trade. Annobon [004] in the Gulf of Equatorial Guinea and James Island [043], renamed Kunta Kinteh Island, in Gambia were major departure points from the Caribbean islands to the United States. In the Pacific, the Solomon Islands [082] suffered human trafficking, and Tokelau [091] was partly depopulated by Peruvian human traders or "blackbirding" cargoes commissioned by mine owners.

Pirates and privateers have been instrumental in human trafficking in the service of nation-states and large private enterprises. The potentially deadly menaces on the sea hide boats and the treasure on island bases such as Tortuga [093] and the Norman Islands [059] inspired novels like Robert Louis Stevenson's *Treasure Island* (1883). Piracy still takes place today in the Gulf of Aden and along Somalia's seaboard, as islands continue to support illegal drug trafficking and smuggling.

Deregulated Ones

Contracts, laws, and constitutions exist within a certain social, economic, and political structure. From this perspective, "offshore" islands play an important role in establishing deviant institutions, removed from the normalized economic structures, policed states, and tax systems. The absence of regulations has allowed alternative systems and entities to venture into collective entropy. With a guarantee of remoteness—and consequently invisibility—islands are the perfect territory for income and inheritance tax evasion and money laundering. They have become the site of an invisible exercise of global capitalism that takes place outside official state jurisdictions.

The very large assortment of islands located in the Caribbean Sea, including Barbados [008] and Saint Martin [074], are offshore financial centers hiding behind a facade of white sand beaches. Outside national boundaries (and therefore free of oversight), these offshore islands maintain

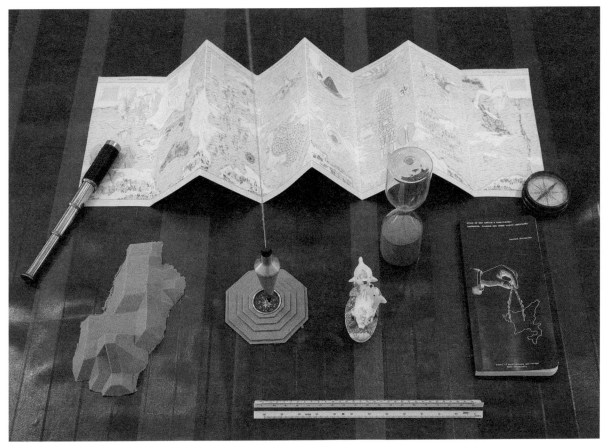

From the exhibition "Islands, Archipelagos, and Other Liquid Territories," 2015.

a "waterwall" that keeps transactions secret. The Isle of Man [042], a self-governing island dependent on the British Crown but technically outside its legal jurisdiction, benefits not only London's financial markets but the City of London Corporation, an offshore island inside Britain.

Hiding from public view? Why not also enjoy "an idyllic island paradise for yourself?"[05] Owned by Virgin Group CEO Richard Branson, Necker Island [057] is a perfect specimen of a private isle luxury resort for the happy few to enjoy. On a larger scale, Paradise Island [065], also private, is a multifaceted real-estate asset that concentrates all of its facilities within a prestigious gated community— theme parks, numerous casinos, hotel suites, and a myriad of multimillion-dollar villas—all primed to give the world's wealthiest 1 percent a "taste of paradise" and the best experience ever.

Those That Have Developed as Intense Laboratories

Islands are generally considered contained by their geography; they are finite and limited by the presence of the surrounding liquid element. Since the invention of the property system, every inch of their surface has been parceled. In the hands of engineers and technocrats, islands are shaped, filled, and cropped to make the most of their finite land, sometimes to the extreme.

Islands of extreme density have iconic architecture, infrastructure, and skylines that resemble stock exchange indexes on a nervous week. Large crowds of cosmopolitan populations bustle through streets and pedestrian walkways. Heavily constructed, densely populated, and intensely lived, this category of islands pushes the limits of the urbanized world. Two international centers of capitalist exchange and expansion, Hong Kong Island [040] and Manhattan [050] have exploded all notions of what an island can be. In this sense, they are active laboratories with significant global influence on the future. In contrast to Santa Cruz del Islote, where there is no space left to bury the dead,[06] Singapore [80] has managed to give shape to its social, economic, and political dimensions, combining urban density with one of the most expensive operations of fabricated landscape.

Another version of island engineering has been explored on Yas Island [101], where the density of buildings supports a concentration of luxurious activities: shopping, entertainment, theme parks, sports, and more shopping. Everything

069

From the exhibition "Tracking Baudelaire," 2013.

you can imagine is wrapped inside a spectacular Formula 1 circuit. Set to revolutionize the future, Yas is an island where there is no time left to enjoy boredom.

Those That Have Deconstructed Landscapes

In Western society, nature and culture are often seen to be in opposition. In many other societies around the world, however, a more symbiotic relationship is thought to exist. From their perspective, we can imagine that the production of landscape might reconcile nature and culture. In the case of an island, the word "seascape" could become a new terminology from which a new perspective on the land/island could emerge. Conversely the construction—and destruction—of the seascape is affecting the presence of islands.

The construction of seascapes has changed the nature of islands. In the case of little Sable Island [071] in the North Pacific, the planting of eighty thousands trees and shrub by the Canadian government supported the goal of creating a green wall so that ships would stop wrecking on the island. The trees rapidly died from the lack of fresh water, but it nonetheless transformed the ecosystem with the survival of a single Scots pine. A similar technique, but with a different purpose, motivated the composition of Castaway Cay [017], developed by Disney Cruise Line as an experience of fantasy and wonder for a public eager to discover settings where their favorite films were shot.

Disappearing Ones

Islands may appear or disappear. Here we refer to islands not as continental, or oceanic geologic formations,[07] but as mythological entities, such as Atlantis and Lemuria, or Mu,[08] which have inhabited our collective consciousness and unconscious awareness in search of a better world. If the "lost island" or "lost continent" belongs to ancient times, we are preparing the ground for new myths in the age of the Anthropocene. With global warming and the rise of sea levels on the one hand and the lack of water and desertification on the other, new territorial conditions and challenges confront island permanence or ephemerality.

The *aqua alta*, or periodical flooding of the historical Adriatic city of Venice [098], provides evidence of a gradual if persistent process of sinking. Many archipelagoes and small island nations in the Pacific, such as Vanuatu [097], are also becoming submerged. These conditions will create another wave of human migration, with hundreds of thousands of ecological or climate refugees.

Hundreds of islands and islets in the Indian Ocean, from the Maldives [049] to Bhola Island [010], in one of the most amphibious territories of the Bangladeshi Delta, are also facing dramatic challenges as the water level wipes out villages.

In a different sort of reversal, Vozrozhdeniya Island [100] is an island no more. Located in the middle of the Aral Sea—a sea that has already disappeared—the island has been stripped of its "island" status and become land.

Coda: Other Heterotopias

In the history of civilization, the ship–island duo, with the ocean as its support, has been instrumental to conceiving the world from another perspective, continuously expanding its limits. Islands and ships are connected; they exist in a symbiotic relationship. They are two sides of the same coin, with the ocean as the surface where the exchange takes place. The island is perceived as a point of reference, serving multiple purposes for navigation. It can be a final destination, or a point of *appui* to refill supplies, or a point of *relache* to take a break.[09] For sailors, islands and their harbors are composed through the nomadic and fragmented accumulation of knowledge and goods as well as their related stories. In that regard, the nomad ship defines a world composed of a series of trajectories and segmented routes.

Following Michel Foucault's concept of heterotopia to define "other spaces,"[10] the ship or the heterotopia problematizes the question of mobility and challenges the limit between an interior and an exterior space, between a nomadic and a sedentary structure.[11] The boat anchors the island to the map of the world. It also allows for the island's discovery as well as its capability to offer escape.

The ship constructs the island as a landmass surrounded by water. Lucky is the one who can shout "Land!" when the fog clears from a beautiful bay welcoming a boat that has spent months at sea. From an etymological perspective, when the ship refers to a mode of transport, it also suggests a condition or quality of being. From this perspective, the term "island-ship" would refer to the condition of living on an island that is permanently on the move; a floating island that would demystify spatial and temporal conditions, the inside and the outside, the sedentary and the nomadic, the fantasy of being here and everywhere at the same time.

Foucault offered another understanding of the boat as a possibility of being deviant through heterotopia. In *Madness and Civilization* (1964) he uses the *Ship of Fools* (1494) by the German humanist Sebastian Brant as emblematic of a society that regards the sea as an allegory of insanity and the boat as a device for the mob to express its inner desire and perversion. Concluding his essay *Of Other Spaces* (1984), Foucault refers to the ship as an essential component of human civilization, without which it could risk losing its imagination and ambition. In the tangled relationship between ship and island, the concept of a ship of fools reaching the shore of an island of fools could serve as a metaphor to keep spaces free from the regulation of hegemonic states, or simply as a reminder that, for civilizations without islands, dreams dry up.

01. The map takes its name from Gilles Deleuze, "Desert Islands," (1946), rpt. in *Desert Islands and Other Texts, 1953–1974*, ed. David Lapoujade, trans. Michael Taormina (Los Angeles: Semiotext(e), 2004).

02. Epeli Hau'ofa, "Our Sea of Islands," *The Contemporary Pacific* 6, no. 1 (Spring 1994): 147–161.

03. Edouard Glissant and J. Michael Dash, *Caribbean Discourse: Selected Essays* (Charlottesville: University of Virginia Press, 1989).

04. *Celestial Emporium of Benevolent Knowledge* is a fictitious taxonomy of animals proposed by Jorge Luis Borges in an essay called "John Wilkins' Analytical Language," in *Selected Nonfictions*, ed. Eliot Weinberger (New York: Viking, 1999), 229–232. The essay was originally published as "El idioma analítico de John Wilkins" in *La Nación* (in Spanish), Argentina, on February 8, 1942, and later republished in Jorge Luis Borges, *Otras Inquisiciones* (Buenos Aires: Emece Editores, 1964).

05. Sir Richard Branson remarks, "Necker Island is my home and favorite hideaway. I invite you to explore this idyllic island paradise for yourself and to be inspired by its beauty. I hope someday to be able to share it with you." See http://www.virginlimitededition.com.

06. Santa Cruz del Islote, located off Colombia's Caribbean coast, is unofficially the world's most crowded island, with more than 100,000 inhabitants per square kilometer.

07. Island categorization here is provided by scientific classification, reused by Deleuze in "Desert Islands," 9.

08. In Plato's myth of an ideal state, Atlantis is described by Critias and located in the middle of the Atlantic Ocean. Lemuria and Mu are the names given to a lost continent located in either the Indian or Pacific Ocean. The concept of a lost continent was first introduced by adventurer Augustus Le Plongeon in the 19th century, who used the submerged body to explain human migration and the "mystery of Easter Island."

09. For the concept of *point de relache* and *point d'appui* as qualifying the role of islands in the colonial period, see Matt Matsuda, *The Empire of Love* (New York: Cambridge University Press, 2012).

10. Michel Foucault, "Of Other Spaces," trans. Jay Miskowiec, *Diacritics* 16 (Spring 1986): 22–27.

11. See Cesare Casarino, *Modernity at Sea* (Minneapolis: University of Minnesota Press, 2002).

Image Credits
All images © MAP Office.

Molten Entities

**Timothy Morton
with artwork by
Olafur Eliasson**

An island appears to be separate, but we all know that (with a few exceptions) they are joined to the rest of the earth below the surface of the water. At the moment of writing, during which my home country of the United Kingdom is considering seceding (again) from Europe (the UK is very much the Texas of Europe), it seems more than a little appropriate to point this out.

But there are truly separated islands—the "islands of ice," otherwise known as icebergs. These are islands whose separation from their surrounding liquid medium has become a geopolitical issue of the greatest significance. Despite the predominance of relationism, it is not true that in every case we should maintain that "No man is an island," following John Donne. Interrelation is not necessarily always good: just consider the oppressive effects of some authoritarian forms of communitarianism.

This is an essay about the relation of a thing to the entities that surround it and compose it. It is always best to think of boundaries as molten. As an ontological category, the term *molten* requires some relaxation of the supposed Law of the Excluded Middle and a modal logic to cope with threshold states that strict Western logic tends to make illegal. Logic and ontology do not help icebergs. Paradoxically, what helps is not to claim that, in fact, beings are entirely inviolate, but rather that their ontological uniqueness is predicated on an intrinsic fragility, a molten quality that is intrinsic to their ontological (rather than simply ontic or phenomenal) structure. Graham Harman's image of the molten core of an object speaks to this: where does that core stop? Is it not correct to suggest that, unless we impose artificial metaphysical constraints on this core, it extends all the way to the molten edge?

In November 2015 the artist Olafur Eliasson displayed a large block of ice from Greenland at the Paris Climate Change Conference (COP21). The project was called *Ice Watch*. Eliasson was hoping to show how the ice invites us humans into something like a dialogue or dance. The ice is not simply an unformatted surface waiting for us humans to make it significant. The molten edges of the ice block, displaced in a Paris square, become a way to think about how beings are intrinsically in motion because they are intrinsically melting, fragile. Do we really want to reduce the iceberg to its surrounding context or its atomic parts? It seems as if human geophysical forces are doing a very good job of just that.

Being a thing doesn't mean having solid edges, then. In fact, it means the opposite; being a thing means having ambiguous edges. Did you think I was going to say "no edges"? The idea that "No man is an island" is obviously very popular right now as a progressive concept. Collectivity and relation aren't always on the left, you know. Edmund Burke opposed the French Revolution precisely by deploying a notion of the ponderous weight of tradition, a massive accumulation of precedent and relations going back to the legendary founding of Britain. At that moment, sitting in a room with a little island consisting of a blank sheet of paper and drawing up a constitution on it was the radical thing to do. Again, it's not obvious that we should be dissolving islands, and again, global warming is cooperating beautifully with eliminative materialism to make sure that quite a few islands really don't exist fairly shortly. A case in point is the island of Tuvalu in the Pacific, whose government ministers staged an underwater cabinet meeting in protest of this imminent fact.

The trouble is, philosophy seems to want to get rid of islands by reducing them to smaller parts, or by conceptualizing them as being themselves smaller parts of a larger system (archipelagoes seem sexier). Yet at the very same time, philosophers want to get rid of ambiguity, which is the only way islands actually get to be islands. Double trouble! Philosophy is hell-bent on an island logic consisting of the never formally proved Law of Noncontradiction and its niece, the Law of the Excluded Middle. According to the Law of Noncontradiction, either you are an island or you are not: you cannot be both at the same time. But there are plenty of logical circumstances in which it's perfectly reasonable to be true and false at the same time—moments at which trying to reduce the paradox this entails results in much more virulent paradoxes, for example. And there are plenty of moments in which it's perfectly okay to allow for shades of grey between black and white, which is what the Law of the Excluded Middle forbids. Many biological beings are like that: they are heaps of other stuff, and philosophy just isn't good with heaps. It tends to want heaps not to exist, and it uses these laws to get rid of them. Unfortunately, these laws were hardwired into social space at the start of the Neolithic, and that means that the laws themselves are part of the actual reasons why actual islands are dissolving!

If you look at the coastline of an island from space, you will see something fairly regular—perhaps it's rather triangular. When you look close up, say from a hang glider, you will see all kinds of curves and folds that you didn't see from space. And when you crawl around the surface of the coastline as an ant about three millimeters long, you will find something very different again—not just impressionistically different, but extensionally different: the circumference will be a different length. Indeed there may be circumstances—ways of measuring that island—that cause its circumference to be infinite. This is rather like what happens when you examine something like a Koch Curve, the fractal shape in which triangles are populated with smaller versions of themselves to infinity. One ends up with a shape that is bounded yet infinite. The Koch Curve is strangely "more than itself" at every point. An island is a cornucopia, or TARDIS, that

contains more of itself on the "inside" than it appears to have on the outside. This is because they always exceed how they appear, even to themselves. They melt out of themselves, without moving *in* space or time and without being pushed by anything. Space and time are qualities of that molten ooze, and every single thing has a different kind of molten, temporal ooze. If you have been to Iceland you will know that this welling-up quality is not only ontologically correct, it is how islands come into being—liquid rock in various states of cooling.

Measurement is not outside of the realm of phenomena, which we so often reify or dismiss as "subjective" or "experiential." Measurement happens with measuring gear relating to a certain world or realm of projects: the ant is trying to get from this crevice to that crevice; you are a NASA scientist mapping global warming; she is having fun in a hang glider above the coast of Iceland. These phenomenal manifolds are also island-like—independent yet perforated and open beings. The idea that islands are things that we can point to *in* preformatted space is an artifact of our anthropocentrically scaled worlds and projects relating to islands. We want to land on them. We want to sail to them to extract their spices. The spice race—otherwise known as the early Renaissance—was the first space race. Europeans invented perspective geometry on a Cartesian-type plane precisely to navigate their way around the Cape of Good Hope to get to the islands that, until then, were a medieval fantasy of luxury—a sort of earthly paradise, as they used to say, east of Eden. The bringing into existence or realization of this dream was indeed a project that required mapping islands, as well as routes to get to them, on a flat plane with spatial coordinates established in advance. But as we should have learned from Einstein by now, that kind of flat plane is just a human-scaled, good enough to be getting on with region of a much more interesting universe, useful for conquering and subjugating non-Europeans and nonhumans.

Then there is lava's way of measuring the ocean, pouring into it and hardening into all kinds of rock. Then there is the ocean's way of measuring the lava, seething around it, steaming and hissing. *Measuring* comes from the word *metron*, which is an abstraction based on a verb that actually means pacing. Before it is about pacing things out according to a preformatted human-scaled grid, it is about pacing, period. Iceland gets the measure of us: it paces us as we try to climb up it or drive around it.

Movement such as pacing can happen because things are moving all by themselves, just by being different from themselves at every point, as we've been exploring. The minimum of movement is a shimmering or vibrating without being pushed; a melting. It's not that things don't exist—the problem is not this island that I need to liquidate into lots of tiny, static solid islands called atoms . . . The issue is that *exist* doesn't mean to be a definite thing that you can point to directly. Exist means to be profoundly ambiguous, such that ambiguity is a fantastic signal of interpretive accuracy, within some specific ambiguity tolerance threshold. Things melt out of and around themselves at the ontological level—not at the level you can see or write a check for but at the level at which you think about how things exist. This kind of accuracy has not to do with imposing your (Neoplatonic Christian) will on things or the Badiouian upgrade, cutting into a continuum because you are the Decider, the event maker, the almighty human equipped with the right tools at the right time. This kind of accuracy comes logically before all that: it is more like listening or attending or tracing around the surface of the edges of an island with six delicate legs. I bet that ant encounters parts that are both the island and not the island with every step she takes. Imagine her crawling around the surface of a rock on the seashore in a tidal pool: now that's accurate.

Relating isn't some wondering way to fasten islands into chains to make them more exciting. *Relating* is how a thing is, all by itself, because it slips and slides like lava over itself without being pushed. *Relating* is how a thing listens—to itself, first and foremost; how a thing shimmers or volcanoes and oozes all over itself. *Relating* can happen because every thing is a molten island. Everything is an Iceland.

Olafur Eliasson and Minik Rosing, *Ice Watch*, 2014. Place du Panthéon, Paris, 2015. Photo: Martin Argyroglo. © Olafur Eliasson and Minik Rosing.

Timothy Morton

Of Ecology, Immunity, and Islands: The Lost Maples of Big Bend

Cary Wolfe

The title of this essay is taken from Lost Maples State Natural Area, in the Hill Country of Texas, west of San Antonio, a place named for some of the most southerly occurring maple trees in the United States. My focus, however, is on the lost maples (and other "relict" species, such as oaks) that live in isolated sections of Big Bend National Park, in Texas. Established as a national park in 1944, Big Bend is a UNESCO Biosphere reserve. A Rhode Island–sized area located within the Chihuahuan Desert, it is a dramatic landscape made up of five distinct ecological zones, bordered by the river for 118 miles. The "arcing linear oasis," as a National Park Service brochure puts it, forms "a ribbon of green that cuts across the dry desert and carves deep canyons." Because of its geological and climatological complexity, Big Bend is a site of remarkable biodiversity, home to some 1,200 different species including 430 bird and more than 50 endangered, threatened, or otherwise listed species. Some of these, such as the Carmen Mountain Whitetail Deer, exist nowhere else in the United States.[01]

As one of the most isolated, least-visited—and darkest—places in the lower 48 states, Big Bend is in many ways an island of biodiversity in the vast, arid land that is west Texas.[02] But in another sense, the Big Bend area is not isolated at all, because it sits on the US/Mexico border in an era that has attracted considerable national debate about emigration across the border from points south. This sense is reflected in the curious recent history of a border crossing at the east end of the park, at Boquillas del Carmen, which had been closed in 2002 in the wake of the 9/11 attacks because of anxiety over "homeland security" but was reopened in 2013.[03]

And yet, as Margret Grebowicz notes in her wonderful little book The National Park to Come, Boquillas del Carmen is itself a kind of island: "the village itself would not exist were it not for the park, because it is completely isolated from the rest of Mexico by the protected land which surrounds it, three distinct Mexican wilderness areas under protection, together comprised in the `sister park' to Big Bend."[04] Two islands, then, are linked by the ebb and flow of world-historical events.

Like Grebowicz, I want to explore these two registers together—the ecological and the political—and how the conceptual apparatus of the island functions at their point of articulation in the place that is Big Bend. We tend to think of islands in horizontal and nautical terms, but with Big Bend we find another kind of island: the island of the Chisos Mountains—the southernmost mountains in the United States—that sit in the center of the park, rising to a height of 7,800 feet.[05] As the park's brochure describes it, "if the Rio Grande is Big Bend country's linear oasis, then the Chisos Mountains are its green island in a sea of desert," a horizontal oasis in a scorching, inhospitable landscape, creating a

distinct microclimate in terms of both temperature and moisture. These "sky islands" inhabit a geological terrain, as John McPhee writes in Basin and Range, that is not "corrugated, like the folded Appalachians, like a tubal air mattress, like a rippled potato chip . . . Each range here is like a warship standing on its own . . . as if they were members of a fleet without precedent."[06] Because the basins separating such sky islands are typically quite vast and dry, McPhee continues, "Animals tend to be content with their home ranges and not to venture out across the big dry valleys." As one of his interlocutors explains, "The faunas in the high ranges here are quite distinct from one another. Animals are isolated like Darwin's finches in the Galápagos."[07]

The same is true of the flora in these sky islands; nowhere more so than in places like Boot Canyon in Big Bend, which, because of its particular geology and aspect, is an island within an island. Book Canyon is part of the Moist Chisos Woodland Formation, which consists of only about 800 acres (along the northeastern slope of the Chisos) in a park comprising over 800,000 acres. As one naturalist's guidebook notes, radiocarbon dating in Big Bend shows that 15,000 to 20,000 years ago the vegetation in Big Bend's desert valleys was much like what we find in the Chisos today, suggesting that conditions in the area during the Pleistocene were much moister than they are now. About 10,000 years ago, the climate in Big Bend began to change from relatively high levels of precipitation to scant rainfall, becoming dryer as time went on.[08] One result of this is the presence of so-called relict species, which can live nowhere else in the park, such as Big Tooth Maple, Arizona Cypress, Quaking Aspen, and several species of Oaks, which were stranded in Boot and Pine canyons with the retreat of the last ice.

What we find here, then, is an island that is both spatial and temporal; the trees are an index of geological time and climate change against which the vagaries of human time and human civilization—such as the closing and opening of the Boquillas Crossing—may be contextualized. But they are also traces that register the presence of an absence: not just the absence of the ecosystems in which the Maples, Oaks, and Aspens are typically found, much farther north, but a much more profound absence that challenges the commonplace notion in ecological thought that "everything is connected"—an absence that challenges, that is, the notion of "world," in which islands would just be nodes, points of interconnection in a larger, encompassing fabric of life.

To get at what I mean, I want to linger over Jacques Derrida's counterintuitive contention, contained in his remarkable reading of Robinson Crusoe in the second volume of The Beast and the Sovereign seminars, that "there is no world, there are only islands." Taking up, as he has before, his engagement of Martin Heidegger on the question, "what do beasts and men have in common?" Derrida offers in reply this quite remarkable passage made up of a movement through three possible theses:

> 1. Incontestably, animals and humans inhabit the same world, the same objective world even if they do not have the same experience of the objectivity of the object. 2. Incontestably, animals and humans do not inhabit the same world, for the human world will never be purely and simply identical to the world of animals. 3. In spite of this identity and this difference, neither animals of different species, nor humans of different cultures, nor any animal or human individual inhabit the same world as another, however close and similar these living individuals may be (be they humans or animals), and the difference between one world and another will remain always unbridgeable, because the community of the world is always constructed, simulated by a set of stabilizing apparatuses, more or less stable, then, and never natural, language in the broad sense, codes of traces being designed, among all living beings, to construct a unity of the world that is always deconstructible, nowhere and never given in nature. Between my world . . . and any other world there is first the space and time of an infinite difference, an interruption that is incommensurable with all attempts to make a passage, a bridge, an isthmus, all attempts at communication, translation, trope, and transfer that the desire for a world . . . will try to pose, impose, propose, stabilize. There is no world, there are only islands.[09]

Derrida's assertion might seem counterintuitive, but it will seem less so if we remember that in the terms of biological systems theory, "there is no world" precisely for the reasons we may trace back to Jakob von Uexküll's work on human and animal *umwelten* and forward to those who work on the biology of consciousness and cognition, such as Humberto Maturana and Francisco Varela, whose theory of "autopoiesis" demonstrates that what counts as "world" is always a product of the contingent and selective practices deployed in the embodied enaction of a particular autopoietic living system, which is always *closed* and self-referential on the level of its particular mode of "organization" but *open* to its environment and its perturbations on the level of "structure."[10] "If we deny the objectivity of a knowable world," they ask, "are we not in the chaos of total arbitrariness because everything is possible?" The way "to cut this apparent Gordian knot," they write, is "to bypass entirely this logical geography of inner versus outer" by noting that, for example,

> the operational closure of the nervous system tells us that it does not operate according to either of the two extremes: it is neither representational nor solipsistic.

> It is not solipsistic because as part of the nervous system's organism, it participates in the interactions of the nervous system with its environment. The interactions continuously trigger in it the structural changes that modulate its dynamics of states . . .

> Nor is it representational, for in each interaction it is the nervous system's structural state that specifies what perturbations are possible and what changes trigger them.[11]

Crucial here—and easy to miss—is that *time* is constitutive in this ongoing navigation of the system/environment relationship, as the phrase "dynamics of states" suggests. And this is true, not only ontogenetically but phylogenetically, in evolutionary terms. Indeed, as theoretical biologist and MacArthur Fellow Stuart Kauffman argues, the world is "enchanted" precisely because there are no "entailing laws" that govern, in Newtonian fashion, the evolution of the biosphere and its various forms of life. As Kauffman puts it, even before we reach the level of what he calls "Kantian wholes" such as mega fauna and flora, we have to ask:

> Has the universe in 13.7 billion years of existence created all the possible fundamental particles and stable atoms? Yes. Now consider proteins. These are linear sequences of twenty kinds of amino acids that typically fold into some shape and catalyze a reaction or perform some structural or other function. A biological protein can range from perhaps 50 amino acids long to several thousands. A typical length is 300 amino acids long. Then let's consider all possible proteins length 200 amino acids. How many are possible? Each position in the 200 has 20 possible choices of amino acids, so there are 20×20×20 200 times or 20 to the 200th power which is roughly 10 to the 260th power possible proteins of length 200. Now let's ask if the universe can have created all these proteins since its inception 13.7 billion years ago. There are roughly 10 to the 80th particles in the known universe. If they were doing nothing, ignoring space-like separation, but making proteins on the shortest time scale in the universe, the Planck time scale of 10 raised to the—43 seconds, it would take 10 raised to the 39th power times the lifetime of our universe to make all possible proteins of length 200 just *once*. In short, in the lifetime of our universe, only a vastly tiny fraction of all possible proteins can have been created. This means profound things. First, the universe is vastly non-ergodic. It is not like a gas at equilibrium in statistical mechanics. With this vast non-ergocity, when the possibilities are vastly larger than what can actually happen, history enters.[12]

Of course, Kauffman argues, this principle applies even more radically at the level of "Kantian wholes," and from this

View of Boot Canyon with oaks, maples, and aspens showing their fall color, Big Bend National Park, Texas.

vantage, what we confront in the lost maples of Boot Canyon is, precisely, a materialized "trace," as Derrida would put it, whose inscrutability haunts the present with retentions from an evolutionary past and protentions of an evolutionary future whose radical alterity resides in the temporalized complexity of recursive system/environment relations. In other words, there is no "there" there; there is no "world"—not in the sense of the world not being "real" but in the sense of a philosophically realist account of the world not being real. (And it is the utter confusion of these two claims—an ontological claim and an epistemological claim, the question of materialism and the question of realism—that has caused so much confusion in the contemporary theoretical landscape, as if disagreeing with the position called "philosophical realism" automatically means believing that the material world isn't real.)[13] No one dispatches this problem more elegantly and lucidly than philosopher Richard Rorty in *Objectivity, Relativism, and Truth*, where he points out that philosophical "idealism" and philosophical "realism," which

seem opposites, are in fact two sides of the same coin called philosophical "representationalism." As Rorty puts it,

> for representationalists, 'making true' and 'representing' are reciprocal relations: the nonlinguistic item which makes *S* true is the one represented by *S*. But antirepresentationalists see both notions as equally unfortunate and dispensable . . . More precisely, it is no truer that 'atoms are what they are because we use "atom" as we do' than that 'we use "atom" as we do because atoms are as they are.' *Both* of these claims, the anti-representationalist says, are entirely empty.[14]

Nevertheless,[15] in the face of this complexity and infinitude registered by both Derrida and Kauffman, we are forced to make decisions all the time about what Derrida calls the "killing" and the "letting die" of various forms of life, human and non-human—including, for example, the "letting die" of the Big Tooth Maple and the Carmen Mountain

079

Cary Wolfe

Whitetail Deer through the ongoing global warming that will, in time, force areas such as Boot Canyon beyond a fatal threshold for these species in terms of both temperature and aridity. As Derrida puts it in *Philosophy in a Time of Terror* (2003),

> Can't one terrorize without killing? Does killing necessarily mean putting to death? Isn't it also "letting die"? Can't "letting die," "not wanting to know that one is letting others die"—hundreds of millions of human beings, from hunger, AIDS, lack of medical treatment, and so on—also be part of a "more or less" conscious and deliberate terrorist strategy? We are perhaps wrong to assume so quickly that all terrorism is voluntary, conscious, organized, deliberate, intentionally calculated.[16]

This leads, in turn (in both Derrida's discussion and in my own), to the question of community (Who do we "put to death"? Who do we "let die"? Who is protected?) and to the immunity and autoimmunity with which this question is—for Derrida and others, such as Roberto Esposito and Donna Haraway—ineluctably bound up. These are precisely the sorts of considerations that Grebowicz is interested in, when she argues that the idea of the national park produces a kind of phantasmatic form of democratic community, which then gets naturalized by particular concepts of "nature" and "wilderness." As she puts it,

> nature not only becomes a useful locus for the democratic ideal; it allows us to imagine that democracy is not a form of modern politics, but some original human state. The idea that this kind of original experience, this opportunity to be "found," should be available to everyone and not just the elite creates the effect of a people who can become truly, once and for all, themselves, speaking as themselves in this, the final form of social organization, final because it is original.[17]

It is worth exploring for a moment, I think, the extent to which this characterization might apply to a figure who is certainly one of the most important and penetrating philosophers to probe the relationship between *c*ommunity and *im*munity, especially in the context of attempting to think a form of "affirmative" biopolitics that would take seriously the claims of non-human life: namely, Italian political philosopher Roberto Esposito. Like Derrida, Esposito realizes that "the idea of immunity, which is needed for protecting our life, if carried past a certain threshold, winds up negating life," so that "not only is our freedom but also the very meaning of our individual and collective existence lost: that flow of meaning, that encounter with existence outside of itself

that I define with the term *communitas*."[18] And like Derrida, he sees the semantics of the "person" and the "individual" as inadequate to the task of thinking questions of community, democracy, and so on: "One cannot base a philosophy of community on a metaphysics of the individual," he writes.[19] Indeed, he argues,

> What else is community if not the lack of "one's own"? . . . This is the meaning that is etymologically inscribed with the very *munus* form which *communitas* is derived and that it carries within itself as its own nonbelonging to itself, as a not belonging, or an impropriety, of all the members that make up community through a reciprocal distortion, which is the distortion of community itself . . . If community is nothing but the relation—the "with" or the "between"—that joins multiple subjects, this means that it cannot be a subject, individual, or collective.[20]

But if community is in this sense "impossible," as he puts it—if indeed it is nothing but the conjunctive *and*, as it were, formal relation of difference of the "with" or the "between"—then it is not at all clear how the question of community countenances the entire semantic nexus of "lack," "guilt," "debt," "perversion," and so on that eventuates in Esposito's key claim that "melancholy is not something that community contains along with other attitudes, postures, or possibilities but something by which community itself is contained and determined," resembling "a fault or wound that community experiences not as a temporary or partial condition but as community's only way of being."[21] The problem is not just that such a formulation would seem to thrust us back into the domain of "the person" and "the individual" (Isn't it only persons, whether human or non-human, that experience melancholy and guilt?)—an especially acute problem for a thinker who argues, "a single destiny binds the world, the whole world, and its life. Either the world will find a way to survive together, or it will perish as one."[22]

Rather, the primary problem can be brought into sharper focus by remembering the distinction Derrida makes in many places in his early work between "lack" and "absence"—an absence generated by the force of iterability, the trace, *différance*, and so on: an absence that must be thought "without *nostalgia*," as he puts it in "*Différance*."[23] Rather than launching into a long discussion of Derrida's early work at this juncture, I will rely here on Matthias Fritsch's able summary in a piece focused very much on politics and political theory, specifically on Chantal Mouffe's attempt to ground a theory of constitutive social antagonism and its centrality to democracy in the Derridean infrastructure of *différance* and iterability. Fritsch writes,

Différance names the empty gap, the differential relation, between elements without which they cannot function. Secondly, however, the deferral aspect of *différance* also signals that the differentiation process never comes to a close, but is begun anew with each new instance of an element's use or occurrence . . . A necessary infinity of distinguishing references enters the system, which is not a quasi-system in the sense that its structurality consists in nothing other than its use or its event . . . The future to come thus implies that identity is infinitely divided against itself, and hence, in open-ended and unforeseeable ways, infiltrated with the otherness needed to establish it.[24]

And what this means (and it's why Derridean "*différance*" cannot be assimilated to Schmitt's friend/enemy distinction, as Mouffe wishes) is that "the relation between identity and its other is not exclusionary of a clearly demarcated `outside,' as for Derrida identity is not so much marked by excluding defined others, but by the infinite porosity of a supposed inside and outside, and hence its constant re-negotiation."[25]

A few crucial points follow from this. First, time is thus constitutive of the problem of the system/environment relationship for Derrida as it is for systems theory—a point that Martin Hägglund has made well in his book-length study—which is why Derrida writes that the play of *différance* designates "the unity of chance and necessity in calculations without end," precisely as described earlier by Kauffman.[26] Or, to combine the terms of systems theory and deconstruction, the formal element of a system can never be characterized by any kind of basal simplicity because its meaning depends upon the real-time dynamic state of the system in which the element functions—what Derrida would call the moment of the element's "performativity" or "iteration." For Derrida, this constitutive role of what he calls "the becoming-space of time or becoming-time of space" mitigates against all forms of sovereignty, conceived as what he calls "ipseity" or the "self-same," which are fatefully imbricated in this dynamic once they performatively attempt to enact or declare themselves as such. As he writes in *Rogues*, sovereignty "always contracts duration into the timeless instant . . . Sovereignty neither gives nor gives itself the time, it does not take time."[27]

Secondly, a related point that derives from this first: Esposito may be right that our "mortal finitude" assumes the form of "reciprocal 'care'" and that "care, rather than interest, lies at the basis of community."[28] But what Esposito seems to both invite and ignore—invite by his seemingly Derridean insistence that community is nothing but the spacing of the "with" and "between" of individual subjects, and ignore by his reinscription of what Derrida would call a phantasmatic

"being-able" that sets up such finitude as a "fault," "wound," or "perversion," a lack rather than an absence—is a more profound understanding of what I have elsewhere called "double finitude": our finitude not just as embodied and vulnerable beings who need care but also as ones who, to enter into communicative relations and social bonds with others at all, are by necessity subjected to the "not me" and "not ours" of semiotic systems characterized by *différance* and the trace that, as Derrida puts it, must "be extended to the entire field of the living, or rather to the life/death relation, beyond the anthropological limits of 'spoken' language."[29] It's not just human beings, in other words, who are subjected to the finitude of *différance* and the trace—any creature that engages in communicative, semiotic behaviors is—and that means that this second form of finitude is not held in reserve for a "human" who can thereby be ontologically separated from other forms of life.

Third—and crucially—this has profound implications for Esposito's rendering of the immunitary paradigm of biopolitics, which in this light seems to reify the inside/outside relation in arguing that "whereas *communitas* opens, exposes, and turns individuals inside out, freeing them to their exteriority, *immunitas* returns individuals to themselves, encloses them once again in their own skin. *Immunitas* brings the outside inside, eliminating whatever part of the individual that lies outside."[30] What such a characterization misses is not just the "infinite porosity" and "constant re-negotiation" of the inside/outside relation noted by Fritsch above, but also what I have called the "second-order" turn of systems theory, which holds that—contrary to the understanding of autopoietic systems as solipsistic—the operational closure of systems and the self-reference based upon it arise as a practical and adaptive necessity precisely because systems are not closed: that is, precisely because they find themselves in an environment of overwhelmingly and exponentially greater complexity than is possible for any single system. To put it another way, systems have to operate selectively and "blindly" (as Luhmann puts it), not because they are closed but precisely because they are not, and the asymmetrical distribution of complexity across the system/environment difference is in fact what forces the strategy of self-referential closure and autopoiesis.[31] Indeed, the second-order turn, as I have argued elsewhere,[32] is to realize that the more systems build up their own internal complexity through recursive self-reference and closure, the more linked they are to changes in their environments, to which they become more and more sensitive. They can buy more time in relation to environmental change, as it were, but there is also more to which to respond.

From this vantage, we can now see more clearly the cascade of problems that eventuates from Esposito's seemingly innocent and commonsensical assertion that "we have always existed in common"—an assertion that not only seems counterfactual in light of the question of "world" as rearticulated through work in biological systems theory reaching back to Uexküll but that also begs the question, "from what Archimedean vantage point is such an assertion to be made, surmounting as it appears to do, the constraints and finitude of self-reference?" But what if we begin instead not with commonality but with difference and alterity, the finitude and situatedness from which we all blindly set out, and, with Donna Haraway, see that "immune system discourse is about constraint and possibility for engaging in a world full of 'difference,' replete with non-self"? From this perspective, immunity doesn't mean isolation: it "can also be conceived in terms of shared specificities; of the semipermeable self able to engage with others (human and non-human, inner and outer), but always with finite consequences; of situated possibilities and impossibilities of individuation and identification; and of partial fusions and dangers."[33]

In this light, we can appreciate the more-than-metaphorical resonance of Derrida's assertion that "Not only is there no kingdom of *différance*, but *différance* instigates the subversion of every kingdom."[34] And this is precisely why he suggests "the thinking of the political has always been a thinking of *différance* and the thinking of *différance* always a thinking *of* the political, of the contours and limits of the political."[35] We are thus back to the question of sovereignty as what Derrida calls the "self-same" and "ipseity," "the power that *gives itself* its own law . . . the sovereign and reappropriating gathering of self in the simultaneity of an assemblage or assembly, being together or 'living together,' as we say."[36] We are back, in fact, to the questions Grebowicz is interested in in *The National Park to Come*: questions of nation and national boundaries and of how those map and are mapped onto a certain notion of "nature" and "wilderness" as "places where the political and the natural collapse into each other in a way that makes both democracy and wilderness policy appear transcendent, as if they belonged to the realm of natural, not civil, law."[37]

It is this political imaginary, I have been arguing, that lurks beneath Esposito's attempt to conjugate an "affirmative" biopolitics of "life," the "common," and "community," and it is decisively subverted by close attention to ecology in the sense that I have elaborated it above—an ecology in which "there is no world," an ecology of the "not us," the "not ours," and the "not now"—a shift in perspective that has particular resonance in the geopolitical setting of Big Bend National Park. To put it another way, fundamental to an "everything is connected" idea of nature or ecology is the sovereign presumption that there is some Archimedean point from which one could see that "everything is connected," a vantage from which (to reach back now to the first-generation systems theory of Gregory Bateson) the "map" might be presumed to coincide with the "territory,"[38] which is to say the presumption that one could escape the performativity, iterability, and autopoietic self-reference for which the "island" (especially in Derrida's remarkable second year of *The Beast and the Sovereign* seminars) is an especially powerful figure.[39] After all, this is precisely why Derrida is so resistant to the discourse of "globalization," which is "simply alleged and not even there, and where we, we who are worldless, *weltlos*, form a world only against the backdrop of a nonworld."[40] Indeed, he asserts, "sovereignty is a circularity, indeed a sphericity."[41] In other words, we usually think that the "one world/everything is connected" idea of ecology and sovereign "national boundaries" are opposites, but what I have tried to show here is that they are, in fact, two sides of the same coin.

01. Roland H. Wauer and Carl M. Fleming, *Naturalist's Big Bend* (College Station: Texas A&M University Press, 2002), 21–22.

02. Big Bend has been designated a gold-star-level International Dark Sky Park by the International Dark Sky Association. See Margret Grebowicz, *The National Park to Come* (Stanford: Stanford University Press, 2015), 88, fn. 32.

03. Ibid., 3.

04. Ibid., 44.

05. Wauer and Fleming, *Naturalist's Big Ben*, 6.

06. John McPhee, *Basin and Range* (New York: Farrar, Straus, and Giroux, 1981), 47.

07. Ibid., 48.

08. Wauer and Fleming, *Naturalist's Big Bend*, 6–7.

09. Jacques Derrida, *The Beast and the Sovereign*, vol. 2, trans. Geoffrey Bennington (Chicago: University of Chicago Press, 2011), 8–9.

10. Jakob von Uexküll, *A Foray Into the Worlds of Animals and Humans, with A Theory of Meaning*, trans. Joseph D. O'Neil (Minneapolis: University of Minnesota Press, 2010). Humberto Maturana and Francisco Varela, *The Tree of Knowledge: The Biological Roots of Human Understanding*, trans. Robert Paolucci (Boston: Shambhala, 1998). For more on how these questions cross-pollinate with Derrida's work, see my *Animal Rites: American Culture, the Discourse of Species, and Posthumanist Theory* (Chicago: University of Chicago Press, 1998), 78–94; and *Before the Law: Humans and Other Animals in a Biopolitical Frame* (Chicago: University of Chicago Press, 2013), 60–86.

11. Maturana and Varela, *The Tree of Knowledge*, 135, 169.

12. Stuart Kauffman, "The Re-Enchantment of Humanity: Implications of 'No Entailing' Laws," unpublished manuscript.

13. For a subtle and thoroughgoing critique of this confusion, one that traces some of its adventures in the history of philosophy, see Raoni Padui, "Realism, Anti-Realism, and Materialism," *Angelaki: Journal of the Theoretical Humanities* 16, no. 2 (2011): 89–101.

14. Richard Rorty, *Objectivity, Relativism, and Truth: Philosophical Papers*, vol. 1 (Cambridge: Cambridge University

Press, 1991), 4. As Rorty puts it, "what shows us that life is not just a dream, that our beliefs are in touch with reality, is the *causal,* non-intentional, non-representational links between us and the rest of the universe." [159] The anti-representationalist "believes, as strongly as does any realist, that there are objects which are *causally* independent of human beliefs and desires" [101]; she "recognizes relations of *justification* holding between beliefs and desires, and relations of *causation* holding between those beliefs and desires and other items in the universe, but no relations of *representation*." [97] On this view, the anti-representationalists accept "the brute, inhuman, causal stubbornness of the gold or the text. But they think this should not be confused with, so to speak, an *intentional* stubbornness, an insistence on being *described in a certain way,* its *own* way." [83] See also 47–49, 54–55, 116–17. Emphases in the original.

15. For a detailed exploration of this question, see the last two chapters of my book *Before the Law.*

16. Jacques Derrida, *Philosophy in a Time of Terror: Dialogues with Jürgen Habermas and Jacques Derrida,* ed. Giovanna Borradori (Chicago: University of Chicago Press, 2003), 108.

17. Grebowicz, *The National Park to Come,* 25.

18. Roberto Esposito, *Terms of the Political: Community, Immunity, Biopolitics,* trans. Rhiannon Noel Welch (New York: Fordham University Press, 2013), 61.

19. Ibid., 16. See also, in particular, Esposito's essay "The Person and Human Life," in *Theory after 'Theory,'"* ed. Derek Attridge and Jane Elliott (New York: Routledge, 2011), 205–20.

20. Ibid., 29. For Derrida's conjugation of the *munus,* see Jacques Derrida, *Rogues: Two Essays on Reason,* trans. Pascale-Anne Brault and Michael Naas (Stanford, CA: Stanford University Press, 2005), 35.

21. Esposito, *Terms of the Political,* 28.

22. Esposito, *Terms of the Political,* 76.

23. Jacques Derrida, "*Différance,*" in *Margins of Philosophy,* trans. Alan Bass (Chicago: University of Chicago Press, 1982), 27. Emphasis in the original.

24. Matthias Fritsch, "Antagonism and Democratic Citizenship (Schmitt, Mouffe, Derrida)," *Research in Phenomenology* 38, no. 2 (2008): 179–80.

25. Ibid., 181.

26. Derrida, "*Différance,*" 7. See Martin Hägglund, *Radical Atheism: Derrida and the Time of Life* (Stanford, CA: Stanford University Press, 2008).

27. Derrida, *Rogues,* 46, 109.

28. Esposito, *Terms of the Political,* 25–26.

29. Jacques Derrida and Elisabeth Roudinesco, *For What Tomorrow: A Dialogue,* trans. Jeff Fort (Stanford, CA: Stanford University Press, 2004), 63. For more on "double finitude," see the introductory chapter to my *What Is Posthumanism?* (Minneapolis: University of Minnesota Press, 2010).

30. Esposito, *Terms of the Political,* 49.

31. See Niklas Luhmann, *Social Systems,* trans. John Bednarz, Jr., with Dirk Baecker (Stanford, CA: Stanford University Press, 1995), 12–58. Further references are contained in the text. In this connection, Esposito's characterization of Luhmann's rendering of the immunitary paradigm is entirely symptomatic, when he writes that Luhmann's model focuses on "an internal self-regulation of systems that is *completely independent and autonomous* with regard to environmental pressures," which has the effect of "breaking *any possible relationships with the outside* but also of *calling into question the very idea of "outside."* [40] Emphasis added.

32. Namely, in *What Is Posthumanism?,* xx–xxv.

33. Donna J. Haraway, "The Biopolitics of Postmodern Bodies: Constitutions of Self in Immune System Discourse" (1989), rprt. in her *Simians, Cyborgs, and Women: The Reinvention of Nature* (New York: Routledge, 1990), 214, 225.

34. Derrida, "*Différance,*" 22.

35. Derrida, *Rogues,* 39.

36. Derrida, *Rogues,* 11. Emphasis in the original.

37. Grebowicz, *The National Park to Come,* 29.

38. As Bateson puts it, borrowing from the "general semantics" of Korzybski, "the map is not the territory," and "what gets onto the map, in fact, is *difference,* be it a difference in altitude, a difference in vegetation, a difference in population structure, difference in surface, or whatever." Gregory Bateson, *Steps to an Ecology of Mind* (New York: Ballantine, 1972), 449, 451. That is to say, all maps are about self-referential schemata and the systems of differences they do (and do not) make available to observation.

39. Derrida, *The Beast and the Sovereign,* vol. 2. For an explicitly political exploration of the question of performativity, see Derrida's well-known essay, "Declarations of Independence," in *Negotiations: Interventions and Interviews, 1971–2001,* ed. and trans. Elizabeth Rottenberg (Stanford: Stanford University Press, 2002), 46–54.

40. Derrida, *Rogues,* 155. Emphasis in the original.

41. Derrida, *Rogues,* 13. See also, in this connection, his contention that "before the purely geometrical forms named *circle* and *sphere*, I still have difficulty imagining, in this super-preliminary moment, any democracy at all." [10] Emphasis in the original.

Image Credits

079: Image courtesy of the author.

Cary Wolfe

How to Hide an Island

Stefan Helmreich

What happens when waves, moving across the sea, encounter an island? In the language of physical oceanography, wave fronts refract, bending as they approach an island, owing to underwater contours that signal shallowing water depths. Waves also diffract, curving around islands, as around obstacles. The interference patterns that result are sorts of shadows—rippling phantoms that outline or point inward toward the islands that create them.[01]

The structure of such shadows can enter navigational apprehension in a range of ways, from naked eye assessments to radar renderings. One notable capture of wave shadows comes in the form of Marshall Islands "stick charts," diagrams of wave and swell patterns used by Marshallese navigators until about World War II to plan canoe travels around the islands of Micronesia. These diagrams, made of coconut fronds and shells, come in lots of varieties, including ones centered on wave patterns around single islands. Anthropologist John Mack offers that these are "less representations of space" than "representations of *experience* of space"[02]—experience emanating from and embodied in the habits of practiced wayfinders who are trained to feel, in their bodies and boats, the analog materiality of wavy motion. (Mack's opposition between representations of space and experience of space is perhaps too stark. Latitude–longitude charts, sextant-enabled navigation, and radar readings of seascapes all enable and assume specific sorts of mariner experience—particular conjunctures of perception and cognition.)

If emanations of wave patterns can reveal the existence of an island, might technological tinkering with such shadows—perhaps canceling out radiating waves through the production of overlapping waves of opposite phase (creating destructive interference)—hide such islands? Such a possibility is at the center of recent investigations into cloaking, a technique that naval engineers have been exploring to engineer ships that can hide their own wakes, and with which coastal engineers have been experimenting in order to generate surface calm around buoys (making buoys less subject to the turbulent roil of rough seas).[03] Cloaking techniques may also be applied to modulating wavescapes around islands.

Hiding islands, of course, is an enterprise that recalls a range of mythic maritime and science-fiction fantasies about islands as places of isolation and seclusion, as vanishing paradises and utopias, as zones of illicit activity, and as sites of secret scientific and social experimentation.[04] Poet and novelist James Hamilton-Paterson, in an appreciation of islands, writes that, "One seldom looks at an island without also imagining it disappearing behind a bank of fog or storm clouds which at length clear to reveal an empty ocean."[05] Cloaking an island would seem to materialize a long literary tradition of imagining islands as temporary, enchanted way stations in time, as lost worlds, or as figments of maritime

imagination.[06] Cloaking, of course, has a more recent pop cultural resonance: it was first named in the 1960s science fiction television program *Star Trek*, which dreamed up the "cloaking device" as a mechanism that could render spaceships invisible in deep space.[07]

What do scientific projects of maritime cloaking look like? They begin with scientists at the Institut Fresnel in Marseille, France, who, along with colleagues in Liverpool, published a paper in 2008 entitled "Broadband Cylindrical Acoustic Cloak for Linear Surface Waves in a Fluid."[08] In this research report, the authors propose a system for bending liquid waves around land obstacles in ways inspired by experiments in electromagnetic and acoustic cloaking, in which electromagnetic and acoustic waves are bent around solid objects.[09] The authors propose a cloaking infrastructure that might be made of specially shaped and sized pillars submerged in concentric rings around the circumference of an island. The pillars themselves would be made of a metamaterial, a composite of metals (and possibly plastics) engineered to have built-in properties not found in naturally occurring materials, such as the capacity to block, absorb, bend, or amplify very specific wavelengths of electromagnetic or other radiation.[10] The ring infrastructure proposed by the Fresnel-Liverpool team guides waves coming toward an island into a whirlpool that spirals around the island, dissipating and then redirecting the wave energy back outward, canceling out incoming waves. (Think of this as something like providing islands with noise cancelling headphones.) In imagining the uses of such a structure, the authors remark, "our design could be used to protect off-shore platforms or coastlines from ocean waves such as tsunamis." A popular science report on the paper and its experimental model promises readers, "Hiding Islands and Platforms from Tsunamis, Now a Possibility."[11]

A 2014 paper by Massachusetts Institute of Technology (MIT) mechanical engineer J. N. Newman, "Cloaking a Circular Cylinder in Water Waves," elaborates on the Fresnel-Liverpool model and offers a streamlined explication of the theory and aim of cloaking:

> In the diffraction of water waves by fixed bodies, the scattered waves propagate outward in the far field and attenuate with increasing distance from the structure. "Cloaking" refers to the reduction in amplitude or complete elimination of the scattered waves. . . . This may have practical applications, particularly to reduce the mean drift force on offshore structures.[12]

The Fresnel-Liverpool and MIT cloaking projects stage islands not so much as sites of secrecy but as places to be kept stable, safe, and secure. Here, cloaking is not so much (or only) meant to hide islands from people but (also) from

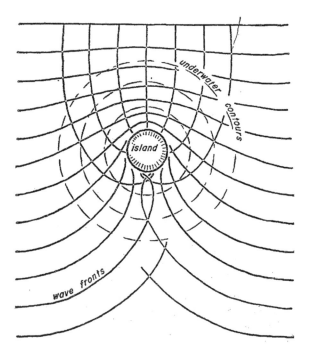

the sea itself. Islands become doubly isolated. Far away from the mainland as well as sheltered from the very sea that once emplaced but now ignores them, it is as though the cloaking device has played a Jedi mind trick on passing waves: "This is not the island you're looking for." In such enterprises, waves—already treated (along with wind, currents, upwellings) as part of an oceanic infrastructure (for travel, commerce, or energy exchange)—are sculpted into further infrastructural form.

Waves become candidates for recruitment into projects in what Pierre Bélanger calls "landscape as infrastructure," where infrastructures, defined by this landscape architect as collective systems of managing "water, waste, food, transport, and energy" are tuned to take account of and explicitly incorporate preexisting "biophysical resources, agents, and services" such as geothermal processes, wildlife migrations, and watershed flows.[13] Waves become physical processes folded into systems of communication and control.

But something more complex is going on in the case of cloaking, since the physical properties of waves are not simply being harnessed but are being engineered into new forms. In cloaking projects, waves become components in "environmental infrastructures." Anthropologist Casper Bruun Jensen writes that environmental infrastructures are "assemblages where the 'natural' and the 'social' mix and take new shape." He offers rivers as one example, which, as environmental infrastructures, operate in shifting ratios and for different constituencies and at different times, as organic machines for distributing energy and wealth, as mobile lattices for multispecies encounters, and as channels for the fluvial transformation of what will count as habitable islets, marshlands, and more.[14] For environmental infrastructures, what is artificial and what is natural is beside the point: more consequential are the new sorts of things and powers that emerge from shifting arrangements of materials, bodies, ideas, and agents.

The making of wavescapes into environmental infrastructures is something I want additionally to call the creation of *infranature*. Whereas environmental infrastructure describes and tracks the generation of novel and unpredictable natural/cultural forms and captures the undoing of divides between the artificial and natural, infranature keeps analytically audible the continued durability of the concept of nature, especially as it may exist for many scientists, engineers, and architects. For people outside academic conversations about the shifting ontologies of nature and culture, the making infrastructural of waves will not fully yank these entities out an order of nature. Infranature names those processes commonly understood to be organic, biological, meteorological, geological, and oceanic that, tailored to social projects and endeavors, may be only partially lifted out of the realm of the implicitly natural. With *infranature*, nature as organic "first nature" is not superseded by the "second nature" of the built environment: rather, second nature becomes recursively folded back into first nature. If the supernatural is that which is transcendent—above nature, outside of history—then the infranatural names that which becomes immanent—inside the putatively natural order of things.[15]

In other words, wavescapes become technologized even as they are still at home in a naturalized world. They become a channeled kind of "subnature," that genre of nature that often stands as antithetical to architectural endeavor (the zone of "dust, mud, gas, smoke, debris, weeds, and insects") but that might be reclaimed, repurposed, even domesticated.[16] Waves become architectural materials—materials that, conjoined with metamaterials, might be employed to create new kinds of spaces, places, and experience.

The kinds of islands imagined by cloaking scientists are ideal-typical islands. Indeed, they are mostly artificial islands—engineered structures such as offshore platforms. One can imagine cloaking-device/artificial-island packages pitched as maritime engineering planning units, packages that might be used to create new kinds of oil-drilling platforms, ocean-sited resorts, or airports.

In *The Invisible Islands*, a 2013 artwork by MAP Office, artists Laurent Gutierrez and Valérie Portefaix offer a map of 33 islands ringing Hong Kong, islands that historically have been home to "surveillance and port defense (from China to the U[nited]K[ingdom]), storage of all sorts (opium, guns, and gold), aqua- and agriculture, refugee communities (drugs addicts, escapees), etc."[17] Gutierrez and Portefaix's

Top: A Marshallese "stick chart" called a wappepe, representing wave patterns around a central island. Bottom: Farhat et al., metallic model of a cloaking infrastructure. Opposite page: Wave refraction around a circular island (waves are moving down the page).

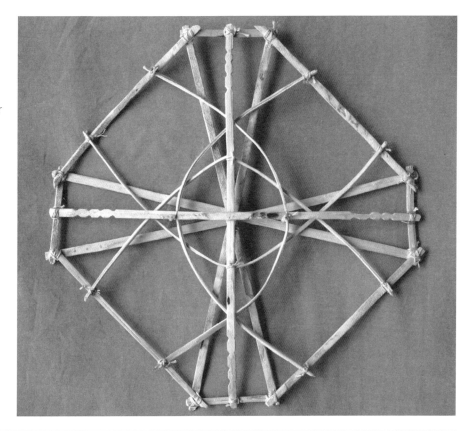

islands have been invisible—administratively, legally, and culturally. Cloaked islands would add a physical, oceanographic manifestation to this array of invisibilities, with kinetically modified waves modulating what can serve as experiences of space.[18]

In their call for submissions, the editors of *New Geographies* ask after "the new limits of islandness." I suggest that, with cloaking, the surrounds of islands—the water and the waves—may be getting pulled into the domain of the infrastructural, or infranatural, as waves become shaped, through cloaking, into artificial sculptures designed to negate themselves. What kind of *islandography* (to play on

Marc Shell's coinage of *islandology*) is in the making here?[19] If the word *geography* points to "earth writing" and *oceanography*, to "ocean writing," reckoning with "wave writing"— call it *undulography*[20]—seems necessary in fashioning a new kind of cloaked islandography. But this is an undulography that cancels itself out, an ~~undulography~~ that, rather than marking a "shift towards the fluid and the continuous that seems to spell the dissolution of the fundamental boundedness, isolation, and determination of the island,"[21] in fact reinforces island boundaries, bending natural phenomena such as waves into media that fortify, rather than dissolve, island isolation.

01. Willard Bascom, *Waves and Beaches: The Dynamics of the Ocean Surface* (Garden City, NY: Doubleday, 1964).

02. John Mack, *The Sea: A Cultural History* (London: Reaktion Books, 2013), 118, emphasis in the original. See also Joseph Genz, Jerome Aucan, Mark Merrifield, Ben Finney, Korent Joel, and Alison Kelen, "Wave Navigation in the Marshall Islands: Comparing Indigenous and Western Scientific Knowledge of the Ocean," *Oceanography* 22, no. 2 (2009): 234–45.

03. Adrian Cho, "Proposed Cloaking Device for Water Waves Could Protect Ships at Sea," *Science* 2 (March 2, 2012), http://www.sciencemag.org/news/2012/03/proposed-cloaking-device-water-waves-could-protect-ships-sea. See also Mohammad-Reza Alam, "Broadband Cloaking in Stratified Seas," *Physical Review Letters* 108 (February 24, 2012): 084502, which suggests a mode of canceling water waves beneath buoys by sculpting portions of the ocean floor so that they realize shapes that attenuate wave action underwater.

04. John Gillis, *Islands of the Mind: How the Human Imagination Created the Atlantic World* (New York: Palgrave Macmillan, 2004).

05. James Hamilton-Paterson, *Seven-Tenths: The Sea and Its Thresholds* (London: Faber and Faber, 2007), 64.

06. Think also about the case of islands which appear on maps but turn out not to be there. From the elusive islands of old sea-charts to today's phantom islands of Google Earth (which sometimes turn out to be digital artifacts), these have a long maritime history. See http://www.dailymail.co.uk/sciencetech/article-2236952/Phantom-island-shown-Google-Earth-does-exist-Australian-scientists-discover-outcrop-Pacific-voyage.html.

07. The term *cloaking device* was coined by D. C. Fontana in her screenplay for an episode of *Star Trek* called "The Enterprise Incident,"

which first aired on September 27, 1968.

08. M. Farhat, S. Enoch, S. Guenneau, and A. B. Movchan, "Broadband Cylindrical Acoustic Cloak for Linear Surface Waves in a Fluid," *Physical Review Letters* 101 (September 26, 2008): 134501.

09. See Colin Barras, "Invisibility Cloaks Could Take Sting out of Tsunamis," *New Scientist*, September 29, 2008, www.newscientist.com/article/dn14829-invisibility-cloaks-could-take-sting-out-of-tsunamis; and Dan Talpalariu, "Hiding Islands and Platforms from Tsunamis, Now a Possibility," *Softpedia*, September 30, 2008, http://news.softpedia.com/news/Hiding-Islands-and-Platforms-From-Tsunamis-Now-A-Possibility-94486.shtml.

10. On cloaking objects at microwave frequencies, see D. Schurig, J. J. Mock, B. J. Justice, et al., "Metamaterial Electromagnetic Cloak at Microwave Frequencies," *Science* 314, no. 5801 (2006): 977–80; and Michael Selvanayagam and George V. Eleftheriades, "Experimental Demonstration of Active Electromagnetic Cloaking," *Physical Review X*, vol. 3, no. 4 (2013): 041011. On acoustic cloaking, see L. Zigoneanu, B. I. Popa, and S. A. Cummer, "Three Dimensional Broadband Omnidirectional Acoustic Ground Cloak," *Nature Materials* 13, no. 4 (2014): 352–55. The intended applications of these cloaking projects are left general in these articles, although funding from the Office of Naval Research and the Army Research Office suggests interest in their development from military quarters.

11. The term *metamaterials* first appears in print in Rodger M. Walser, "Electromagnetic Metamaterials," *Proceedings of SPIE*, vol. 4467, *Complex Mediums II: Beyond Linear Isotropic Dielectrics*, July 9, 2001, 10.1117/12.432921. In 2001, the U.S. Defense Advanced Research Projects Agency founded the Metamaterials program. One institutional anchor for this program is at

the University of California, Berkeley. The University's Multidisciplinary Research Program of the University Research Initiative (MURI): Scalable and Reconfigurable Electromagnetic Metamaterials and Devices describes metamaterials on its website as a "new class of ordered nanocomposites that exhibit exceptional properties not readily observed in nature. These properties arise from qualitatively new response functions that are: (1) not observed in the constituent materials and (2) result from the inclusion of artificially fabricated, extrinsic, low dimensional inhomogeneities. At the heart of the metamaterial advantage lies the physics of 'small-scale.' The physics at small scale is different than in bulk owing to, for instance, quantum confinement, exchange-biased ferromagnetism, and effective media responses, which can result in enhanced electromagnetic properties." http://xlab.me.berkeley.edu/MURI/muri.html. One may now await the adaptation of critical theory of the "new materialism" to this metamaterial moment; see for example, Jane Bennett, *Vibrant Matter: A Political Ecology of Things* (Durham, NC: Duke University Press, 2009).

12. J. N. Newman, "Cloaking a Circular Cylinder in Water Waves," *European Journal of Mechanics–B/Fluids* 47 (2014): 145–50.

13. Pierre Bélanger, "Landscape as Infrastructure," *Landscape Journal* 28 (2009): 1–9. Compare with Gary Strang, "Infrastructure as Landscape," *Places* 10, no. 3 (1996): 8–15. Strang discusses how artificial constructions such as canals and telecommunications networks might themselves be imagined as given parts of the biophysical environment.

14. Casper Bruun Jensen, "Experimenting with Political Materials: Environmental Infrastructures and Ontological Transformations," *Distinktion: Scandinavian Journal of Social Theory* 16, no. 1 (2015): 27. Jensen's discussion of rivers draws from Richard

088

White, *The Organic Machine: The Remaking of the Columbia River* (New York: Hill and Wang, 1995); and Hugh Raffles, *In Amazonia: A Natural History* (Princeton, NJ: Princeton University Press, 2002). See also Sara B. Pritchard, *Confluence: The Nature of Technology and the Remaking of the Rhône* (Cambridge, MA: Harvard University Press, 2011). For further critical discussion of how organic process and landscape are enlisted into projects of infrastructure, see Ashley Carse, "Nature as Infrastructure: Making and Managing the Panama Canal Watershed," *Social Studies of Science* 42, no. 4 (2012): 539–563. For a discussion of the functionalism assumed by some studies of infrastructure (consider Bélanger, above), see "Andrea Ballestero on Infrastructure, Sponges, and Aquifers," Center for Energy and Environmental Research in the Human Sciences @ Rice, blog, January 19, 2016, http://culturesofenergy.com/andrea-ballestero-on-infrastructure-sponges-and-aquifers. Thanks goes to Caterina Scaramelli for thinking with me on this point.

15. For one influential articulation of "first nature" as the biophysical, organic world and "second nature" as the built environment, see William Cronon, *Nature's Metropolis: Chicago and the Great West* (New York: W. W. Norton, 1991).

16. David Gissen, *Subnature: Architecture's Other Environments* (New York: Princeton Architectural Press, 2009).

17. Laurent Gutierrez and Valérie Portefaix, "Islands and Other Invisible Territories," in *Art in the Anthropocene: Encounters among Aesthetics, Politics, Environments and Epistemologies*, ed. Heather Davis and Etienne Turpin (London: Open Humanities, 2015), 223. Compare with Angus Peter Campbell, *Invisible Islands* (Glasgow: Otago Publishing, 2006), a collection of Calvinoesque and Borgesian fables about imaginary islands off the coast of Scotland.

18. Building on the Marshallese materials with which Mack develops the notion of an "experience of [wave] space," we should recall what happened to the Marshallese after World War II. The 1954 detonation of a hydrogen bomb at Bikini Atoll by the United States left generations of Marshallese—particularly in the Rongelap and Utirik atolls—sick from exposure to radioactive fallout. A history of Marshallese wave experience will look different when it takes into account the hydrogen bomb shockwave and its terrible genealogical consequences. See Holly M. Barker, *Bravo for the Marshallese: Regaining Control in a Post-Nuclear, Post-Colonial World* (Belmont, CA: Wadsworth Learning, 2004).

19. Marc Shell, *Islandology: Geography, Rhetoric, Politics* (Stanford: Stanford University Press, 2014).

20. The Greek-derived word kymography, which might suggest itself, is already taken, used to describe the tracing of cardiac pulse waves. On undulography, which mixes Latin and Greek elements, see Stefan Helmreich, "Old Waves, New Waves: Changing Objects in Physical Oceanography," in *Fluid Frontiers: New Currents in Marine and Maritime Environmental History*, ed. John Gillis and Franziska Torma (Cambridge: White Horse Press, 2015), 76–88.

21. Daniel Daou and Pablo Pérez-Ramos, call for papers, *New Geographies 08—Island*, October 2015.

Image Credits

Stefan Helmreich

On Seeing and Believing: Islands of Chaos and the Key Question of Scientific Visualization

Nina Samuel

Seeing is Believing.
—Benoît Mandelbrot, *The Fractal Geometry of Nature* (1982)

Throughout history, islands have been discussed—and distinguished—in relation to the mainland. Writing in 1880 on the distribution of animal and vegetal inhabitants living on these geological formations, evolutionary biologist Alfred Russel Wallace identified two distinct categories of islands, linked to "two distinct modes of origin": "they have either been separated from continents of which they are but detached fragments, or they have originated in the ocean and have never formed part of a continent or any large mass of land. This difference of origin is fundamental."[01] Yet the attempt to categorize islands is more complex. Hybrid forms like peninsulas and "island-continents"[02] break the dichotomy of mainland and island.

Writing a few years after Wallace, H. G. Wells expanded upon the dual classification of islands by introducing a factor of time. He detected three classifications: "recent continental" islands, "ancient continental" islands, and "oceanic" islands, which he described as "isolated peaks rising from the beds of deep oceans, with no particular connection, geological or zoological, with any mainland."[03] It had been these isolated islands in particular that had inspired the fantasies of storytellers throughout time, Wells's own *Island of Doctor Moreau* (1896) prominent among them.[04]

These attempts at classifying islands reveal two inherent conundrums. The first involves a tension between detachment and connectedness. The second, because an island's connection to the mainland is usually hidden below the water level, involves a riddle of hidden origins: the history of an island is, at turns, not at all, only partially, or temporarily observable.

These conundrums are both related to questions of visibility. Where are the limits of the island? What are the properties of its edges, or coastline, separating the realm of the sea from the realm of land? In 1967 mathematician Benoît Mandelbrot published the essay "How Long is the Coast of Britain?" in the journal *Science*, investigating these questions from the viewpoint of mathematics.[05] It was not the mainland of islands that had become interesting for scientific investigation but rather their borders. Mandelbrot argues that coastlines are self-similar and infinite in mathematical terms. The apparent paradox that mathematics reveal when they use a fundamentally finite object to discuss the idea of the infinite has its point of origin a few decades earlier. The concept of the infinite border of an island, which Mandelbrot developed from the 1960s on, corresponds to the notion of functions without derivatives. These functions, whose special features are values that spring back and forth between two constants *ad infinitum* (which makes them impossible to draw precisely) had put the discipline of mathematics into deep crisis at the end of the 19th century.[06] Prior to this time, mathematicians had called these deviations from classical assumptions about elementary concepts of geometry a "lamentable plague,"[07] had referred to them as "monsters" of mathematical logic, and had labeled them outrageous attacks on the intelligence of their precursors.[08] Eventually banished from late 19th-century mathematical discourses, these curves were actually symptomatic of a historic change in mathematics. This change renegotiated the relationship between experience and geometry, between seeing and thinking: functions without derivatives are finite in our perception, yet, conceptually and mathematically, they are of infinite length. Constantly revealing new details under enlargement, they are endlessly complex.

The coastline of an island features as a prominent example of the objects that Mandelbrot began referring to in 1975 as "fractals:" collections of dots, lines, surfaces, or solids "loosely characterized as being violently convoluted and broken up."[09] Fractals exist in between the classical Euclidian dimensions. Mandelbrot labeled this the broken dimension D.[10] This fractal dimension is an index for the varying degree of roughness of fractal structures. It quantifies complexity as a ratio of the change in detail to the change in scale. The dimension D is always a decimal number and distinguishes fractals from Euclidean geometry, in which there are only whole-number dimensions for lines, planes, and solids.

Fractal geometry is closely related to the field of dynamical systems (commonly known as chaos theory), an interdisciplinary area of study that gained enormous popularity and encouraged high hopes for a new applicability of mathematics in science during the mid-1980s and 1990s.[11] Throughout his work, islands formed an important core of Mandelbrot's theoretical considerations. Two different meanings of "island"—one figurative and one abstract—compete for primacy, each pointing to an antipodal power of visual representation in the thinking process. An investigation of both meanings provides an invitation to perambulate the fractal islands of Benoît Mandelbrot, one of the best-known producers of digital images in scientific and industrial research.[12] The question of the visibility of islands and their relation to the mainland plays a crucial role on this field trip. The review of the historical role of the island in Mandelbrot's work leads to a reflection on the shift that chaos theory brings to our thinking about the shapes of nature and about the meaning of those shapes for visual representation within the scientific thinking process.

Islands of Chance

In the history of scientific visualization, islands provide a striking example of the intricate interdependence of have been possible without both analogue and digital computer technologies as instruments of experimental visualization. While fractal islands are abstract mathematical thought experiments in the first place, the technological advances of computer graphics helped to unfold their imaginative power.

In his first book introducing the term "fractal" to a wider audience (1975), Mandelbrot published a series of four computer-generated black-and-white cubes in tiered arrangement.[14] The cubes are constructed from a grid with a mountainous surface on top. The accompanying text raves about their evocative quality: "Constantly, I lapse into wondering during which trip (or in which travel film) I actually saw the last view in the sequence, with its vista of small islands scattered like seeds at the tip of a narrow peninsula."[15] Coastlines and islands were amongst the first shapes in nature that Mandelbrot projected into his computer-generated images. Similar "scenic cubes" appear in Mandelbrot's first fractal computer animations from the early 1970s. Presented as "imaginary continents," one sees those three-dimensional relief structures slowly rotating in front of a black background. Produced by Mandelbrot and his programmer Hirsh Lewitan at IBM (where Mandelbrot worked from 1958 until his last days), the films were never released and were mainly used for educational purposes within academia. It is in these early animations that Mandelbrot openly plays with the confluence of the worlds of science and science fiction. The words "The Island of Dr. Mandelbrot (with apologies to H. G. Wells 1896)" appear on the screen for a few seconds, emphasizing the importance of the island metaphor in his work. While Dr. Moreau aspires to create humans from animals, Dr. Mandelbrot uses mathematics to create nature. With gentle, endearing irony, he related his own work to that of a long line of scientists seen as godlike, if weird, creator figures.[16] There is a hint in these first animated simulations of a classic dream of the early pioneers of computer graphics—namely, that they might, with the aid of the computer, create a new world, a second reality.

From early on, the goal of Mandelbrot's visual experiments was to connect mathematics with nature. Using chance as a generator, he was able to produce shapes resembling different sorts of natural formations that cannot be comprehended by means of Euclidean geometry. Looking back, Mandelbrot often described how the sight of these first computer-generated shapes was perceived with a shock of recognition that operated in a manner similar to déjà vu:

> It is impossible to forget the sleepless nights we spent producing the pictures with programs that we had diverted from their intended purpose so as to be able to use them at all. . . . The device was very cumbersome, but when the shapes came out, what a revelation! The pictures were so

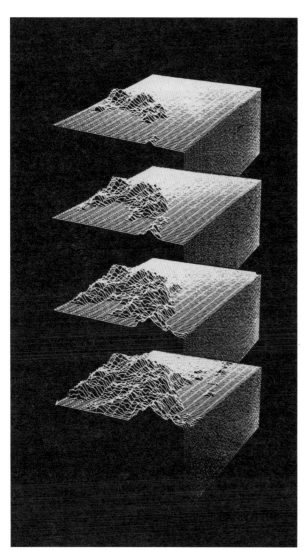

Benoît Mandelbrot and Sigmund Handelman, *Some Views of an Imaginary Continent*, 1975.

imagination, optical illusion, and existence that characterizes, on the one hand, the dichotomy of land and sea and, on the other, the relationship of visibility and invisibility in the realm of representation. Islands form a paradigmatic battleground between scientific method and mythological narrative. The early history of cartography records a telling example of this tension. The islands Gerhard Mercator envisioned in 1569 consisted of outlines drawn into a world populated by sea monsters. His islands are embedded in narratives of discovery and conquest—a melting pot of science and fiction.[13] This visual and epistemological tension inscribed within the notion of islands has not weakened with the arrival of digital visualization; on the contrary, it has gained new relevance. Fractal geometry and the emergence of a theory of complex dynamics in the 1970s would not poor. . . . Even so, there was an overwhelming feeling that what we had drawn was right.[17]

One of the shapes that had inspired this euphoria was a rather modest formation of two black spots with a few smaller surrounding ones of variable size and with uneven contour lines. Reports such as this document the "Columbus feeling" frequently referred to in descriptions of early computer use.[18] At this time, image processing required lots of calculation time. After a long waiting period, images came as surprises. Mandelbrot described how his eye had been overwhelmed with such a strong sense of excitement that, once the new shapes were finally visible, he attempted to relate them to something familiar as a way to ease the tension: "Although we hadn't expected it, relief set in: the curve described the coast of New Zealand and Bounty Island."[19] In another text he noted the image's similarity to cartography was hard to overlook: the top island was reminiscent of Greenland; with a quarter turn, the one on the left looked like Africa; and after a turn of 180 degrees, one could see New Zealand with Bounty Island in the mass of specks.[20] In that same year, Mandelbrot published similar chance shapes in another context, noting that he had now discovered Greece, the mirrored Sea of Okhotsk, the Gulf of Siam, and western Scotland.[21] Mandelbrot relied on an associative interpretive logic in dealing with such ambiguity, cheerfully rotating his images in search of familiar shapes.

It is important to keep in mind, however, that Mandelbrot's imaginative technique to create analogies between mathematics and images did serve as an analytic tool as well. Having spent years testing the effects of various dimensional values in order to determine how he might achieve the greatest simulation of "nature," Mandelbrot arrived at an important mathematical thought solely on the basis of a visual impression. Looking at some of his pictures while preparing the manuscript for what would become *Fractal Geometry*, he once again had the sense that he was looking at landforms. All of a sudden, "I screamed: Stop it, stop it! . . . I see an island, I see a continent. It's amazing—this is Spain, this is Great Britain . . . and then Scandinavia!"[22] Since he had previously used the fractal dimension of 1.3 for such distinct impressions of nature, he now conjectured that these pictures must also have the value 4/3 (rounded to 1.3). That Mandelbrot's intuition was correct was ultimately proved in 2000 by the mathematicians Gregory F. Lawler, Oded Schramm, and Wendelin Werner.[23] This gap between hypothesis and proof was not untypical of Mandelbrot, whose creative, associative way of looking led him to conjectures rather than to rigorous mathematical statements. Lawler himself compared Mandelbrot's approach to that of the archaeologist who digs and makes exciting discoveries but leaves it to others to provide the explanation or the context—or in Lawler's words: "If he had not produced the questions, other people would have not found the answer."[24]

The creation of visual analogies—the pursuit of "analogical seeing"—was the engine that drove Mandelbrot's research and helped him to connect mathematics and images, mathematics and nature. However, his unconventional methods also got him into trouble, more than once. In the years of his first experiments with fractal coastlines, producing pictures took all night. Mandelbrot's speckled geographies were often thrown away the next morning by computer-room operators who, lacking Mandelbrot's flourishing geographical imagination, were unable to relate the shapes to anything familiar and thus believed them to be misprints. This unstable existence and constant threat of being extinguished connect Mandelbrot's figurative islands with his abstract ones.

Islands as Evidence

Publishing can be a cumbersome business. In 1980, when Mandelbrot retrieved the copy-edited proof of his manuscript from the *Annals of the New York Academy of Science*, he could not believe his eyes. Without asking, the editors had modified the central image of the article. They had erased the little specks surrounding the bulbous shape that constituted his main visual argument: "Horrors! It is now free of

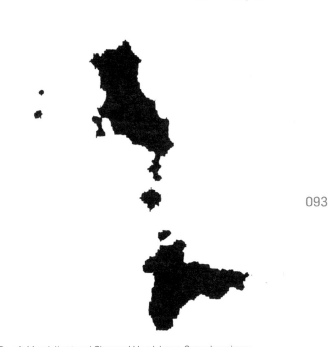

$$D = 1{,}3$$

Benoît Mandelbrot and Sigmund Handelman, *Some Imaginary Coasts*, 1975.

093

Nina Samuel

specks! . . . Clearly, gremlins in the printing business had . . . repeated that evil deed."[25] The image published there for the first time would later be given the name Mandelbrot Set to honor its inventor and would soon make him world famous, inside and outside the mathematics community. In the mid-1980s, it became the most well-known emblem of chaos theory and one of the first scientific icons in the digitalization era. On various occasions, Mandelbrot dubbed the messy speck structure of his images from the Mandelbrot Set "islands," or "offshore islands."[26] Because those islands constituted self-similar replicas of the whole shape, they played an extraordinary role in his fractal theory.[27] However, the small specks were deceptively similar to interference or printer smudges, and they were repeatedly retouched by conscientious computer lab and printshop employees. For that reason, in the years 1980–1981, Mandelbrot got into the habit of posting warnings on his output equipment: "Do *not* clean off the dust specks, they are *real*."[28] According to his own reports, the fact that his early fractal pictures were in constant danger of being erased had infuriated him on many occasions.

The deeper theoretical reason for the resemblance of his visualized fractals with computer errors or dirt is their specific geometric texture, which is in opposition with Euclidean geometry. To stress this distinction, he also called his geometry a science of non-shapes—a "morphology of the amorphous."[29] It suggests that one ought to devote oneself to the irregular shapes beyond the reach of the compass, inasmuch as they are "grainy, hydra-like, in between, pimply, pocky, ramified, seaweedy, strange, tangled, tortuous, wiggly, wispy, wrinkled."[30] This equates his geometrical concept of roughness, which revolutionized our thinking about the shapes of nature.[31] It is summarized in his assertion that "clouds are not spheres, mountains are not cones, coastlines are not circles."[32] According to Mandelbrot, to understand and imitate nature, we need to search off the beaten tracks of Euclid's geometry and have to be "motivated to sniff out the ramifications of those specks of dirt."[33]

The concept of island that is established in fractal geometry differs from the dual scheme of continental and oceanic islands in that the frontier between the ocean and the island is deconstructed. Fractal islands are not finite entities; rather, they are endlessly fissured and rough. Fractal islands are elusive. They reside in the hybrid area between order and disorder. Their borders are infinitely complex and intricately entangled with the surrounding sea. How can one tell where the sea starts and where the island stops? The closer one zooms in on the border area, the more jagged it appears. The fractal concept of island challenges the common notions of boundary and of finite entity. While the border between fractal island and ocean clearly exists, it

can only be approximated—never located in an exact mathematical sense.

Key to understand the epistemic challenge within the fractal islands is taking a closer look at the relation between visualization technique and mathematics. The Mandelbrot Set is at heart nothing but a series of numbers that can be graphically represented within the complex number field. Because complex numbers consist of two components (one real and one imaginary), the picture space of a digital graphic that sits in a coordinate system with its x and y axis allows us to produce a correlation between the invisible equation and the visible surface: each pixel on the screen corresponds to one precisely defined complex number. That said, the discrete, grid-like structure of digital visualization technology has also generated its own zones of insecurity for this correlation: while a nonlinear dynamic structure generally takes up an infinite and continuous space, if it is to be represented digitally, on a computer, it has to be reduced and approximated. Since the calculations inevitably have to be performed with a finite number of iterations, the resulting images always bear traces of a compromise. The encounter between formally infinite mathematics and the finite abilities of the computer (owing to its limited processing power) necessarily produced indefinite areas. As a consequence, pictorial details that seem unrelated or "far apart" on an image may well be connected or "very close" as far as their provable mathematical properties are concerned. In short, visibility and existence in a mathematical sense—what can be seen and what can be rigorously proven—are not the same. This also complicates the relation between detachment and connectedness. The gap between appearance and 'reality' became a serious challenge for Mandelbrot's investigation of his "mathematical islands."

One of the hardest mathematical questions in the early years of Mandelbrot's experimentation concerned the gaps between the surrounding island-speckles and the mainland—the large round shape with the small bulbs in the central part of his set, which Mandelbrot sometimes called a "continent." These components, and especially the mysterious spaces between them, raised serious issues about the mutual dependency of the world of mathematics and the image technologies that generated them. The specks of islands seemingly detached from the main body of the set were declared, in a fateful confusion of image and proof, as a "fact," although this assertion was clearly unproven, as it was not supported by any mathematical theorem. In the accompanying text to Mandelbrot's image, he stated: "A striking fact, which I think is new, becomes apparent here: [the] Figure is made of several disconnected portions."[34] True to his credo regarding the predominance of visual judgment—"seeing is believing"[35]—he had trusted his eyes.[36]

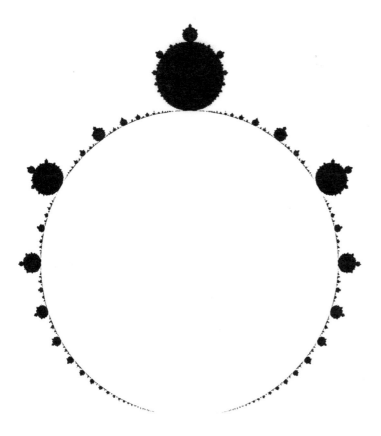

The mathematicians Adrien Douady and John Hubbard would, however, provide counter-evidence in 1982. In an article in *Comptes Rendus*, they determined that fine lines connected the specks with the main body but that at this earlier point in history they could not be made visible: "These islands are in fact attached by threads that evade the computer."[37] Douady compared the complex problem of making these structures visible with trying to see tiny mountain rivulets from an airplane flying overhead.[38] When Mandelbrot was making his experiments, it was technically impossible to draw the connecting lines, or filaments, with the existing graphic programs. There was a built-in impenetrability between the two "planes" of the digital image, its visible surface and the indiscernible columns of numbers that generated the picture (i.e., the operational undersurface that processed the formula).[39] Accordingly, an unbridgeable divide was created between the "islands" and the "continent."

Nonetheless, in 1980, because his detached island-speckles were of such tremendous importance for his mathematical theory, Mandelbrot reinserted the deleted picture details by hand in offprints of the article that he sent to

colleagues.[40] Since he did not see any connecting lines and had unlimited faith in his computer, he did not believe they existed—a belief he reinforced in the drawing. Suddenly, Mandelbrot's "seeing is believing" became "drawing is believing." The digitally produced shape had to be authenticated through drawing in order to exist and to be trusted. By means of his own successive acts of reinterpretation, the same pictorial details mutated from a hint to a proof and finally ended up as the main result: a material trace became mathematical *evidence*.

Nevertheless, the story of the Mandelbrot Set is not one of subjective naiveté, or of confusing pictures with reality. On the contrary, the story raises the question of how one arrives at understanding through computer graphics in an exemplary way. It clearly shows how difficult it can be to maintain a distance between what the eye can see and what can be proved analytically. As the story of a struggle for agreement between observation and theory, it illustrates equally clearly how necessary it is for the eye to be schooled in pictures and how risky thinking inspired by pictures can be. In short, it says something about the fundamental ambiguity of visual perception.

095

Nina Samuel

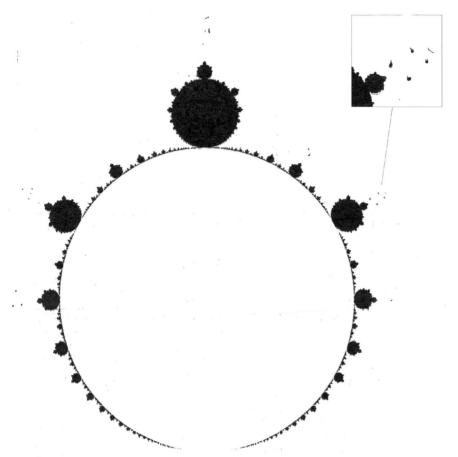

Benoît Mandelbrot, offprint from the first publication of the Mandelbrot Set, 1980, with specks drawn in by hand.

Chaos and fractals introduce an antidichotomic turn to our thinking about the shapes of nature. Characterized by their own geometric in-betweenness, which is manifest in their broken dimension D, they operate structurally between oppositions and resolve their conflict. In fractal theory, islands are used as paradigmatic entities that exemplify this tendency. Fractal islands introduce rough, irregular shapes that had not been recognized earlier as worthy of geometrical investigation. In this sense they celebrate the form of the antiform. Likewise, in chaos theory, order and disorder are not conceived as antagonists but rather as part of a transitional zone that invites exploration. Referring to mathematical inventions of the 19th century, islands as finite objects served as an initial point for fractal theory to introduce the idea of an infinite borderline. While fractal islands are finite–infinite objects, they are also connected–detached. Mathematically speaking, they are connected with the mainland of the Mandelbrot Set, yet they can also be considered detached: their bridge to the mainland is infinitely complex, so that reaching one of these islands would take an endless amount of time. An imagined pedestrian would never reach

her destination. Hence, they undermine the traditional categorization of continental and oceanic islands.

* * *

Islands, in Mandelbrot's work, exemplify the use and the power of pictures in science in a twofold manner. On the one hand, there is the attempt to generate figurative cartographies of chance and stimulate the viewer's imagination: pictures can release a productive, imaginative power that advances our thinking. On the other, images also posses a seductive and potentially ungovernable energy, one that encourages frictions between vision and thought and potentially even causes egregious errors. These two sides of pictures are inseparable and equally necessary. Mandelbrot's "seeing is believing" fails to give due credit to the particular role that the visual plays in the process of scientific cognition. If seeing amounts to nothing more than believing, it can hardly function as a thinking tool. On the contrary, seeing should be doubting. It must stir the imagination if it is to generate new insights. In that way pictures can serve as the raw material for thinking, or as thought thresholds for the mind.

01. Alfred Russel Wallace, *Island Life, or the Phenomenon and Causes of Insular Faunas and Floras. Including a Revision and Attempted Solution of the Problem of Geological Climates*, 2nd ed. (London: Macmillan, 1895), 242–43.

02. Ibid., 418.

03. H. G. Wells, "The Influence of Islands on Variation," *Saturday Review* 80 (August 17, 1895): 204–05.

04. H. G. Wells, *The Island of Doctor Moreau* (Garden City, NY: Garden City Publishing, 1896).

05. Benoît Mandelbrot, "How Long is the Coast of Britain? Statistical Self-Similarity and Fractional Dimension," *Science* 156 (1967): 636–38.

06. Compare Martin Gardner, "In Which 'Monster' Curves Force Redefinition of the Word 'Curve,'" *Scientific American*, December 1976, 124–33; with the more detailed, Klaus Thomas Volkert, *Die Krise der Anschauung: Eine Studie zu formalen und heuristischen Verfahren in der Mathematik seit 1850* (Göttingen: Vandenhoeck & Ruprecht, 1986); Klaus Thomas Volkert, "Die Geschichte der pathologischen Funktionen: Ein Beitrag zur Entstehung der mathematischen Methodologie," *Archive for History of Exact Sciences* 37, no. 1 (1987): 193–232; and Herbert Mehrtens, *Moderne–Sprache–Mathematik: Eine Geschichte des Streits um die Grundlagen der Disziplin und des Subjekts formaler Systeme* (Frankfurt am Main: Suhrkamp, 1990).

07. Charles Hermite to Thomas Joannes Stieltjes, May 20, 1893, published in *Correspondance d'Hermite et de Stieltjes*, vol. 2, ed. Benjamin Baillaud and Henry Bourget (Paris: Gauthier-Villars, 1905), 318.

08. Henri Poincaré, *Science et Méthode* (Paris: Flammarion, 1908), 132.

09. Benoît Mandelbrot, "Intermittent Turbulence and Fractal Dimension: Kurtosis and the Spectral Exponent 5/3+B," in *Turbulence and Navier Stokes Equations*, ed. Roger Temam Lecture Notes in Mathematics 565 (New York: Springer 1976), 121.

10. For his broken Dimension D—the "Hausdorff Dimension," an important feature of fractals—Mandelbrot adapted a definition formulated in Felix Hausdorff, "Dimension und Äusseres Mass," *Mathematische Annalen* 79 (1919): 157–79.

11. For a historical overview of chaos theory, see Ralph Abraham and Yoshisuke Ueda, eds., World Scientific Series on Nonlinear Science, series A, vol. 39, *The Chaos-Avantgarde: Memories of the Early Days of Chaos Theory* (Singapore: World Scientific, 2000). Fractals and chaos had been popularized widely though the publication of heavily illustrated books, see for example Heinz-Otto Peitgen and Peter H. Richter, eds., *The Beauty of Fractals: Images of Complex Dynamical Systems* (Berlin and Heidelberg: Springer, 1986). Fractals and chaos are closely related. You could say fractals provide the geometry of chaos and chaos expands fractals in time. Fractals originated in mathematics and geometry, while chaos is more closely linked to physics.

12. This text is based on and uses excerpts from Nina Samuel, ed., *The Islands of Benoît Mandelbrot: Fractals, Chaos, and the Materiality of Thinking* (New York: Yale University Press, 2012); Nina Samuel, *Die Form des Chaos: Bild und Erkenntnis in der komplexen Dynamik und der fraktalen Geometrie* (Paderborn: Wilhelm Fink, 2014).

13. On Gerhard Mercator and his map *Nova et Aucta Orbis Terrae Descriptio ad Usum Navigantium Emendate Accommodata*, see Gloria Meynen, "Die Insel als Kulturtechnik (Ein Entwurf)," *Zeitschrift für Medienwissenschaft* 2, no. 1 (2010): 79.

14. Benoît Mandelbrot, *Les objets fractals: Forme, hasard et dimension* (Paris: Flammarion, 1975), 113.

15. Mandelbrot, *Les objets fractals*, 112; see also Benoît Mandelbrot, *Fractals: Form, Chance, and Dimension* (San Francisco: W. H. Freeman and Company, 1977), 221.

16. For this motif, see Horst Bredekamp, "Der Mensch als 'zweiter Gott': Motive der Wiederkehr eines kunsttheoretischen Topos im Zeitalter der Bildsimulation," in *Bilder bewegen: Von der Kunstkammer zum Endspiel*, ed. Jörg Probst (Berlin: Wagenbach, 2007), 106–20.

17. Benoît Mandelbrot, "Les inattendus des fractales," *Pour la Science* 234 (April 1997): 10–11; Monte Davis, "Profile of Benoît B. Mandelbrot," *Omni Magazine*, May 2, 1984, http://users.math .yale.edu/mandelbrot/web_pdfs/profile.pdf.

18. See Peter Glaser, "Das Kolumbus-Gefühl. Entdeckungen in einer virtuellen Welt," in *Computerkultur, oder The Beauty of Bit & Byte*, ed. Michael Weisser (Bremen: TMS-Verlag, 1989), 19–40.

19. Mandelbrot, "Les inattendus des fractales," 10–11.

20. Mandelbrot, *Les objets fractals*, 116.

21. Benoît Mandelbrot, "On the Geometry of Homogeneous Turbulence, with Stress on the Fractal Dimension of the Iso-surfaces of Scalars," *Journal of Fluid Mechanics* 72, no. 2 (1975): 405.

22. Benoît Mandelbrot, interview with the author, April 2008.

23. Gregory F. Lawler, Oded Schramm, and Wendelin Werner, "The Dimension of the Planar Brownian Frontier is 4/3," math/0010165, 2000, http://arxiv.org/abs/math/0010165. The three mathematicians received a Nobel Prize for their mathematical proof.

24. Gregory F. Lawler, e-mail correspondence with the author, February 2, 2012.

25. Benoît Mandelbrot, *Fractals and Chaos: The Mandelbrot Set and Beyond* (New York: Springer, 2004), 22.

26. Ibid., 14.

27. Self-similarity was already key in the founding text of fractal geometry. See Mandelbrot, "How Long is the Coast of Britain? Statistical Self-similarity and Fractional Dimension."

28. Mandelbrot, *Fractals and Chaos*, 22.

29. Mandelbrot, *The Fractal Geometry of Nature*, 1.

30. Mandelbrot, *The Fractal Geometry of Nature*, 5.

31. See John Brockman, "A Theory of Roughness: A Talk with Benoît Mandelbrot," *EDGE* 151 (2004): 1–7, www.edge.org.

32. Mandelbrot, *The Fractal Geometry of Nature*, 1.

33. Mandelbrot, *Fractals and Chaos*, 23. Views critical of his equation of fractals and nature can be found in David Avnir et al., "Is the Geometry of Nature Fractal?" *Science* 279, no. 5347 (1998): 39–40; and Steven G. Krantz, "Fractal Geometry," The Mathematical Intelligencer 11, no. 4 (1989): 12–16.

34. Benoît Mandelbrot, "Fractal Aspects of the Iteration of z → λz (1-z), for Complex λ and z," in *Nonlinear Dynamics*, ed. Robert H. G. Helleman, *Annals of the New York Academy of Sciences* 357 (New York: New York Academy of Sciences, 1980), 250.

35. Mandelbrot, *The Fractal Geometry of Nature*, 21.

36. Mandelbrot remarked elsewhere, "before beginning to understand what fractals are, one should know what they look like." Benoît Mandelbrot, "Fractals and the Geometry of Nature," in *1981 Britannica Yearbook of Science and the Future* (Chicago: Encyclopaedia Britannica, 1980), 168.

37. Adrien Douady and John Hamal Hubbard, "Itération des polynômes quadratiques complexes," *Comptes Rendus* (Paris) 294, no. 1 (1982): 123.

38. Adrien Douady, telephone interview with the author, January 7, 2005.

39. For a discussion of the "two planes" of the digital image, see Frieder Nake, "Das doppelte Bild," *Bildwelten des Wissens: Kunsthistorisches Jahrbuch für Bildkritik* 3 (2005): 40–50.

40. Mandelbrot, *Fractals and Chaos*, 37.

Image Credits

092: Benoît Mandelbrot, Les objets fractals (Paris: Flammarion 1975), 113.

093: Benoît Mandelbrot, Les objets fractals (Paris: Flammarion 1975), 116.

095: Benoît Mandelbrot, "Fractal aspects of the iteration of z → λz (1-z) for complex λ and z," in *Non-linear Dynamics*. ed. Robert H. G. Helleman, *Annals of the New York Academy of Sciences* 357 (1980): 250.

096: Scan from John Hubbard. Private collection. Zoom-in detail: Bard Graduate Center. Decorative Arts, Design History, Material Culture, New York, NY.

Nina Samuel

A Stroll between
Fields and Objects

Stan Allen,
in conversation
with Daniel Daou &
Pablo Pérez-Ramos

New Geographies: We would like to begin by looking back a few years, to 1997 and the publication of your article "From Object to Field."[01] This was a critical text in architectural theory, as it signaled a shift from geometry to algebra in architectural design: in other words, a shift from strategies based on the division of wholes to strategies based on the aggregation of parts. More importantly for our project, the characterization of the field as fundamentally horizontal implied ideas about continuity and surface, which made that essay key in discussions around the relationship between architecture and landscape in the years that followed. In 2009, however, as the Dean of the Princeton School of Architecture, you organized the conference "Landform Building,"[02] where the accent shifted from the field back to the object—to the specific building. Can you talk about this *stroll* from the object to the field, and back again, to the object?

Stan Allen: I like your use of the term *stroll*. Maybe it was a bit of a random walk. From my current perspective though, it is a false dilemma to have to choose between objects and fields. At this point in our work, there are projects that are invested in the idea of the object, and there are projects invested in the idea of the field. Sometimes there's even an overlap within specific projects: objects arrayed in a field also need to be designed. So one simple answer is that these are both techniques that are available to us as architects and there are times when field strategies are appropriate, and there are times when object strategies are appropriate. I don't see a conflict in keeping both strategies in play.

In our recent project for the 2016 Venice Biennale, for example, we ended up working with field strategies. That decision came from the specifics of the challenge we were given: the re-use of the Albert Kahn-designed Packard Factory in Detroit—a vast piece of industrial architecture, now in ruins. What is extraordinary about the Packard Plant is the delirium of serial production that belonged to the first machine age. A repetitive field of identical slabs, columns, and windows is a counterpart to the cars that rolled off the assembly line. We didn't approach the project with any preconceptions; instead, the artifact we were confronted with led us to a field strategy. I would say that, to a large degree, we are dedicated to taking projects on their own terms, and sometimes that brings us back to field strategies.

There is, however, a larger arc that speaks to the thematic of your journal in terms of fields, process, and ecology. I first used the term *field conditions* in a studio I taught at Columbia in 1994. My engagement with field conditions was driven in those early years by a reflection on the problem of urban context, and it preceded my engagement with landscape and ecology. It was a couple of years later that I moderated a panel at the Storefront for Art and Architecture in New York on Dutch architecture. Inevitably, landscape had to figure into my thinking about the Dutch architecture of the 1990s. That's where I met Winy Maas, and I first used the term *artificial ecologies* in a piece I wrote on the work of MVRDV around 1996. So the starting point was architecture and urbanism, and an early intuition about process and ecology. The specific engagement with landscape came a little later, out of the collaboration with James Corner that started in 1999. This is to say, I had been thinking about these ideas in slightly different forms before landscape really became a protagonist in our work.

By the time we organized "Landform Building" in 2009, the term *landscape urbanism* had been around for over a decade, and the conference aimed to be not so much a rejection of landscape urbanism as an opportunity to rethink the interdisciplinary claims of landscape urbanism in relationship to the specific agency of architecture. Two of the attractions of landscape in the 1990s were its affiliation with the surface strategies in architecture and its potential to create smooth connectivity among multiple programs. But architecture—in my mind at least—is necessarily composed of objects and boundaries. So there was a shift in my thinking around that time motivated by a desire to say that architects had learned certain lessons from landscape through the experiment of landscape urbanism. But there was also a danger of losing the specific agency of architecture—an agency that is invested in the creation of boundaries, partitions, and free-standing objects, as much as movement, connectivity, surface, and flows.

I would hope that this process, from 1994 to 1997 to 2009, all the way to the present, is not so much about the oscillation between fields and objects as it is a kind of incremental building on both concepts. So when we returned self-consciously to the object (I am thinking here about the project I did in 2010 for the New Maribor Art Gallery), there was a sense that we could incorporate the lessons from landscape and field conditions into a building that was more of an object: a building invested in its iconic presence as an institution in the city, and a building that both structurally and programmatically is as much about sectional differentiation and modulated space as it is about the city as a network of flows.

NG: We would like you to elaborate further on the concept of *boundary*, which you have already mentioned along with the object. In order to do so, we would like to quote Kenneth Frampton, who ended his 1999 Raoul Wallenberg Lecture, "Megaform as Urban Landscape," by citing Vittorio Gregotti, who says: "The origin of architecture is not the primitive hut, but the marking of ground, to establish a cosmic order around the surrounding chaos of nature."[03] In the 2011 *Landform Building* volume, which followed the conference, you echo Gregotti when you write that architects need to remember that "the marking out of territory and the separation of a protected interior space from nature are founding acts of architecture; if architects are experts in anything, they are experts at limits and boundaries."[04] How do you position these ideas in an intellectual context where architectural thinking on the large scale is governed by systemic approaches based on flows and connectivity?

SA: This was another important component in that shift we were discussing. In the 1990s and early 2000s, there was a fascination with smooth connectivity, with flows, with emerging questions about chaos and complexity theories, all underwritten by the work of [Gilles] Deleuze and [Félix] Guattari. And at the same time, there was this very attractive idea that architectural connectivity could parallel the rise of digital media and global interconnectivity. In architecture schools there was a kind of blanket assumption that connectivity was always better than separation.[05]

I think that as we entered the 21st century—and in particular, after September 11, 2001—a number of people started looking at this assumption with skepticism. Skepticism from an architectural point of view, I would say, but also from a political point of view. Michael Hays, for example, used the term *ideological smoothing* as early as the 1990s, pointing out that the fascination with smoothness and connectivity plays right into the hands of global capitalism, a system that demands smoothness and connectivity, not limits, boundaries, and separation. If you looked at the world post-September 11, it also became very clear that this utopia of connectivity was simply that: a utopia. The facts on the ground were about bloody conflicts over boundaries and borders. If architecture cannot account for that, then what? If you ignore the question of boundaries, boundaries will come back to haunt you.

It is really about understanding how to take architecture's expertise on the boundary—on walls and separation, on marking out territory—and use it as a powerful tool to reconsider and reconfigure both boundaries and borders. It has to do with rethinking the critical power of separation. Boundaries can exclude, but they can also mark out free space for play or invention. As architects, we should be experts at boundaries and their multiple configurations. We need to critically focus on the knowledge that belongs to the discipline of architecture, as opposed to loosely accepting the utopian idea that "everything is connected" will always be a good thing.

NG: And what about boundaries and encounters between design disciplines? The disappearance of boundaries has also entered the conversation on this type of differentiation. In

relation to the blurring of disciplinary boundaries heralded in mainstream discourse, you have asserted that the most interesting work happens where disciplines come together in the spaces of *transdisciplinarity*—a word used deliberately in opposition to *interdisciplinarity*. Can you explain your ideas behind this?

A Vertical Botanic Garden, US Pavilion, Venice Biennale, 2016. Bird's eye view of site.

SA: Yes. Both *Landform Building* and our Maribor project had to do with recovering the agency of architecture. For a few years we had been working on large-scale urbanism and landscape, and it is just a fact of life that you do not do one of these projects without a large team of experts. You need expertise in areas where architects may not be so knowledgeable: you need hydrologists, civil engineers, ecologists, finance people, etc. What I am critical of is a kind of weak interdisciplinarity where architects try to become experts in, say, economics or sociology. What I mean by transdisciplinarity is the interchange that happens when everybody is very clear about their own area of expertise and can enter into a conversation. The most interesting conversations are always with others who are also experts in their field. It's only then that areas of overlap and exchange appear. Instead of working between disciplines, where perhaps no one is an expert, you start from a clear disciplinary basis and work *across* disciplines to create new territory.

Stan Allen

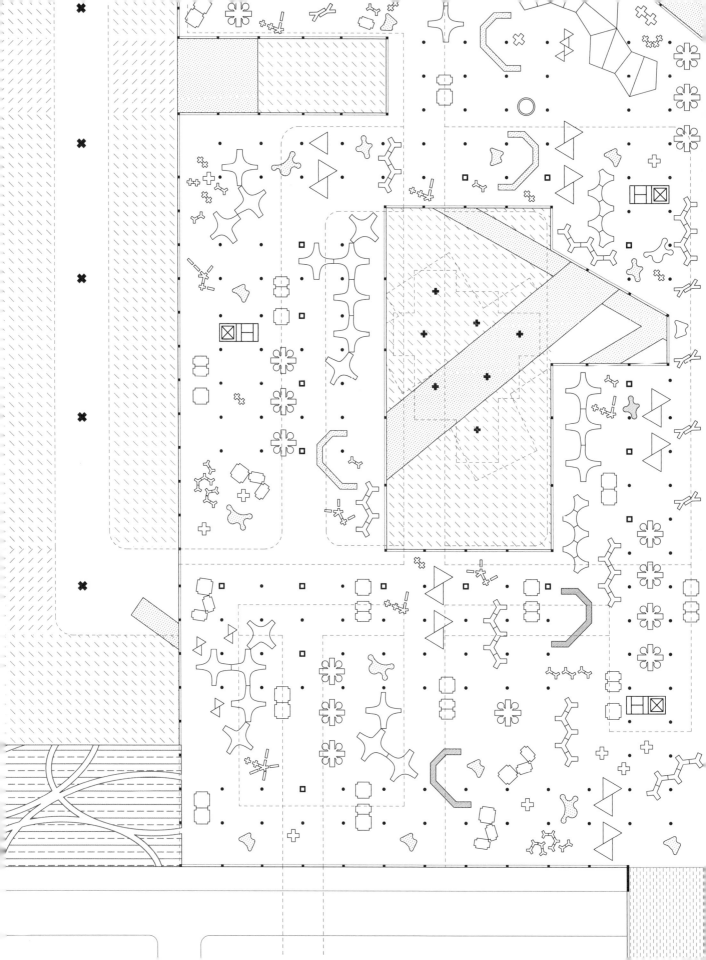

NG: In 2004 James Corner published the essay "Not Unlike Life Itself" in reaction, partially, to Michael Speaks's 2002 essay "Design Intelligence."[06] In seeking to recover the cultural efficacy of the discipline and ensure its professional survival, both Corner and Speaks advocated leaving behind theory and the negativity of criticism in favor of a more opportunistic "design intelligence."

George Baird offers a good reconstruction of what came to be known as the post-critical debate, fueled by Corner and Speaks, in his 2004 overview article "Criticality and its Discontents."[07] Baird linked the dissatisfaction with architecture's reliance on critical theory back to the 1995 piece "Whatever Happened to Urbanism," in which Rem Koolhaas complains that "according to [Jacques] Derrida we cannot be Whole, according to [Jean] Baudrillard we cannot be Real, according to [Paul] Virilio we cannot be There."[08] He goes on to suggest that urbanism has to become a way of thinking that "simply accepts what is there." It is a very clear call to eschew the perceived negativity of critical theory.

Corner's piece is important because, when he says that ecological metaphors are as "topical for business and management as they are in biology, and that designers have to adopt them if they are to survive," he is effectively bridging ecological metaphors with the survivalist notion of design intelligence. In fact, we interpret the title of his essay as suggesting a form of "capitalist realism," to quote Mark Fisher, where the market is ecology, and ecology is "life itself."[09] Part of our goal with this issue of *New Geographies* is a critical revision of the way in which the metaphors of ecology have been naturalized and instrumentalized within the debate around disciplinarity. Again, in "From Object to Field," you quote from Robert Morris's "Anti Form" (1968): "European art, since Cubism, has been a history of permuting relationships about the general premise that *relationships should remain critical.*" You continue, "Perhaps a more radical shift is required."[10] What exactly are you suggesting?

SA: Your question brings up a lot of different issues. Let me speak to three of them. First of all, I was part of those debates in the early 2000s around the post-critical. I was a participant in the 2000 "Pragmatist Imagination" conference at the Museum of Modern Art in New York (MoMA) and, in the larger scheme of things, my allegiances are with Speaks and Corner. I thought that debate was already belated at that time, and it certainly still is today. None of the protagonists are going to change their ideas. I think in the end it's better to simply speak of competing research projects. So for many reasons, I don't want to revisit that debate.

The one thing I would probably insist on, together with Bob Somol and Sarah Whiting, is that I have never identified with the post-critical, but instead with the projective. Architecture is not so much about maintaining a distance, a critical view vis-à-vis reality, as much as it is about the potential of imagining and implementing alternative realities. In order to propose an alternative reality, of course, you have to have a critical reading of the present, but that's just the first step; architecture is fundamentally projective, oriented toward the future.

Part of my skepticism also has to do with a sense of history: the critical theory of the 1980s and the 1990s did its work. It was crucial at that time, but today we need to build on that work. We can move forward with new theoretical models, not continually cover the same ground. There is an interview with Paul Rabinow in which he says that "architects are no longer the technicians or engineers of the three great variables: territory, communication, and speed." He goes on to say, "I do not think that there is anything that is functionally—by its very nature—absolutely liberating. Liberty is a *practice* . . . It can never be inherent in the structure of things to guarantee the exercise of freedom. The guarantee of freedom is freedom."[11] That is a healthy attitude to me; it's not about simply giving in to things as they are, but saying the potential for change and resistance is located in the citizens and users, not in the architect. There are, quite frankly, much larger forces at work, within which architecture is relatively powerless. So in that sense, I am certainly sympathetic to both Corner and Speaks, in terms of being opportunistic. We have to be opportunistic precisely in order to

Opposite page: A Vertical Botanic Garden. Plan detail.

Stan Allen

find those moments where, as architects, we can create the potential for the citizens to resist and change the status quo.

Again, for me, it is important to be very specific about the agency of architecture within the larger scheme of things. Koolhaas likes to point out that architects are simultaneously very powerful and completely powerless. If one understands where architects can be powerful and where architects are powerless, one has a much clearer approach to these questions.

Now, to turn to the notion of ecology and, as you say, the instrumentalization of ecology. In architecture we use the word *ecology* without actually examining the debates that play out within ecological circles. When you look at those discussions, you realize that there is not one ecology but several. Is ecology a hard or soft science? Is it philosophy, literature, or an ethic? Just as there are within our discipline, there are fierce ongoing debates among ecologists. Take, for example, the question of whether nature, if left to itself, would return to a steady state or remain in constant flux. This question has real-world consequences. Decisions about environmental policy or forest management can depend on where you stand in this debate, and ecologists cannot agree among themselves. So while I agree we need to be cautious about the instrumentalization of ecology, I would argue that it is precisely the instrumentality of ecology—its deep connection to urgent issues on the ground today—that makes it a useful resource for architects. The rich interplay of theory, research, and practice it contains is not a bad model for our field.

NG: Now that you've touched on the subject, we would like to talk about the transition from ecological models to geological ones. Although the word ecology does not appear in "From Field to Object," the text is considered a keystone in the engagement of complex systems ecology in design. For the past two decades, architects and designers have used ecology as a master model to explain the interrelationship between the city and the landscape, often emphasizing change and process at the expense of permanence and form. You, by contrast, have rejected the entrenched assumption that ecological (and biological) metaphors are the only ones that can plausibly involve architecture in today's interpretations of context or the environment. Instead, you propose a shift toward the geological, which involves a stronger notion of permanence and form. Why?

SA: There are two components to that shift. In your first question, you spoke about the "Field Conditions" piece from the 1990s as marking a shift from the culture of geometry, topology, division, and deformation to a methodology that has to do with algebra, addition, and part-to-whole relationships. That was generous of you, but I don't think the field shifted along with me. I have an ongoing debate with Scott Cohen around this. He is fond of quoting Valerio Olgiati, who says that architects can be divided into "adders" and "dividers." Scott is a divider; I'm an adder. Both camps are alive and well. Again, we have here two parallel research projects, and having both makes the debate more interesting. So I would say that addition is simply a direction which has proven useful and interesting to me. I think one should be quite honest about where sensibility and aesthetic preference enter in: I like flat, faceted surfaces as opposed to curvilinear form—although I would also insist that they are more logical in as much as they are easier to construct.

What I would argue is this: for the past two decades at least, the biological metaphor has been dominant—the appeal to animate form, ecology, and dynamic shapes. For me at least, it goes back to the 1990s, when Greg Lynn was first using digital software at Columbia to model biomorphic processes in design. At that time we talked a lot about the "stopping problem." If you have this language of flowing movement and deforming geometrical primitives, when do you decide to stop? At what moment do you determine the flow is going to be frozen? I think Greg was quite honest. He said, "well, you do it when it looks right." But that always seemed, to me at least, somewhat unsatisfying. You had these moving systems, and at

104

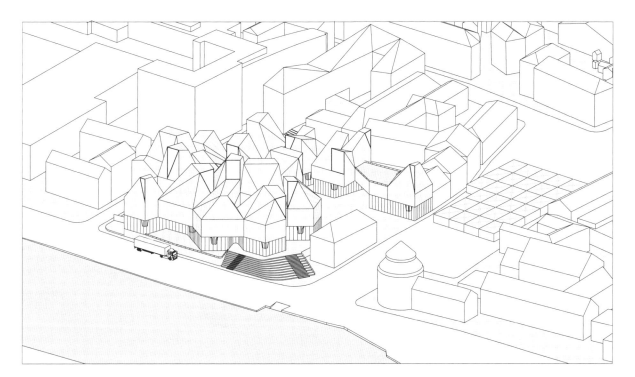

New Maribor Art Gallery, axonometric in context.

a certain point you froze them, and at that point the process inevitably became metaphorical: the movement is implied or depicted but never actual.

And in this sense the computer-driven work of the 1990s is actually very similar to the deconstructivist work of the previous decade, which was about implied collisions and fragmentation. I remember, for example, during the installation of the deconstructivism show at MoMA in 1988, Zaha Hadid wanted to mount one of her models as if it had crashed through one of the museum's partitions. In order to do that, they had to cut out the sheetrock on both sides, very carefully place this (actually quite delicate) model in the opening, plaster the hole back up, and then meticulously repaint the wall. The result was a still picture of the violent act of an architectural model crashing through the wall. The idea that architecture becomes a snapshot of some sort of movement or process is something that persisted from deconstructivism right through the digital and those invested in flows, movement, and animation. You always had a condition where some sort of dynamic process was interrupted at a certain arbitrary moment and then frozen. My work has never been about that sense of implied or arrested movement, and perhaps it is inevitable that I turned to geology. Architecture is hard, stubborn, and mineral; persistent in time and slow to change. I would say that architecture is less like "life itself" and more like the ground, or the platform upon which the dynamism of life unfolds. That's one part of the geological argument.

As for the second part: if you can argue that architecture is invested in permanence and stability, then you can also argue for what Jane Bennett, in her brilliant book *Vibrant Matter*, calls a *vitalist materiality*.[12] For me to insist on the fundamentally mineral character of buildings and cities does not necessarily consign them to the realm of dead matter but rather requires that both life and materiality be reconceived. For Bennett, it is simply unproductive to divide the world into animate life on the one hand and inanimate matter on the other. She proposes instead that we pay close attention to rates of change. She looks at things like the history of metallurgy and suggests that you can think of metal—a supposedly hard, inert material—as something that's alive and moving, and this is happening at the molecular structure. It's happening when materials deform or crack, it's happening in the slow transformations of rock and soil over time through uplift or erosion.

105

Stan Allen

Pilgrimage Church, Neviges,
Germany, Gottfried Böhm, 1968.

This is a really rich, interesting way to rethink architecture's relationship to materiality, and it gets us out of the phenomenological essentialism of materials as inert and unchanging. Instead it views matter as endowed with a kind of life, a vitality, that is visible in the crystalline forms of the geological. And if you do that, you have to give up the model of human subjects imposing their will over inanimate objects and pay closer attention to the life of things.

NG: About this tension between the dynamism of processes and the inescapable fixity of architecture, we would like to discuss the question of processes vis-à-vis specificity. This volume is critical of process narratives in contemporary landscape and urbanism that put the accent on open-endedness, uncertainty, emergence, indeterminacy, and so on. In the last decade, one of the drawings that has been most widely used to illustrate these narratives of open-endedness is the "Emergence through Adaptive Management" diagram of ecological succession that first appeared in your proposal for the Downsview Park competition, which you did in collaboration with James Corner's Field Operations and ecologist Nina-Marie

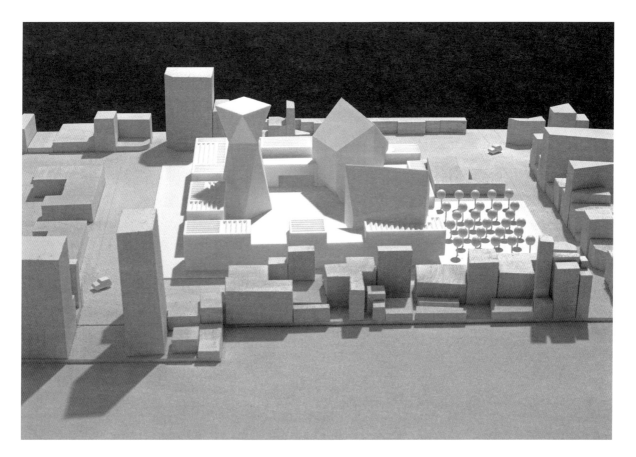

Lister. In this diagram a diverse and complex ecosystem seems to simply emerge, or "naturally" occur. You have used this project, however, to discuss the idea of "directed indeterminacy," according to which the highest conditions of flexibility are always reached through specificity. Can you please talk a little bit about this?

Tainan Art Museum, bird's eye view of site.

SA: Yes, around the time of the Downsview Park competition there was a lot of fascination with emergent systems and self-organization: the idea that somehow the logic will just bubble up from conditions that are out there in the field, and that the architect's job is simply to identify those conditions and put them in relationship with one another. This was true of all the entries to some degree.

But if you look at the literature of ecology, you realize that dynamic ecological systems can only flourish in relation to very specific initial conditions. If there is not enough information embedded in the system, there won't be anything to trigger change, and the system will just die. Conversely, if there is too much information in the system, there will be cycles of overload, and the system may crash. There is a sweet spot in the middle where there is sufficient information in the system to trigger the dynamism, change, feedback loops, and interactivity that will lead to adaptation processes and increasing levels of diversity within the system. But if you do not have a sufficient degree of precision and specificity in the system to begin with, that process will never take off.

At Downsview we proposed a very specific set of initial conditions, which had to do with movement and circulation, how we sculpted the landscape surface, and where we had located major programmatic elements. This initial state of the project was a designed condition; it did not emerge bottom-up from the on-site conditions. It was imposed by us as architects, from the outside. It's from this point on that the possibility of an emergent field

Stan Allen

arises. Part of the knowledge we possess as architects, landscape architects, and urbanists is that there are configurations that are fundamentally more open to change and more adaptive than others. Part of what we do in our work is study and understand different kinds of configurations at this scale. We argued that we hit the sweet spot at Downsview—that the initial moves we made would have been sufficient to trigger a series of changes that would have grown the landscape over time.

Now, another part of the answer concerns whether those conditions are visible; some of them are. For instance, the specific depth and dimension of the corrugations in the areas for water retention: principles of hydrology and soil chemistry and porosity determine that this slope works and that slope doesn't, that certain plants will grow here and other plants won't. You could probably make similar arguments about program: people will or will not congregate here. These are very specific design decisions with concrete consequences in the world.

But there is another aspect to consider, which is that somebody has to manage that ecology. It means that we have to design the process and think about the organizational structure of something like a public trust or public–private partnership that is going to take care of the park during its long lifespan. In other words, while some design decisions are physical, others have to do with the organizational logic of the system. This is part of the expanded field of expertise that is needed today to deal with large-scale projects. It's about management, organizational know-how, and communication. All of these are implied in the "design" of one of these large-scale urban assemblages, or pieces of landscape.

NG: We have talked about disciplinarity and criticality. For our last question, we would like to talk about imagination, and about topology as a potential heuristic model for architecture. In *The Topological Imagination*, Angus Fletcher talks about what he calls the "ethics of scale."[13] He explains that topology has never been concerned with magnitudes: it merely relates to properties of surface regardless of size. We think this is a poignant observation, especially since, as you mention, there is a difference between thinking in the abstract and making decisions in the real world, which has consequences.

We recently discovered the mathematical field of mereotopology, which is a hybrid of topology (the study of qualitative properties such as convergence, connectedness, and openness, that remain unvaried under certain transformations) and mereology (the study of part-to-part relationships). So mereotopology studies not only the relationship of parts to parts and wholes, but also the properties of the boundaries between parts. In this sense, and to conclude our stroll between fields and objects, would you feel that "mereotopological imagination" would more fairly characterize the sort of parallel project you spoke about earlier?

SA: [*Laughs*] Well I have to admit, the first I heard of the term was when I looked over your notes for the interview, so thank you for that. It certainly is something that interests me, and I'll give two quick responses.

Many times I have had this experience of taking a book on topology or some other scientific field and thinking, "this is going to be great." You expect it to be full of suggestive diagrams and images, and then you open it and it's full of equations! And it doesn't mean anything to us. I'm flippant about this, but in a way it is a real issue. Historically (and despite the use of the computer, I think this is still the case), nothing gets into architecture except through the filter of the graphic—by way of diagrams or drawings. If you can't draw it, it doesn't have architectural agency. I know this is changing, but for us, even though everything we do is on the computer, and we occasionally use scripting, at a certain point it results in a drawing. And as I investigated mereotopology, despite a lot of suggestive concepts, I just didn't find it very rich, graphically. We have to remember that architecture is still a crude medium compared to the fluidity of mathematics.

Jeff Kipnis used to say that architecture is continually defining itself as a defective form of another discipline—architecture as defective sociology, architecture as defective sculpture, architecture as defective philosophy, or in this case, architecture as defective mathematics. I think that was a plea on Kipnis's part to ask whether there is another habit of mind that we might cultivate as architects. Which is to ask, what is the specific intelligence of architecture on its own? Is it, for example, graphic instruments and the development of drawing techniques that might allow us to work with complex topological forms, not necessarily expressed in equations and pure mathematics, but which create significant architectural consequences and consequences in the world? That is a necessary part of architectural expertise and deserves closer attention.

But the key word here is imagination, actually. In many instances we fall into these political discussions that are based on the impossibility of reconciling different points of view. One of the things that the creative disciplines can do is extend the horizon of imagination. We can propose relationships and possibilities that actually haven't been articulated yet. I do insist that architecture has to deal with serious pragmatic conditions in the present, but there's an aspect of our discipline that is involved in expanding the horizon of the imagination, and we always want to hold onto that possibility.

01. Stan Allen, "Field Conditions," in *Points + Lines* (New York: Princeton Architectural Press, 1999).

02. The "Landform Building: Architecture's New Terrain" conference took place at the Princeton School of Architecture in April 2009 and was followed by the 2011 publication of a book with the same title.

03. This citation of Vittorio Gregotti can be found in Kenneth Frampton, *Megaform as Urban Landscape: 1999 Raoul Wallenberg Lecture* (Ann Arbor: University of Michigan, 1999), 42.

04. Stan Allen, "From the Biological to the Geological," in *Landform Building: Architecture's New Terrain*, ed. Stan Allen and Marc McQuade (Baden and Princeton, NJ: Lars Müller Publishers, Princeton University School of Architecture, 2011), 34.

05. See Michael Hays, "Architecture Theory, Media and the Question of Audience," *Assemblage* 27 (August 1995): 45.

06. James Corner, "Not Unlike Life Itself: Landscape Strategy Now" *Harvard Design Magazine* 21 (Fall/Winter 2004): 32–34, and Michael Speaks, "Design Intelligence: Part 1, Introduction," *A+U* (December 2002): 10–18.

07. George Baird, "'Criticality' and Its Discontents," *Harvard Design Magazine* 21 (Fall/Winter 2004): 16–21.

08. Rem Koolhaas, "Whatever Happened to Urbanism?," in *S, M, L, XL* (New York: Monacelli Press, 1995), 967.

09. Mark Fisher, *Capitalist Realism: Is There No Alternative?* (Winchester, UK: Zero Books, 2009).

10. Quoted in Allen, *From Object to Field*, 101. Emphasis added.

11. Simon During, ed., *The Cultural Studies Reader* (London and New York: Routledge, 1993), 135.

12. Jane Bennett, *Vibrant Matter: A Political Ecology of Things* (Durham: Duke University Press, 2010).

13. Angus Fletcher, *The Topological Imagination: Spheres, Edges, and Islands* (Cambridge, MA: Harvard University Press, 2016).

Image Credits

101, 102, 105, 107: SAA/Stan Allen Architect.

On the Limits of Process: The Case for Precision in Landscape

Anita Berrizbeitia

For almost three decades, process-based design and its related terms, such as the open-ended, the indeterminate, the aleatory, the dynamic, the fluid, the adaptive, the resilient, have been at the forefront of landscape architecture. Positioned as inherent to the medium, these concepts have foregrounded landscape's becoming, and, reflecting shifts in cultural and disciplinary contexts, have operationalized time and change for different ends. In the late 1980s, the early work of Michel Desvigne, Georges Hargreaves, and Michael van Valkenburgh, for instance, lodged a critique against "imported" formalism in design. Formal concerns receded, giving way to process-based aesthetics of time, change, chance, and impermanence that were closely related to phenomenology. A second cultural shift based on new paradigms in ecological thinking (from an equilibrium-based model to a continuously adaptive model of nature) privileged landscape's capacity to self-generate, and resilience rather than poetics became the key operative goal of design.[01] More recently, the focus on sustainability and ecological services has propelled the idea of the performative—the ability of landscape to carry out work—through which the notion of process has assumed a problem-solving role. Finally, with the emergence of digital technologies, time and process can now be modeled. Paradoxically, the processual logic of algorithms produces an aestheticization of process that is as formalistic as those rejected decades ago.

In parallel with these developments, other concepts and attitudes emerged that sought to propose alternatives to this mainstream view of process as open-ended phenomenon. George Hargreaves—in his own design work and also with co-editor Julia Czerniak in their 2007 volume *Large Parks*—introduced the concept of scales of landscape management as a way to shape a more nuanced articulation of temporality in the landscape medium, especially as it relates to public space. Other landscape theorists have argued for a middle ground between perceived oppositions in order to critique what they identify as a new set of false dichotomies—the fully open versus the static, the performative versus the aesthetic—derived from prevalent discourses on process.[02] More recent concepts such as "the curation of ecologies" and "managed succession" are currently being explored by landscape architecture students and practitioners as plausible ways of mediating the relationship between process and design.

Although process and its related concepts have been extremely fruitful to expand the field of landscape architecture and its modes of practice, they also have a less promising side. As methods they have run their course and are now in urgent need of revision. Often today, process becomes a conceptual glass wall—an impediment to propositional design and experimental risk taking—to the point where we are about to see a one-size-fits-all, flattening-out of design.

In this scenario, as long as key performative indicators are present—the wetland, the porous pavement, the graphs that catalog the plant and animal species—everything is okay.

Yet from the vernacular to the infrastructural, design unceasingly proves that highest conditions of flexibility (today's "adaptability" or "resilience") are always reached through great precision and specificity: in order for something to be adaptable, it has to be precisely designed to be adaptable and not just be undesigned. Even more importantly, the idea of process is limiting today because it works against the agency of design as a political and social project, which entails imagination and critical thinking. The future of design lies not in focusing on the things that will happen anyway but in giving shape to things that would not otherwise happen, and yet need urgently to happen.

The precisely designed, then, is presented here as a counterpoint to loose, process-oriented thinking. Although precision is typically associated with top-down agency, with the imposed, the static, the stable, it also exists in the bottom-up, the evolved, the dynamic, and in the active form (or formation). That is, an expanded notion of precision yields an expanded notion of form that internalizes process.

Three recent projects suggest that the question of form in landscape is already being re-examined: the Quinta Normal de Agricultura in Santiago, Chile; the Louvre-Lens Museum in Lens, France; and the gridded plantations in Bordeaux, Saclay. These projects, as well as many others by Michel Desvigne Paysagiste's practice, demonstrate how shape, materiality, and geometry work to negotiate a dialectic between the precisely formed and the process-based in landscape, and between past histories and future uses on the site. The transactional attribute of form in these projects suggests that form is not only a thing-in-itself (with its own visual power) but that, in addition, it operates as an interface between its own condition of autonomy—producing an atmosphere, an ambience, a milieu—and those exterior conditions—such as connectivity to larger urban networks, logistics of territory, accessibility, and so on—that act upon it. In other words, the widespread notion that "form follows," which compromises the agency of form on a multitude of external forces, is tempered with the recognition of the necessary autonomy of form, with its possibility of being apprehended as such.[03]

The renovation of the *Quinta Normal de Agricultura*—a 19th-century garden created to acclimatize European species of the temperate zone into the semi-arid environment of Santiago de Chile—took place between 2009 and 2011 and was designed by Danilo Martic and Teodoro Fernández. The project addressed the contradictory purposes of preserving a horticultural collection of majestic trees and transforming the grounds into a public park in a densely populated and

Danilo Martic and Teodoro Fernández, *Quinta Normal de Agricultura*, Santiago de Chile, Chile, 2011.

largely neglected part of the city. This entailed the installation of a durable, paved surface over what was previously the soft, porous ground of the garden, which could potentially harm the root zone of the trees. The primary, and most precise, design intervention consists of a series of surfaces built in stone, wood, and stone dust, all of which together do not amount to more than 12 inches in thickness. This enables social occupation of the space alongside preservation of the pre-existing trees. Here we see not only the visual and programmatic power of a surface precisely described but also the power of form as performative of the interface. Its formal, expressive character and its precise definition as a series of thinly laminated surfaces that negotiate between the trees lends expression and a sense of boundedness without restriction to this public park. The ground—with its hybrid geometries that are self-referential (autonomous) and, at the same time, respond to the location of the trees—appears and performs as a surface of contact between old forest canopy and new public realm. Precise form need not be dismissed as static or formalistic; rather, it can be embraced as an enabler of the evolution of urban space, from a previous mono-functional condition (in this case, a private institutional garden) to a multipurpose public space within a contemporary metropolitan area.

Another highly precise ground is that of the Museum Park Louvre-Lens, a collaborative project by SANAA (Kazuyo Sejima + Ryue Nishizawa) and landscape architect Catherine Mosbach, constructed on a 62-acre former coal-mining site. As has been often stated, the design registers the traces left by the mining economy (such as the landforms of displaced earth and the tunnels), preserves the vegetation of exotic species that emerged in its disturbed and toxic soil,

and sets up a series of curated successional ecologies in its gardens. But it is reductive to describe the designers' intentions only in terms of the site's mining past and the resulting anthropogenic ecologies.

What is evident here is a series of intentional distortions and reinterpretations that bring all the forces that have been at work—past, latent, active—to coalesce through a negotiation that critically calibrates their presence. Invoking the words *condensation*, *contamination* (of form and uses), *initiation*, and *consolidation*, Mosbach describes the conceptual framework for her project.[04] More importantly, she also uses the word *transfiguration* because it describes what the project achieves: a transformation into a different state. The slight curvature of the brushed aluminum facade and the wet pavement from the almost constant rain that falls in the region produce soft, blurred reflections that bring the larger landscape, the horizon, and the sky into the space of the site, separating it from the rest. Architecture and landscape collaborate to draw in an entire milieu, an ambiance, a delicate presence that diverts attention away from the politics of dominant urban institutions and toward that particular place and moment in time.

Michel Desvigne's proposition of landscape as an intermediate nature is another example of precise form that works as interface. Although often described as indeterminate, deferred, and open-ended, it is impossible to overlook the fact that Desvigne's work is, at the same time, full of definition, most often through the use of specifically dimensioned grids and other Euclidean geometries (paradoxically disdained today as static). To write this work off as only process is to disregard so much more that is present in it.

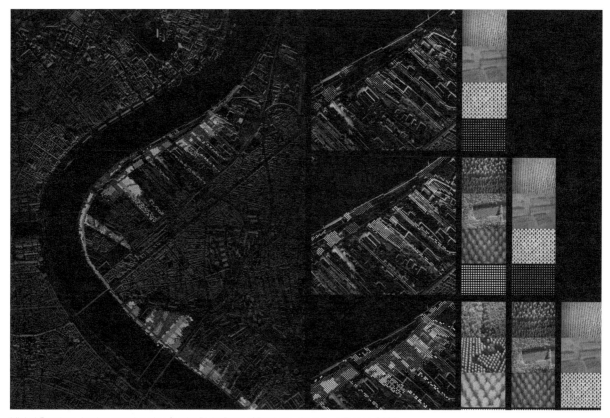

Michel Desvigne, implementation plan for the Right Bank of Bordeaux, Bordeaux, France, 2000.

From the beginning of his career, Desvigne received unusual commissions for landscapes that did not yet exist as sites of intervention when the contracts were signed. Such commissions include Bordeaux, Saclay, and Euralens. Because these projects have taken many years (if not decades) to be fully implemented, they have required new forms of client–designer agreements and, in the absence of programs and real budgets, new forms of working. While this projection in time may classify the work as "process-based" design, Desvigne resists the conventional image of process as a spatially unarticulated landscape, such as those more typically associated with sites in an indeterminate programmatic and administrative state. From the project-scale proposals such as the Governor's Island competition in New York, the building terrace at Keio University, Tokyo, or the garden for the Walker Art Center in Minneapolis, to the larger, phased regional landscapes of Bordeaux, Lens, and Saclay, gridded forms serve to structure space, time, and program in an integrated and visible manner. Legibility and a visible coherence in the landscape are, for Desvigne, constitutive of a *res publica* in that they construct alternative ways of occupying and giving form to a place. Such forms of occupation are both retrospective—they trace past agricultural and geological structures; and projective—they are denaturalized

through distortions and hybridizations. Related to legibility, coherence, and *res publica* is also an insistence on the elaboration of "presence,"[05] which counters the normative and modernist conceptions of grids as spatial and visual structures that reject narratives. However, unlike looser vector-based, process-design approaches, Desvigne's highly specific geometries bridge different temporal regimes on the site and constitute an interface between a present post-industrial (Bordeaux, Lens) or post-agricultural (Saclay) condition of fallow land and a yet-to-be-determined future.

These landscapes are processes of rapidly replicating form, where precise recursive gestures create the possibility that we can apprehend structure. The designs are not clearly bounded: there is no hard boundary condition that separates the positive form of the design from its constitutive negative. Rather, there is gradual variation between the existing context and the proposed intervention. The landscape is understood as a continuum, and the design emerges as a precise and abrupt intensification in the gradient of relationships, which creates a transition between inside and outside. Intermediate natures are, then, not indeterminate natures but highly specific spaces of negotiation between past traces, geographical structure, agricultural practices, and the vision for a future public realm.[06]

113

Anita Berrizbeitia

SANAA (Kazuyo Sejima + Ryue
Nishizawa) and Catherine
Mosbach, Museum Park Louvre-
Lens, Lens, France, 2012.

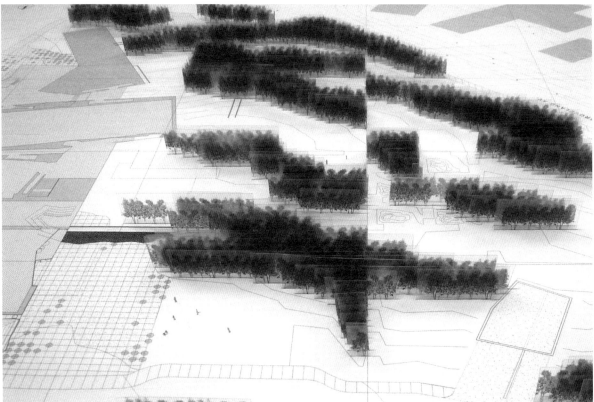

<u>Top</u>: Michel Desvigne, Keio University, Tokyo, Japan, 2005. <u>Bottom</u>: Michel Desvigne, Walker Art Center, Minneapolis, 2005.

Boundary, then, like form, requires a more nuanced definition as a dialectical condition. Though boundaries enable conceptual and experiential autonomy from that 'other' which is not landscape, they also engage this otherness in order to define the particular terms of relationship (such as what is left outside and what is allowed to be continuous). Such a notion counters the recent veneration of unarticulated flux, fluidity, and change, where everything is posited in equal terms as "urban," in favor of a negotiated interaction that recognizes the necessary difference between things, enabling a new imagination to emerge. While still standing for control, definition, determination, and other precision-based notions epitomized by the idea of boundary, form-as-interface modifies that notion in at least two ways. On the one hand, it cancels the agonistic closeness of the boundary, and on the other, it puts the emphasis on the interaction—on the dialectic between two sides.[07] In other words, the boundary is a condition that belongs to none of the sides (such as a wall) and is therefore a moment of separation, whereas the interface belongs to both sides and is therefore a moment of negotiation.

To be clear, I am not advocating here that we leave aside what remain as core environmental and social responsibilities of the field, which are also those that the world today requires. What I am arguing for, nevertheless, is that landscape architecture not be reduced to satisfying these responsibilities alone. The projects just described are located in socially and economically underserved communities with little prospect of growth or change in the short term. These projects do not represent public spaces in the service of a robust capitalism already in existence. Yet they demonstrate that landscape architecture's greatest effectiveness derives from exceeding the base conditions of sustainability, through the self-conscious command over form, geometry, and materiality as both autonomous and relational. These belong to disciplinary concerns that other fields which share the same environmental agendas (such as restoration ecology or civil engineering) do not, and cannot, have. Yet, what is at stake is not just the identity of the field but also the legibility of a socially constructed space that emerges through a deeper commitment to the exploration of form. The precisely designed form reveals rather than obscures. Its high definition communicates, draws in, mediates, and enables.

Early versions of these arguments were presented in lectures delivered at the University of Virginia in 2015 and at the Harvard University Graduate School of Design in 2016. I am grateful to colleagues at both schools and especially to Pablo Pérez-Ramos, coeditor of this issue of *New Geographies*, for valuable discussion and comment.

01. Equilibrium models of nature defend the idea that disturbances and fluctuations are automatically corrected by negative feedback mechanisms, whereas more adaptive models based on complexity tend to accept natural disturbances as common and necessary. See, for example, David Keller and Frank Golley, "Community, Niche, Diversity, and Stability," in their edited volume *The Philosophy of Ecology: From Science to Synthesis* (Athens: University of Georgia Press, 2000), 101–10; Nina-Marie Lister, "Sustainable Large Parks: Ecological Design or Designer Ecology?" in *Large Parks*, ed. George Hargreaves and Julia Czerniak (New York: Princeton Architectural Press, 2008), 35–58; and Donald Worster, "The Ecology of Order and Chaos," *Environmental History Review* 14, nos. 1–2, *1989 Conference Papers, Part 2* (Spring–Summer, 1990): 1–18.

02. Julia Czerniak's formulation of *appearance* versus *performance* constituted a key moment, marking a sort of "great divide"

between operative and aesthetic capacities in landscape design that is very much present today. See Julia Czerniak's introduction, "Appearance, Performance: Landscape at Downsview," *CASE Downsview Park Toronto*, ed. Julia Czerniak (Cambridge, MA: Harvard University, Graduate School of Design, 2001), 12–23. For the claim of a midway position between the fully open and the static, see Anita Berrizbeitia, "Scales of Undecidability," in the same volume (116–25). In her essay "Sustaining Beauty: The Performance of Appearance," *Journal of Landscape Architecture* (Spring 2008): 6–23, Elizabeth Meyer also strengthened the linkage between performance and appearance at a moment when they were still understood as independent.

03. According to Louis Sullivan, "form (ever) follows function"; according to biologist D'Arcy Wentworth Thompson, "form follows forces"; according to modernist landscape architect James C. Rose, "form follows plants"; and according to today's process-based landscape design, "form follows performance."

04. Catherine Mosbach, "Atmosphere, Atmosphere, Do I Look Anything Like Atmosphere," lecture delivered at the symposium "On Atmospheres: Spaces of Embodiment" organized by Silvia Benedito at Harvard University, Graduate School of Design, Cambridge, MA, February 4, 2016.

05. Anita Berrizbeitia, in conversation with Michel Desvigne, as part of Berrizbeitia's lecture "On the Limits of Process: The Case for Precision in Landscape," delivered at Harvard University Graduate School of Design, Cambridge, MA, April 14, 2016, http://www.gsd.harvard.edu/#/media/anita-berrizbeitia-on-the-limits-of-process-the-case-for.html.

06. Michel Desvigne, introduction to *Intermediate Natures: The Landscapes of Michel Desvigne* (Basel: Birkhäuser, 2009), 13.

07. Marc Shell distinguishes between the Latin and Norse roots of the English word *island*, the Latin *insula* meaning "land insulated by and defined against a surrounding medium," and the Norse meaning "water-land"—literally the coast, the point where water and land happen at once. Unlike the more boundary-oriented Latin notion, the Norse meaning is closer to the idea of interface, as the moment where two worlds happen at once. See Marc Shell, "Defining Islands and Isolating Definitions," in *Islandology* (Stanford, CA: Stanford University Press, 2014), 13–25.

Image Credits

117

Anita Berrizbeitia

The Limits of Limits: Schmitt, Aureli, and the Geopolitical Ontology of the Island

Douglas Spencer

Models of fluidity, process, self-organization, and complexity today enjoy near-hegemonic status in the fields of architectural, landscape, and urban design. As against the putatively top-down practices of planning and the authorial mastery of modernist design, we are led to believe that a progressive turn to more bottom-up, networked, ecologically sensitive, and "new-materialist" principles is underway. The advocates of this turn are, however, in thrall to the same models as are to be found in the history of neoliberal thought and as are frequently employed in the achievement of its political and economic agendas.[01]

The writings of the architect and teacher Pier Vittorio Aureli appear to offer a clear and decisive critique of this development. Perhaps most appealingly, Aureli's account of the architectural archipelago offers a way for architects and architecture to counter the purely economic logic of neoliberal processes of urbanization—particularly where the urban comes to stand, as with Landscape Urbanism, for the purely processual—through the assumption of a political project. The field conditions of urbanism as connective landscape are countered, by the Italian architectural theorist, with the self-sufficient autonomy and formal limits of architecture as island.

Aureli's politics of architectural form are, though, questionable in their claim to effectively contest the prevalence of models of the fluid, connective, and self-organizing in design, as well as the broader neoliberal conditions in which they operate. The inadequacies of Aureli's archipelago model, in these terms, are rooted in its indebtedness to the thought of the Nazi jurist Carl Schmitt, with its characteristically agonistic polarizations of land–sea, political–economic, friend–enemy, limited–unlimited, and, especially, in its mythic and fascistic origins.

Landscape Urbanism: From Object to Field

That the urban has, in recent years, been transformed from a form composed of static architectural objects into a "field" of processes, networks, mobility, and infrastructural connectivity constitutes something like a founding principle for Landscape Urbanism. In his 1999 essay "Field Conditions," Stan Allen—a significant figure in the formulation and promotion of Landscape Urbanism—located the emergence of what he identifies as a generalized shift from "object to field" amidst the science, technology, and culture of the post-World War II period.[02] Allen defined this "field condition" as one of "loosely bound aggregates characterized by porosity and local interconnectivity . . . bottom-up phenomena, defined not by overarching geometrical schemas but by intricate local connections."[03] Employing these insights, Allen recommended, would at last place design "in contact with the real."[04]

Contemporary to Allen's essay, Alex Wall's "Programming the Urban Surface" has been equally significant to the theoretical development of Landscape Urbanism.[05] Here, Wall writes that in contemporary urbanization, "infrastructures and flows of material have become more significant than static political and spatial boundaries . . . The emphasis shifts here from *forms* of urban space to *processes* of urbanization."[06] Consequently, he continues, we are now experiencing "a fundamental paradigm shift from viewing cities in formal terms to looking at them in dynamic ways. Hence, familiar urban typologies of *square, park, district*, and so on are of less use or significance than are the infrastructures, network flows, ambiguous spaces, and other polymorphous conditions that constitute the contemporary metropolis."[07]

The paradigms of fluidity, interconnectivity, and process promoted by Allen and Wall are echoed in the conception of "weak urbanism" formulated by Andrea Branzi. This putatively new condition of urbanism, argues Branzi in the essay "A Strong Century," proceeds according to a hermeneutics that is "more ductile and therefore able to absorb the new and confront the surprises and complexities that this produces."[08] The ductile and fluid qualities of Branzi's model of urbanism are further elaborated through his adoption of the sociologist Zygmunt Bauman's concept of a "liquid modernity," of which he writes, "For Bauman, the term 'liquid' positively indicates the idea of a state of material that does not possess its own form (rather, that of its container) and tends to follow a temporal flow of transformations. These conditions converge to describe 'the nature of the current, and in many respects, new phase of the history of modernism.'"[09]

For Charles Waldheim, landscape is the medium through which urbanism achieves the kind of connective and fluidly interactive performance appropriate to contemporary realities. Landscape, as a "performative medium," writes Waldheim in his recent *Landscape as Urbanism: A General Theory*, services the post-Fordist city "through a unique combination of ecological performance and design culture."[10] "Rather than offering an exception to the structure of the city," he continues, landscape "aligns with the return to the project of city-making associated with contemporary service, creative and culture economies."[11] In this fashion, Waldheim argues, landscape succeeds as the discipline of urban design, replacing the now hopelessly retrograde and leaden one of architecture. The turn to landscape is one in which urbanism is "unburdened of all that architectural baggage."[12]

It would be difficult to conceive of anything more diametrically opposed to the position of Aureli than this, invested as it is in the politics of architectural form as the delimited, posed against the connective economies of a landscaped urbanism. Rather than pursuing the economic zeitgeist, or drawing upon ontologies of complexity, he has proposed to redeem what he regards as a foundational politics of architectural form through the *geopolitical* ontology of Carl Schmitt.[13]

Leviathan and Behemoth

In *The Nomos of the Earth* (1950) and *Land and Sea* (1954), Carl Schmitt argues that a new spatial order has emerged in the aftermath of World War II.[14] The great sea powers—England and the United States—have finally established their ascension over the land-based powers of the European continent. For Schmitt, as he posits in *Land and Sea*, "world history" is a struggle between maritime and land or continental powers that he casts, in mythological terms, as the battle between Leviathan and Behemoth, between sea creature and land animal:

> Behemoth tries to tear Leviathan to pieces with its horns and teeth, while in turn, Leviathan tries hard to stop the land animal's mouth and nostrils with its flaps and fins in order to deprive it of food and air. This is a graphic illustration . . . of the blockade to which a sea power subjects a land power by cutting its supplies in order to starve it to death.[15]

The defeat of Germany is made to stand more broadly for the defeat of the behemoth of Europe by the leviathans of England and America. Noting that in some sense, given the all-encompassing nature of the oceans, all land for Schmitt is effectively an island, this final victory of sea over land brings to a conclusion the "spatial revolution" initiated when England "turned her collective existence seawards and centred it on the sea element."[16] Setting out on this course, transforming itself from "a nation of sheep herders" into one of "pirates" in the Elizabethan period, England went on to "win the first round of the planetary, spatial revolution."[17] This revolution brings about, for the first time in world history, a truly global order, with the British Empire at its center. Earlier empires, says Schmitt in *The Nomos of the Earth*, were in some ways interconnected, but these "lacked a global character": "Each considered itself to be the *world*, the *cosmos*, the *house*."[18] Prior to the spatial revolution of modernity there is, then, an effective archipelago of more or less isolated *worlds*, each surrounded by the uncharted and "malevolent chaos" of the sea.[19] With the coming to hegemony of the new maritime powers, the plurality of *worlds* becomes the singular *world*, a truly global condition.

The ascension of the maritime powers brings to a close a centuries-long struggle between land and sea. Over this period, from the 16th to the 19th century, the lines of the first planetary order are clearly drawn. They run between the dry land of the European continent—itself clearly divided between sovereign national states—and the sea, ostensibly belonging to no one but ruled in reality by England: "The dry-land order implies the subdivision into state territories. The high seas, in turn, are free: they know no state and are not subjected to any state or territorial sovereignty."[20] The turn to the sea, then, marks a rupture in the existing *nomos* of the earth, its literal deterritorialization. The conquest of the sea opens up a new spatial condition in which the old practices of land-based sovereignty—the making of clearly bounded worlds—are undermined. The sovereign order of limits is challenged by new powers that operate through the medium of the unlimited.

In plotting out this dichotomy between the limited and the unlimited, played out between land and sea, Schmitt associates the judicial territory of the land with an established order and the unlimited space of the sea with the practice of commercial trade. He notes, in *Land and Sea*, the popularity among the English for maxims such as those of Sir Walter Raleigh: "'Whoever controls the seas controls the world trade; whoever controls world trade holds all the treasures of the world in his possession, and in fact, the whole world.'"[21] "Slogans about freedom, such as 'All world trade is free exchange,'" he writes, "express the zenith of England's maritime and global power."[22] In constructing these polarities and associations—of land and island as the "properly" juridical and political space of man, as opposed to the sea as the chaotic, desacralized, and unlimited realm of trade and commerce—Schmitt is rehearsing themes first established in the same ancient world into which he projects the origins of the struggles between land and sea powers.

Anaximander and the *Apeiron*

The profound significance of monetization for the world of ancient Greece, Richard Seaford has argued in his *Money and the Early Greek Mind: Homer, Philosophy, Tragedy* (2004), is registered in the cosmology of Anaximander (610–546 BCE).[23] Seaford suggests that Anaximander's conception of the *apeiron*—the "unlimited," the primordial, infinite, and unendingly productive source from which all things are constituted—is inseparable from the development of monetization in the ancient Greek world of the pre-Socratic philosopher, particularly that of the commercial city of Miletus in which he lived.[24] Just as money serves as a substrate of trade, the *apeiron* serves as the substrate from which all other things come into being. Seaford further pursues this analogy between "money and *everything* that we know" in Anaximander's conception of the *apeiron*, noting, for instance, that the *apeiron* and money are each said to "contain all things," to "steer" and regulate all things, to be in constant movement and circulation, and to be "undifferentiated, homogeneous."

"The *apeiron*," writes Seaford, "is abstract in the sense that (although it surrounds all things and is their source) it is imperceptible. So too money is both concrete and abstract, visible and invisible." Given the extent of these analogies, Seaford is lead to posit that the relationship between the *apeiron* and money is more than simply analogical: we are "forced to accept [that] Anaximander's cosmos is in some respect a projection of social relations." His hypothesis is that "one factor in the genesis of the notion of the *apeiron*, and of philosophical cosmology in general, was money."[25] Underlying all things is the *apeiron*, and underlying the conception of this is monetization, with its abstract, undifferentiated, and impersonal relations, with its fecund and limitless circulation.

The unleashing of the unsettling effects of monetization are played out in what Seaford describes as a "collision between the unlimit of money and the limit inherent in ritual." The Athenian poet and legislator Solon (a contemporary of Anaximander), was the first, notes Seaford, "to believe that there is a hidden *measure* (of intelligence) that holds the limits of all things, and to recommend the principle of *moderation*." The notion of limit as figured by Solon in the character of Tellos is, argues Seaford, "suggestive of *telos*, whose basic sense of *limit* or *completion* qualifies it to refer to ritual."[26] Likewise in Aristotle's *Politics*, he notes, one can locate the same concern with a wealth that is measured in terms of its adequacy to the "good life," as opposed to the unlimited wealth pursued through the buying and selling of commodities.[27] Ritualized orders of limit and moderation, then, are set against the unlimited pursuit of wealth accumulated for its own sake in the collision to which Seaford refers. This struggle follows, logically enough, from the fact that forms of monetized exchange, as Seaford also shows, were developed out of, and historically succeeded, ritual forms of exchange. From ritualized practices of gift-giving, sacrifice, and expiation—mediating between men and gods—monetization facilitated an abstract circulation of things and values, endlessly exchanged, as the impersonal relations mediating between men.

Bringing us more tangibly to the theme of the island and the archipelago, Seaford notes that in Aeschylus's *Agamemnon*, "the sea, as homogenous and unlimited, evokes the homogeneity and unlimit of money."[28] As he also remarks, in respect of this figuration of the sea as the unlimited, "The (potentially alarming and relatively novel) *man-made* inexhaustibility of money is envisaged as in terms of the *natural* inexhaustibility of the sea."[29] To envisage this association between two expressions of the unlimited would not be difficult, of course, for people increasingly engaged in commercial trade routed through the waters of the Eastern Mediterranean.

The impact of monetization in the world of ancient and classical Greece is registered, in its tragedy and philosophy,

in terms of fundamental oppositions. These appear in Aristotle, as Seaford notes, in terms of a polarization "between community and outsider . . . out of which arise the corresponding polarities self-sufficiency–trade, goods–money, limit–unlimit, moral–immoral, natural–unnatural."[30] Following Seaford's reading of *Agamemnon*, we can add to this series land–sea—a polarization between the self-sufficient and self-contained limit of the settled territory—the *island*—and the unsettling commercial space of the unlimited sea that surrounds and threatens its order.

The Discreet Charms of Carl Schmitt

The polarities through which Schmitt's geopolitical ontology are performed are then as much ancient as they are reflections on his contemporary situation. His arguments, in fact, rehearse an archaic tragedy dressed up as the truth of global modernity. Following Schmitt, Aureli, in turn, is insistent that only clearly bounded, physically and juridically delimited spatial orders, such as those of the archipelago, can properly sustain the properly political. In adopting Schmitt's geopolitical ontology in this fashion, Aureli revives a definition of the political originally confected to underwrite the appropriation of land and the juridical "rights" of this appropriation. As the philosopher Bruno Bosteels writes of this ontologizing work, "Schmitt first of all presupposes an immediate connection between being and spatiality . . . All being is oriented in accord with an immanent principle of justice and right: 'Right is the rightfulness of being that is given at the origin.' The earth itself, of course, is the primal site for this suturing of being, space, and law as right."[31] It is this essentializing and archaic foundation of a juridical politics of land appropriation, and its defense, that Aureli takes up as appropriate to the question of contemporary processes of urbanization. The outside, the unlimited "sea" of urbanism or landscape, is abjured as inescapably economic. "One can argue," writes Aureli in *The Possibility of an Absolute Architecture* (2011), "that the notion of urbanization presupposes the fundamental substitution of politics with economics as a mode of city governance to the point that today it is reasonable—almost banal—to ask not what kind of political power is governing us, but whether we are governed by politics at all."[32]

Aureli's allegiance to and admiration for what he terms Schmitt's "political realism" determines his definition of the political and the strictness with which it is to be understood as separate and distinct from the economic.[33] Schmitt's account of the political, as taken up by Aureli, is heavily reliant on the former's infamous friend–enemy distinction, as propounded in *The Concept of the Political*, published in 1932. Here Schmitt proclaims that "the specific political distinction to which political actions and motives can be reduced is that between friend and enemy."[34]

121

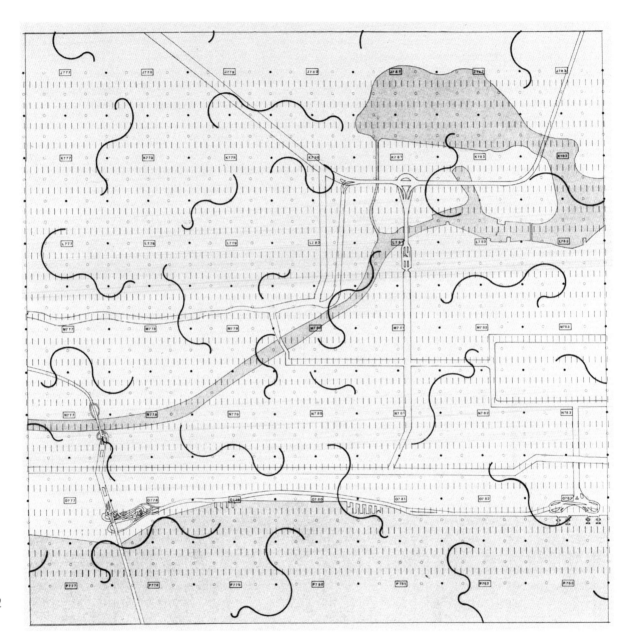

Archizoom Associati, No-Stop City, 1969.

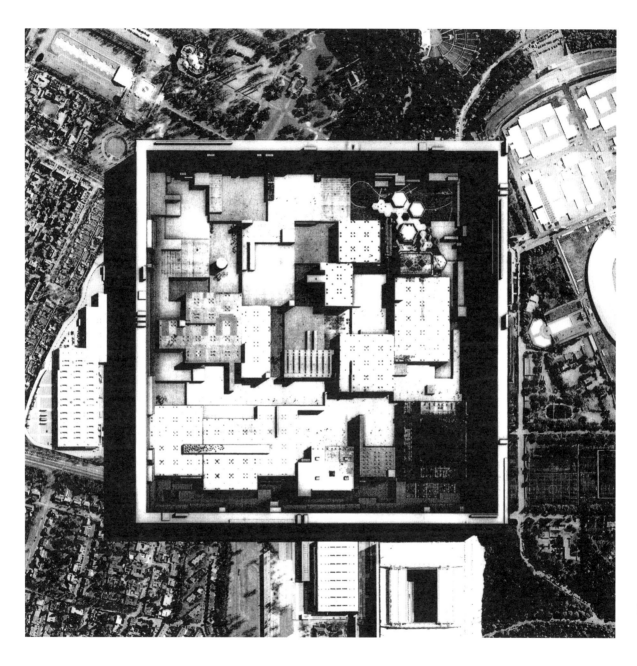

Dogma, A Simple Heart: Urban Study on the
European North West Metropolitan Area, 2011.

Andrea Branzi, *Metropoli Merceologica*, 2010.

For Schmitt the political just *is*, ontologically, the ineluctable struggle between friend and enemy. This struggle marks the perpetual agonism that must exist between sovereign nation states in order that the political exists as such. The necessary and defining expression of this agonism is war: "A world in which the possibility of war is utterly eliminated," writes Schmitt, "a completely pacified globe, would be a world without the distinction of friend and enemy and hence a world without politics."[35] As opposed to liberal notions of competition that might derive from matters of trade, the properly political is dependent on the possibility of armed conflict between sovereign spatial orders. "The friend, enemy, and combat concepts receive their real meaning precisely because they refer to the real possibility of physical killing," Schmitt makes plain in *The Concept of the Political*.[36] As is well known, Schmitt's theories of sovereignty and the political were instrumental to the juridical formulations of National Socialism, particularly during the period of his membership in the Nazi Party. As international relations scholar Benno Gerhard Teschke notes, Schmitt's theory of the political "inscribed Hitler's 'spatial revolution' into a full-scale reinterpretation of Europe's geopolitical history, grounded in land appropriations, which legitimized Nazi Germany's wars of conquest."[37]

Aureli's reading of Schmitt attempts to abstract this agonistic formulation of what is essentially political from its historically specific political context. Indeed, there appears no reference to Schmitt's fascism, anti-Semitism, or membership in the Nazi party in Aureli's *The Possibility of an Absolute Architecture*. Schmitt is described here simply as a "German jurist."[38] For Aureli, it seems, the fascism of Schmitt's politics can be disregarded while its agonism, and its fixation on the appropriation of land, can be repurposed as a universal truth in order to pursue a properly political architectural project.[39]

This project is founded on the formalization of the friend–enemy distinction through an architecture with the function to clearly inscribe limits and boundaries upon appropriated land. Aureli argues that the formal "essentially involves an act of spatial determination, of (de)limitation."[40] Architecture, as a practice of delimitation, generates the inside–outside binary through which the friend can be distinguished from the enemy. Unlike in Schmitt, however, the purpose of this friend–enemy polarization is not to sanction war but to allow us to know and identify ourselves, as such, through an encounter with what we are not: "What counters us inevitably constitutes the knowledge of our own limit, our own form."[41] "The enemy," argues Aureli in a quasi-Brechtian formulation, "estranges us from our familiar self-perception, and gives us back the sharp contour of our own figure."[42] Since form requires delimitation, architecture, as a formal practice of inscribing limits, achieves a political condition only when it is a "composition of parts" and never when it integrates us into the whole of the limitless "sea." In the "composition of parts," writes Aureli, "the concept of the formal and the concept of the political coincide and can be posited against notions such as urban space, urban landscape, and network."[43] Integration with the *apeiron* of urbanism would result in the dissolution of the political and the architectural alike, within a purely economic logic.[44] This dissolution can only be resisted through what Aureli names as the "meta-form of the archipelago."[45]

In *The Possibility of an Absolute Architecture*, Aureli affirms the architectural archipelago as an essentially political form through an account of its periodic historical appearances. This account ranges across the works of figures such as Andrea Palladio, Giovanni Battista Piranesi, Étienne-Louis Boullée, Ludwig Hilberseimer, Oswald Mathias Ungers, and Rem Koolhaas. He praises Koolhaas and Elia Zenghelis's project (as OMA) Exodus, or the Voluntary Prisoners of Architecture, for instance, for its projection of "an exacerbated version of communitarian citizenship based on self-imposed closure."[46] In the work of Ungers, Aureli finds a fully developed "theory of the city as an archipelago."[47] Ungers, especially in the 1977 project for the shrinking city of Berlin, The City within the City—Berlin as Green Archipelago, produces what Aureli understands to be a politically radical project in its refusal of the megastructural form of architecture prevalent in this period. The megastructure is held to integrate architecture with processes of urbanization, dissolving the possibility of the truly political architecture of the limited enclosure; Ungers's project, in contrast, is "composed of islands, each of which was conceived as a formally distinct micro-city."

Aureli also notes the significance of Ungers's earlier research, undertaken with his wife Liselotte, on the history of communitarian (typically Shaker or Anabaptist) settlements in America:

> Religious communities such as the Shakers were characterized by a principle of communal life in which there was no private property; all facilities were for collective use. This resulted in settlements whose form was organized for communal life, with an abundance of common spaces, and in clear contrast to cities, which are shaped by land ownership. Ungers observed that radical communality was possible only within limited settlements.[48]

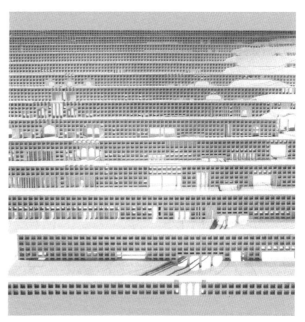

Dogma, A Field of Walls: Project on Giovanni Battista Piranesi's *Campo Marzio dell'Antica Roma*, 2012.

It is this same possibility for a radically autonomous form of life in common that Aureli also locates in the case of "Red Vienna" and the "Hof" superblocks built there in the mid-1930s to accommodate the city's workers. These superblocks collectively constitute a further historical instance of the archipelago. They are situated "within the city as self-sufficient islands in pronounced contrast to their surroundings . . . an archipelago of places for communitarian life."[49]

The Agonies of the Archipelago

As a politics of architecture, Aureli's archipelago is pitched against the economics of urbanism; the island against the sea, the limited against the *apeiron*. The decisiveness with which the political is opposed to the economic derives from the equally decisive function of architecture as, essentially and fundamentally, a practice of formal delimitation. This notion of what is essential and fundamental to architecture derives, in turn, from the Schmittian conception of the *nomos*, a word that comes, states Schmitt, from *nemein*, "a [Greek] word that means both 'to divide' and 'to pasture.' Thus, *nomos* is the immediate form in which the political and social order of a people becomes spatially visible." Elaborating on the meaning of the *nomos* he continues that it can be "described as a wall, because, like a wall, it, too, is based on sacred orientations."[50] The decisive presence of the *nomos* as wall constitutes the foundational act of spatial ordering. It divides inside from outside, friend from enemy.

It is this decisiveness that no doubt endows what Aureli refers to as his "project" with its significant appeal for

Douglas Spencer

those seeking to challenge the hegemony of the various ecoarchitectures and parametricisms, all the relational, infrastructural, and landscape urbanisms, and their relentless reassertions of the fluid, flexible, and self-organizing. To these, "the project" offers a clear and concise set of formulations that appear readily translatable into design thinking and practice. Less often reflected upon, however, are the implications of the politics of agonism on which the archipelago model is premised.

It is seldom noted, for instance, that the political agonism adopted by Aureli is essentially opposed to the possibility of any radical transformation of the social in its totality. The politics of agonism is, by definition, opposed to any form of universalism or internationalism on which any such transformation would depend. It cannot countenance the termination of the friend-enemy distinction, or any movement toward this possibility as a political goal. There must be an ineluctable and untranscendable condition of conflict. For Aureli this is essential to our identity, but it forecloses the possibility of identities that are formed not through the appropriation, settlement, and delimitation of land but on relations of solidarity despite of, and across, boundaries, borders, and walls. As the philosopher Mark Neocleous writes, "For Schmitt the vision of a world without the state, without the political friend-enemy distinction and without war is an absurd and impossible dream. It is also of course a communist, but not a fascist one."[51] While for Aureli the promise of agonism is clearly reoriented to an entirely different agenda from that of Schmitt, the impossibility of even moving toward the overcoming of conflict is, for him, unviable: the overcoming of conflict would annul the political dimension itself (as it is understood here). There can be no dialectical movement of synthesis.[52] But if this is supposed, somehow, to forestall the universalizing managerialism of life, it serves equally to delegitimize any equally universalizing opposition to this prospect. There can only be parts—separate, distinct, and opposed to one another.

In its essentializing tendencies, the formalism through which the identities between the political, the architectural, and the communal are forged is equally problematic. There are no guarantees that small-scale, architecturally delimited settlements will produce or sustain forms of commonality with any even vaguely radical or progressive orientation. As the cultural historian Fred Turner, amongst others, has made plain, the communes of America's West Coast counterculture of the 1960s and 1970s, for instance, were largely organized and populated by affluent white men. The organization of these communes tended to exacerbate patriarchal prejudices, sustain class distinctions, and produce friend–enemy distinctions of the most racist sort between the communalists and the marginalized ethnic groups they encountered.[53]

It might also be noted that gated communities and securitized apartment blocks, with facilities shared in common, are very much the preferred form of dwelling for the urban rich and super-rich wanting to insulate themselves from the chaos of their immediate surroundings. An archipelago of secured enclaves increasingly defines patterns of urban development. The occupants of these are, precisely, enabled through the decisiveness of walls and boundaries to establish their identities in contradistinction to those of the urban masses that surround them. The formal identity between the archipelago and the political agonism of the friend–enemy distinction appears to work then, but to what end?

Aureli's project appears to challenge the essentially neoliberal turn of contemporary urbanization, as well as the models and practices with which architectural, landscape, and urban design have tended to serve it of late. This challenge is, however, in its very definition of the political, absolutely compromised by its Schmittian origins—mythopoetical, archaic, and formalist—at its core. In discounting the possibility that the unlimited—the urban—might itself be a space simultaneously and complexly economic and political, this project effectively concedes the greater part of the territory to the putative enemy. It offers only the possibility of secession from the networks of globalized urbanization that are always already deemed nonpolitical. In doing so, Aureli's politics of form misses what is effectively political in the making fluid, connective, and productive of the urban, especially under the contemporary imperatives of neoliberalism.

Marx and Engels, of course, already understood the process of urbanization and its economic modes of production in explicitly political terms. This process is understood, dialectically, as the ground of any future universal struggle—antagonistic rather than agonistic—against capital, in their *Communist Manifesto*. Many figures within Western Marxism, perhaps most notably Henri Lefebvre, have since taken up and developed their analysis in attempting to understand the politics of urbanization in the late 20th and early 21st centuries. From a different perspective, but equally concerned with the political, Foucault's concept of the "biopolitical" understands the production of subjectivity, especially that occurring within neoliberalism, as a political operation achieved through economic means.[54]

In addition to the politics of urbanization, there is also a politics of design that is effectively obscured by Aureli's position. By the logic of Schmitt's definition of the political, design that is not concerned with the decisive production of limits and boundaries is not political. The production and articulation of networks, the channeling of subjects according to preferred patterns of movement and association, in fact the very act of dismantling limits and boundaries is, though, a political practice. It is the politics of this practice—and its framing as progressive, natural, and ecological, as in the case of Landscape Urbanism—that needs to be contested, rather than discounted *tout court* as a manifestation of the unlimited. The alternative is a politics of regression to an archaically conceived pre-economic condition of autonomy, a monastic politics of retreat that—while now perhaps desirable to some—is evidently attainable only by the most economically privileged.[55] A more ambitious politics would be ready to engage in the no doubt more fraught struggle to understand, and act upon, the spaces of the unlimited as a radically universalizing and collective project.

01. See Douglas Spencer, *The Architecture of Neoliberalism: How Contemporary Architecture Became an Instrument of Control and Compliance* (London: Bloomsbury, 2016).

02. Stan Allen, "Field Conditions," in *Points + Lines* (New York: Princeton Architectural Press, 1999).

03. Ibid., 92.

04. Ibid.

05. Alex Wall, "Programming the Urban Surface," in *Recovering Landscape: Essays in Contemporary Landscape Architecture*, ed. James Corner (New York: Princeton Architectural Press, 1999).

06. Ibid., 234.

07. Ibid.

08. Andrea Branzi, "A Strong Century," in *Weak and Diffuse Modernity: The World of Projects at the Beginning of the 21st Century*, trans. Alta Price (Milan: Skira, 2006), 14–15.

09. Ibid., 20.

10. Charles Waldheim, *Landscape as Urbanism: A General Theory* (Princeton: Princeton University Press, 2016), 5.

11. Ibid.

12. Ibid., 6.

13. I take the term *geopolitical ontology* as a descriptor for the thought of Schmitt from Bruno Bosteels, "The Obscure Subject: Sovereignty and Geopolitics in Carl Schmitt's *The Nomos of the Earth*," *South Atlantic Quarterly* 104, no. 2 (2005): 300.

14. Carl Schmitt, *The Nomos of the Earth in the Law of the* Jus Publicum Europaeum, trans. G. L. Ulmen (1950; rpt. New York: Telos Press, 2006); and Carl Schmitt, *Land and Sea*, trans. Simona Draghici (1954; rpt. Washington, DC: Plutarch Press, 1997).

15. Schmitt, *Land and Sea*, 6.

16. Schmitt, *Land and Sea*, 28.

17. Schmitt, *Land and Sea*, 49.

18. Schmitt, *The Nomos of the Earth*, 51.

19. Schmitt, *The Nomos of the Earth*, 51.

20. Schmitt, *Land and Sea*, 46.

21. Schmitt, *Land and Sea*, 47.

22. Schmitt, *Land and Sea*, 47.

23. Richard Seaford, *Money and the Early Greek Mind: Homer, Philosophy, Tragedy* (Cambridge: Cambridge University Press, 2004).

24. Miletus was unique, notes Seaford, in being at the center of a "commercial network stretching in all directions over much of the known world united . . . by that common currency of precious metals (uncoined or coined) that increasingly provided a measure of value and means of exchange, a substrate of all commercial activity." In ibid., 208.

25. Ibid., 205–08.

26. Ibid., 166. Emphasis in the original.

27. Ibid., 169.

28. Ibid.

29. Ibid., 166. Emphasis in the original.

30. Ibid., 168.

31. Bosteels, "The Obscure Subject," 300.

32. Pier Vittorio Aureli, *The Possibility of an Absolute Architecture* (Cambridge, MA: MIT Press, 2011), 11, 13.

33. Ibid., 235.

34. Carl Schmitt, *The Concept of the Political*, trans. G. D. Schwab (1932; rpt. Chicago: University of Chicago Press, 1996), 26.

35. Ibid., 35.

36. Ibid., 33.

37. Benno Gerhard Teschke, "Fatal Attraction: A Critique of Carl Schmitt's International Political and Legal Theory," *International Theory* 3, no. 2 (2011): 179.

38. Aureli, *Possibility of an Absolute Architecture*, 235.

39. Aureli is, of course, by no means unique in assuming the broad proposition that the politics of Schmitt—despite and not because of his fascism—might offer useful lessons for the political left. For a discussion and critique of this, see Mark Neocleous, "Friend or Enemy? Reading Schmitt Politically," *Radical Philosophy* 79 (September/October, 1996), 13–23.

40. Aureli, *Possibility of an Absolute Architecture*, 31.

41. Aureli, *Possibility of an Absolute Architecture*, 29.

42. Aureli, *Possibility of an Absolute Architecture*, 29.

43. Aureli, *Possibility of an Absolute Architecture*, 31.

44. Aureli, *Possibility of an Absolute Architecture*, x.

45. Aureli, *Possibility of an Absolute Architecture*, xii.

46. Aureli, *Possibility of an Absolute Architecture*, 196–97.

47. Aureli, *Possibility of an Absolute Architecture*, 178.

48. Aureli, *Possibility of an Absolute Architecture*, 199.

49. Aureli, *Possibility of an Absolute Architecture*, 201.

50. Schmitt, *The Nomos of the Earth*, 70.

51. Neocleous, "Friend or Enemy," 23.

52. Aureli makes clear his rejection of the Hegelian dialectic, arguing that "the political realizes the solution of conflict not by a synthesis of the confronting parts, but by recognizing the opposition as a *composition* of parts." *Possibility of an Absolute Architecture*, 29. Emphasis in the original.

53. Fred Turner, *From Counterculture to Cyberculture: Stewart Brand, the Whole Earth Network, and the Rise of Digital Utopianism* (Chicago: University of Chicago Press, 2006).

54. See Michel Foucault, *The Birth of Biopolitics: Lectures at the Collège de France 1978–1979*, trans. Michel Senellart (Basingstoke, UK: Palgrave Macmillan, 2008).

55. This retreat to the monastic, affirmed as an autonmous form of life that might be recovered as an alternative to the current conditions of urbanization, is presented in Pier Vittorio Aureli's *Less is Enough: On Architecture and Asceticism* (Moscow: Strelka Press, 2013). For a critique of this proposition see Douglas Spencer, "Less than Enough: A Critique of Aureli's Project," in *This Thing Called Theory*, ed. Teresa Stoppani, Giorgio Ponzo, and George Themistokleous (London: Routledge, 2016).

Image Credits

122: Courtesy of Archizoom Associati.

123, 125: Courtesy of Dogma.

124: Courtesy of Andrea Branzi.

Douglas Spencer

Toward a
Formless Ecology

Formlessfinder
(Garrett Ricciardi
& Julian Rose)

The earth, our home, is beginning to look more and more like an immense pile of filth.

—Pope Francis, *Encyclical Letter on Care for Our Common Home*

Even as its specific significance remains hotly contested today, the term *climate change* means, by definition, that the climate isn't what it used to be. As the American meteorologist William B. Gail recently pointed out in the *New York Times*, "Nature's longstanding, repeatable patterns—relied on for millenniums by humanity to plan everything from infrastructure to agriculture—are no longer so reliable."[01] Gail argues that as the environment grows fundamentally more extreme and unpredictable, humankind will face an array of devastating effects, from the disruption of the global food supply to an increasing inability to plan for and respond to ecological crises such as floods or forest fires.

Yet even as the last decade has seen a wide range of intellectual efforts to conceptualize nature, from philosopher Timothy Morton's *Ecology Without Nature* (2007) to architectural historian David Gissen's *Subnature* (2009), mainstream design still operates under an idealized notion of a stable and predictable nature.[02] As a result most architectural responses to environmental concerns have remained on the level of representation, broadcasting their concern for environmental responsibility through a set of all-too-familiar tropes—photovoltaics, elaborate louvers and frit patterns, the conspicuous placement of green walls and roofs, and the atoning use of recycled materials.

Recalibrating our thinking about architecture's relation to the environment will not solve climate change in itself, but it will allow us to formulate an architectural response to the new environmental normal of precariousness and wild unpredictability. We believe that architects can put the environment's fundamental instability to work, using George Bataille's notion of the formless as a guide. For the self-described "anti-philosopher," the formless was not a concept that could be defined but a process that could be deployed: in his famous description of the *informe*, he proposed that "a dictionary would begin as of the moment when it no longer provided the meanings of words but their tasks." As the French scholar Denis Hollier has pointed out, Bataille expressed a profound antipathy for architecture,[03] and for this reason his thinking has so far found greater resonance in the field of art, where it has been explored by Yves-Alain Bois, Rosalind Krauss, and others.[04] His hostility, however, was due more to his myopic view of architecture than to any fundamental incompatibility between his ideas and architectural practice. Bataille could only see architecture as form: it was always a metaphor or a symbol, a stand-in for the body, the state, or the institution.

Nevertheless, in his *Critical Dictionary* (the same document that included his notoriously dismissive definition of architecture) he not only praised the formless qualities of space but literally grounded his thinking in what he called a base materialism. The task of the formless, he wrote, was to "declassify" lofty ideas, undermining the abstraction and idealism that shored up traditional thought by confronting them with the raw, messy, and often ugly physicality of the world. The philosopher's mouth, he points out, might be a source of wisdom, but it was also a moist orifice foaming with spit; man might be a noble creature, the only member of the animal kingdom to walk erect with his head held high, but he still has his feet in the mud.[05]

Buildings, too, could be said to have their feet in the mud, and this inherent engagement with the base materiality and brute physical reality of the world could be extraordinarily productive for architecture. The formless is a promising fit for recalibrating architecture's relationship to the environment, precisely because the material reality of our world—an "immense pile of filth," according to Pope Francis—is increasingly formless and because it allows us to not only respond to but perhaps also instrumentalize a wide range of ecological processes—decay, erosion, accumulation, settling, creeping—that have been excluded from architectural thought because they don't fit into our image of what the discipline should be. How might a building redeploy contaminated matter, for example, or respond to something as fundamentally destabilizing as a ground that shifts beneath it? Today's pile of filth could become the foundation of tomorrow's architecture.

When we were commissioned to design an entry pavilion for the Design Miami fair in 2013, we were struck by the fact that much of the region's architecture is able to exist only by struggling against the fundamental instability of sand. The region's geology precludes traditional foundations; most buildings—even parking lots—rest on enormous, raft-like supports floating on loose sand. This condition remains hidden below the surface of most of Miami's architecture, but our design for Tent Pile took advantage of sand's ubiquity and formlessness, finding unexpected potentials and alternative efficiencies in the very qualities that make it an obstacle to typical construction. Its weight offers a counterintuitive stability; its thermal mass generates significant cooling effects, and its very looseness offers new flexibility in tectonics and construction.

The stakes in rethinking architecture in this way are not limited to architecture's relationship to the external world—they also reach the core of the discipline itself. Creating an architecture that can respond to current environmental realities is also an opportunity to, in Bataille's terms, declassify architecture itself. Ecological models are only the latest in a long string of systems of thought—from the ancient orders to Renaissance theories of proportion to contemporary parametric modeling systems—that offer architects an illusion of total control, bringing all aspects of the discipline within one formal framework. This has long resulted in the suppression of messy realities in favor of idealized images. We see this as a capitulation, a literal flattening-out of the field, at the very moment when it should be opening up in all dimensions. Architecture is at its strongest when it doesn't need to deny or exclude, when it can exist in states and places that were previously inconceivable. A formless approach seeks not only to recalibrate architecture's relationship to ecology but to reactivate its role in the world, to make architecture *matter*.

01. William B. Gail, "A New Dark Age Looms," *New York Times*, April 19, 2016, http:// www.nytimes.com/2016/04/19/opinion/ a-new-dark-age-looms.html?_r=0.
02. Timothy Morton, *Ecology without Nature: Rethinking Environmental Aesthetics* (Cambridge, MA: Harvard University Press, 2009); David Gissen, *Subnature: Architecture's Other Environments* (New York: Princeton Architectural Press, 2009).
03. Denis Hollier, *Against Architecture: The Writings of Georges Bataille* (Cambridge, MA: MIT Press, 1992).
04. See, for example, Yves-Alain Bois and Rosalind E. Krauss, *Formless: A User's Guide* (New York: Zone Books, 1997).
05. Georges Bataille et al., *Encyclopaedia Acephalica: Comprising the Critical Dictionary and Related Texts* (London: Atlas Press, 1995), 58–78.

Image Credits

130

Garret Ricciardi and Julian Rose, Entry pavilion, Design Miami fair, 2013.

Nine Islands:
Matters around
Architecture

Neyran Turan

Strata of the world is a jumbled museum.
—Robert Smithson, *Sedimentation of the Mind: Earth Projects* (1968)

Buildings are the very reverse of rocks. They are absolutely in our power, both the species and the situation; and hence arises the excess in which they often abound.
—Thomas Whately, *Observations on Modern Gardening* (1770)

In 1972, *Architectural Design* published an article on the recently built, 50-story One Shell Plaza in Houston, designed by Skidmore, Owings & Merrill. The editors described in detail the lavish materials incorporated in the building, which came from every part of the planet and included primavera mahogany from Guatemala, Italian travertine quarried near Rome, and Persian walnut from Iran. They criticized the building's use of such rare and expensive materials as irresponsible in light of the "increasing worldwide concern over the use and conservation of the earth's natural resources." One material drew particular scrutiny: real leather, used to sheathe the nine-foot-tall walls of the building's 26 elevator cabs. "The architects," the article reported, "wanted no seams or joints horizontally so had to search the world for nine-foot cows"—the largest raised at the time.[01]

In the context of the widespread critique of late modernism and the emerging environmentalism of the 1970s, the tone of this article is not surprising. More striking are the specific connections the article portrays between architectural materiality and resource geographies. How do we understand the materials of architecture in relation to resources today? For some, resources are natural and thus need to be preserved and protected. For others, resources are systemic and thus need to be managed and maintained. In the context of the new geological epoch posited by the Anthropocene, can we conceptualize resources—in this case, materials around architecture—not as merely natural or systemic but geological and geographic? If discussions around materiality in architecture and urbanism usually focus on performance in relation to the material conditions of the building or the city with an instrumental or managerial tone, might a conceptualization of the material as raw matter—both with its (wider) geographic and (deeper) geologic dimensions—bring a new conception of materiality for architecture?[02]

Geologic and Aesthetic

When considering material as matter and resource, the evident historical relationship between the geological and the aesthetic provides important clues. In his book *Romantic Rocks,* literary theorist Noah Heringman shows how the development of the discipline of geology in the Romantic era created a very specific "aesthetic geology," a material and aesthetic appreciation of rocks. To the Romantics, the formlessness of rock compositions dramatized the recalcitrance of raw matter and triggered associations between the Picturesque and geology.[03] Similarly, in his book *Romantic Landscapes: Geology and Its Cultural Influence in Britain, 1765–1835,* Dennis R. Dean points to the unseparated condition of the arts and sciences in the 18th century and demonstrates how the geological developments of the era closely related to that of the Picturesque. More specifically, contrary to seeing the Picturesque as a direct consequence of the enclosure movement in England (the prevailing interpretation), Dean reveals that the "Picturesque was itself a kind of enclosure movement since it endeavored to reduce problems caused by an awareness of geological forces to pictorial dimension."[04] While proposing the Sublime, the Picturesque, and the Geological as three major classifications of the Romantic landscape, Dean sees geological theories as aesthetic constructs in themselves:

> By reducing space to manageable "views," the Picturesque bounds, frames, and subdues its potential energy . . . In general, the Sublime recognizes and delights in present (or latent) force; the Picturesque seeks to deny or contain it; and the Geological stresses the roles of natural forces through time . . . Romantic geological theories are rational attempts to discover origins and processes of the inanimate world—scientific endeavor as it was then understood—but they are also . . . aesthetic constructs designed to affirm a particular version of the geocosm.[05]

What is particularly striking about both Heringman's and Dean's affirmations on the relationship between the geological and the aesthetic is the fact that it was not only that late 18th- and 19th-century landscape painting was affected by the developments in geology but that geology itself was also affected by art and aesthetics. Art historian Marcia Pointon sheds light on this point by exposing the conceptual alliance between geologists and landscape painters, especially during the 19th century. She argues that, while both groups shared a strong interest in developing a new visual language for registering geological features, each also favored imagination over the empiricism and accuracy of topographers:

> Since the accurate recording of features of the landscape without improvement or embroidery was essential to the geologist . . . one might reasonably expect the empirical tradition of the topographer to have had the greatest influence on the development of landscape painting in the nineteenth century, the period when geology becomes

a science of major importance . . . But the topographical artists, whose main tasks had been antiquarian or military (the recording of ancient buildings, harbors and coastlines) used an outline technique which was not well suited to the needs of the geologists . . . Thus, on one level, the growing interest in geology in the 19th century was readily absorbed into an existing tradition remote from topography; and the ground was prepared for an alliance between landscape painting and geology which would operate as much through the imagination as through empiricism.[06]

Pointon's analysis is even more noteworthy when one considers the much-preferred emphasis on empirical research and "evidence" within the design disciplines today, in discussions of environment, landscape, and territory. How can we talk about similar kinds of interactions between aesthetic imagination and the new geological age of the Anthropocene when it comes to understanding material both as resource and recalcitrance of raw matter? Rather than limiting the role of the Anthropocene for design merely to a visualization problem (empirical research of data) or to an issue of mastering or solving (righteous scenario planning or environmental engineering of data and performance), might we see it as an opportunity to prompt renewed relationships between the material and the representational?

As an alternative to relying on prescriptive efficiency measures, one could instead see an emerging body of speculation in the field of eco-criticism and history that understands environment in its temporal and spatial "long-view"—that is, within a longer span of time and larger span of earth, offering an important, expanded interpretation of our relationship to the earth as humans. "To call human beings geological agents," as historian Dipesh Chakrabarty argues, "is to scale up our imagination of the human."[07] As "the distinction between human and natural histories—much of which had been preserved even in environmental histories that saw the two entities in interaction—has begun to collapse," he writes, "it is no longer a question simply of man having an interactive relation with nature" but rather of humans as a "force of nature in the geological sense."[08] Here, one thinks for instance of Timothy Morton's "hyperobjects," which depict environment both within a temporal and spatial long-view; environment as the compilation of immense objects that are vastly spread out in time and space relative to humans. Morton writes:

> Capitalism is a boiling whirlwind of impermanence. It reveals how things are always shifting and changing. But, it isn't the ultimate horizon of meaning . . . Materials from humble Styrofoam to terrifying plutonium will far outlast current social and biological forms. We are talking about

hundreds and thousands of years. Five hundred years from now, polystyrene objects such as cups and takeout boxes will still exist. Humans have manufactured materials that are already beyond the normal scope of our comprehension . . . Plutonium will be around for far longer than all of recorded human "history" so far. If you want a monument, look around you.[09]

Additionally, from historians Jo Guldi and David Armitage's critique of short-termism in historical studies and call for a new conception of the *longue durée* in their book *History Manifesto* (2014), to media theorist Jussi Parikka's geological studies of media—which builds an alternative media theoretical lineage for materials, metals, chemistry, and waste—recent explorations similarly attempt an intellectual shift in our understanding toward a longer span of time as well as a larger and deeper span of earth.[10] The raw materials of the earth, Parikka writes, "articulate the high-technical and low-paid culture of digitality. They also provide an alternative materialism for the geophysical media age."[11] While understanding environment in its temporal and spatial long view, these explorations offer alternative future possibilities for criticality and speculation for building unconventional relationships between the politics and aesthetics of materiality for design disciplines.

Nine Islands

The *Nine Islands: Matters around Architecture* project aims to start such alternative conversations about materiality by focusing on nine expensive building materials. From the recalcitrance of a particular raw matter and its extraction from a specific geographic location, to its processing, transportation, and construction into a desired finished effect in a building, to its demolition and waste, the project aims to open future dialogues in relation to the spatial and temporal long span of architectural materiality.[12] By emphasizing the contrast between the raw and the finished, the project renders architecture's direct relationship with resource geographies visible.

The project consists of an archipelago of nine islands, each of which is represented through an axonometric drawing. Each island is made from a particular, lavish building material (certain types of leather, marble, wood, glass, travertine, gold, limestone, steel, granite, and so on). The upper portion of each island consists of an archetypical building form, achieved through the elementary extrusion of primitive shapes. In opposition to this upper part of the island, the lower part of each consists of a formless landmass, from which the raw matter is extracted (quarry for the marble, tree for the wood, cows for the leather, and so forth).

Opposite page: Neyran Turan, *Nine Islands: Matters around Architecture*.

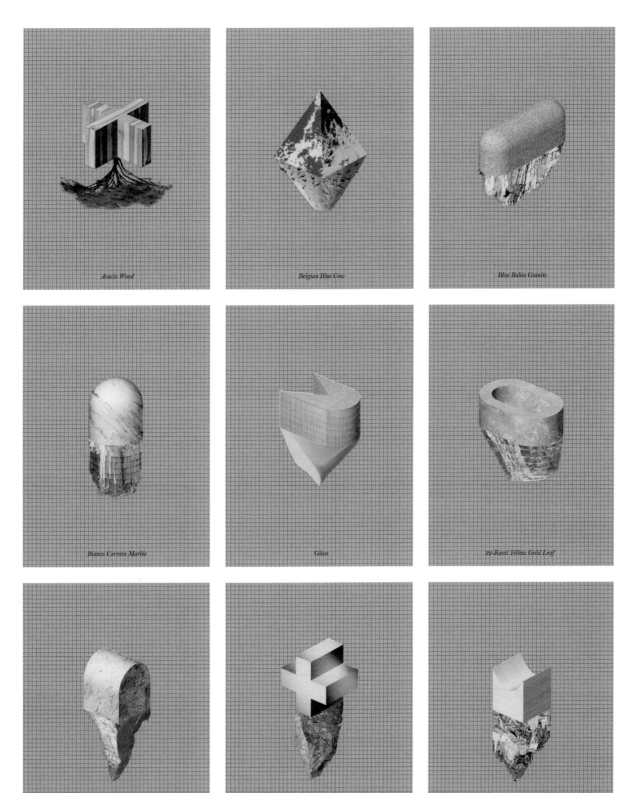

Acacia Wood

Belgian Blue Coxe

Blue Bahia Granite

Bianco Carrara Marble

Glass

22-Karat Yellow Gold Leaf

Bianco Honed Limestone

Steel

Azarshahr Travertine

135

Drawing 5 from NEMESTUDIO'S Architectural League Prize Installation, June 2016.

Accordingly, by juxtaposing the finished surfaces and archaic extrusions of typologically simplified monuments at the top with the vulgar formlessness of the naked landmasses below, each island dramatizes the recalcitrance of a particular raw matter as an object. This juxtaposition of monument and landmass works through two registers: first, the collapse of the finished and the raw aims to call attention to the under-conceptualized space in between; second, by suspending the archetypical slow time of architecture (the extended time-span of a given typology) and the slow time of geology in the objective space of the axonometric, the project presents the "reverse obsolescence" of each island as a resource ruin.[13]

Aiming to couple an inquiry of matter in architecture with its seeming opposites—representation, monumental-ity, and composition—Nine Islands poses an alternative conception of materialism within the discipline. In an era when humans are described as "geological agents,"[14] archi-tecture is both a background and a measure against which the world might be read. Like architecture then, Nine Is-lands represents the world back to itself.

The author would like to acknowledge and thank David Richmond and Patrick Daurio for all of their help with the Nine Islands project.

01. "One Shell Plaza: Tallest Building West of the Mississippi," *Architectural Design* 42, no. 1 (January 1972): 22.

02. For further elaborations on these questions in the context of climate change, see Neyran Turan, "Measure for the Anthropocene," in *Climates: Architecture and the Planetary Imaginary*, ed. James Graham et al. (New York and Zurich: Columbia Books on Architecture and the City Lars Müller Publishers, 2016), 120–128. See also Neyran Turan, "How Do Geographic Objects Perform?," *ARPA*, vol. 3, *Performance* (2015), http://www.arpajournal.net/how-do-geographic-objects-perform.

03. Noah Heringman, *Romantic Rocks: Aesthetic Geology* (Ithaca: Cornell University Press, 2004).

04. Dennis R. Dean, *Romantic Landscapes: Geology and Its Cultural Influence in Britain, 1765–1835* (Ann Arbor: Scholars' Facsimiles & Reprints, 2007), 62.

05. Ibid., 66.

06. Marcia Pointon, "Geology and Landscape Painting in Nineteenth-century England," in *Images of the Earth: Essays in the History of Environmental Sciences*, ed. Ludmilla Jordanova and Roy Porter (Oxford: Alden Press), 95–96. For a similar discussion in the American context, see Rebecca Bedell, *The Anatomy of Nature: Geology and American Landscape Painting, 1825–1875* (Princeton: Princeton University Press, 2002).

07. Dipesh Chakrabarty, "The Climate of History: Four Theses," *Critical Enquiry* 35 (2009): 206.

08. Ibid, 207.

09. Timothy Morton, *Ecological Thought* (Cambridge, MA: Harvard University Press, 2010), 130–31.

10. Jussi Parikka, *The Anthrobscene* (Minneapolis: University of Minnesota Press, 2014); Jo Guldi and David Armitage, *History Manifesto* (Cambridge: Cambridge University Press, 2014).

11. Jussi Parikka, *The Anthrobscene*, 98.

12. The luxury or economy embedded in any particular material is more complex than simply calculating a unit cost, especially if one factors in embodied energy and embodied carbon in relation to the lifecycle of construction materials. Consider concrete, for example. As the most widely used building material, concrete might not make it into the list of most expensive building materials, on first inspection. However, concrete is a mixture of the constituent materials cement, sand, aggregate, and other additives such as plasticizers. The processing and transportation of some of these materials (cement and aggregates, for instance) contribute substantially to the cost of concrete, as well as its energy and carbon impacts. See G. P. Hammond and C. I. Jones, "Embodied Energy and Carbon in Construction Materials," *Proceedings of the Institution of Civil Engineers—Energy* 161, no. 2 (2008): 87–98.

13. Borrowing from Vladimir Nabokov's observation that, "the future is but the obsolete in reverse," in his article "The Monuments of Passaic" from 1967, Robert Smithson used the phrase "ruins in reverse" to refer to the construction sites of the suburban developments in Passaic, which were going to be eventually built. He wrote: "This is the opposite of the "romantic ruin" because the buildings don't *fall* into ruin *after* they are built but rather *rise* into ruin before they are built." Emphases in original. Robert Smithson, "The Monuments of Passaic," *Artforum* (December 1967): 54. For Smithson's reference to Nabokov, see his "Entropy and the New Monuments," *Artforum* (June 1966): 26–31.

14. B. Wilkinson, "Humans as Geologic Agents: A Deep-Time Perspective," *Geology* 33, no. 3 (2005): 161–64. Also see Peter Baccini and Paul H. Brunner, *Metabolism of the Anthroposphere: Analysis, Evaluation, Design* (Cambridge, MA: MIT Press, 2012).

Image Credits

135: Courtesy of the author.

136: Courtesy of NEMESTUDIO.

Neyran Turan

Painterly Formation

Roland Snooks

Painterly formation is a design strategy that engages painterly operations and self-organizing algorithms in a mutual feedback loop. The technique, developed at Studio Roland Snooks, establishes a negotiation between top-down and bottom-up processes. The interaction of the two creates a hybrid character, combining the complex order of behavioral algorithms with the gestural qualities of painterly operations. The brushing of geometry within digital sculpting software and the reorganization of geometry through multi-agent algorithms work in tandem, playing off each other and operating directly on mesh geometry.

This process is part of a larger approach to design that we describe as behavioral formation, which draws from the logic of swarm intelligence. This approach involves encoding design intention within multi-agent algorithms, from which a self-organized intention emerges. In behavioral formation, the strange feedback between direct models and multi-agent algorithms primarily attempts to overcome the global ignorance of those algorithms to develop coherent relationships between form and articulation. This formal strategy privileges the control of surface and topology. The application of digital sculpting techniques and the direct operation of agents on meshes within painterly formation shifts the focus from form to texture. The volatile surface topology that this process generates defines mass rather than surface and is redeployed as a thick texture rather than a controlled spatial operation.

In developing this hybrid of the painterly and the self-organizational, we attempt to escape the indexical characteristics typical of generative processes that rely exclusively on a single system. Painterly formation creates a closeness between the operations as they both operate directly on a common substrate, enabling a fine-grain interaction of the two. The painterly and self-organizational information, once encoded in the polygon mesh substrate, triggers procedural geometric operations, or creates masks for various painterly geometric operations. Operating on a common substrate posits the painterly and self-organizational as isomorphic within this design process.

Painterly formation operates directly on the object, both computationally and conceptually. The operations are not deferred; they do not act as organizational structures to be manipulated later in the design process. Instead the operations are direct and accumulative. This is an attempt to create esoteric formal qualities, arising from a direct concern for the character of the object.

The non-systemic feedback generated by the two operations creates formal tendencies, rather than systemic or indexical consistency, within the object. In this inherently speculative and experimental process, our ambition is to create a strange, nuanced, and rich formal character.

Studio Roland Snooks.
Project team: Roland Snooks,
Marc Gibson.

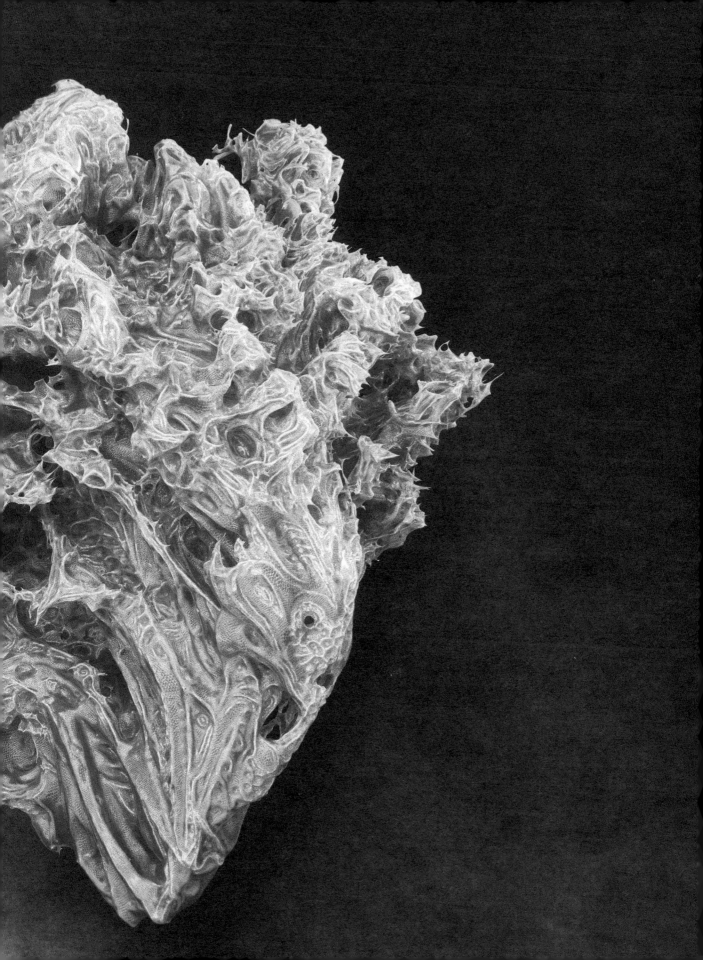

Gardens as Migratory Devices

Kees Lokman & Susan Herrington

Precisely because it is an archetype the garden must be subject to constant reinterpretation; there are as many kinds of gardens as there are concepts of art and work and community, and of relationships to the natural world. Even within a given culture there are many versions of the garden. Yet we somehow recognize them all.

—J. B. Jackson

The term *garden* typically evokes the idea of an enclosed planted space—an idealized version of the world where everything is in its place. A closer look at the origins of the word *garden* in the English language tells us it is derived from the Indo-European root *gher*, meaning to grasp or enclose, with derivatives meaning "enclosure."[01] Yet gardens are also physically connected to the surrounding landscape and therefore facilitate movement—the flow of seeds, nutrients, animals, plants, pollen, and insects. Moreover, the realities of climate change, the shifting of hardiness zones, and the acknowledgement that plants travel and invite travel, whether on their own accord or with human agency, challenge previous conceptions of gardens as bounded spaces. This does not necessarily mean that spatial definition is becoming less important in the design and representation of gardens. Instead it stimulates us to think differently about how to integrate dynamic ecological systems into spatially bounded landscapes.

Over two decades ago, Joan Nassauer introduced the notion of "messy ecosystems and orderly frames" to describe novel landscape designs that communicate human intention while celebrating ecological quality and diversity.[02] For example, by framing naturalistic plantings and untamed patterns with more formal design elements, such as trimmed shrubs, hedges, or fences, it is possible to integrate the aesthetics of "wild" and unfamiliar ecosystems into a familiar design language. According to Nassauer, these "orderly frames are not a means of dominating ecological phenomena for the sake of human pleasure. Orderly frames can be used to construct a widely recognizable cultural framework for ecological quality."[03] Here, formal delineation or enclosure provides a mechanism for spatial definition and ecological diversity in landscapes.

Ideas of movement and migration are increasingly explored in landscape architecture. Brett Milligan, an assistant professor of landscape architecture in the Department of Human Ecology at the University of California, Davis, observes that the notion of bounded elements in a landscape is a fabrication in opposition to the way landscapes really function: "We know that environmental conditions are always changing, but we allow ourselves the fiction of background stability. When we limit our thinking in this way, our political and design responses are circumscribed. (Allot

water rights. Designate a wildlife refuge. Build a wall.) Not surprisingly, they often fail."[04] In other words, when we conceive landscapes or gardens as contained spaces, we limit their capacity to enable natural processes of change and flow that are inherent to works employing biotic material. Milligan suggests that migratory landscapes comprise "patterned movement across space and time," as "qualitatively different landscapes can and do manifest upon a single geographic terrain."[05]

Migratory gardens may well be a propitious strategy in the Anthropocene—an era that demands a rethinking of gardens as part of atmospheric, geologic, hydrologic, and biospheric changes that have resulted from human activity. Maria Hellström Reimer, Director of the national Swedish Faculty for Design Research and Research Education, argues for a new conception of design, "in which many previously disregarded environmental issues such as energy flows, waste handling, biodiversity and human-wildlife coexistence are not only present but conspicuous, calling for more than dutiful attention."[06] Ongoing urbanization, including urban sprawl and accelerated resource extraction are causing habitat fragmentation and environmental transformations across large territories. This suggests that the purpose of gardens should expand from a space dedicated to primarily social functions to a space that also enhances biodiversity and accommodates climate change adaptation strategies. From the movement of plants, to pollinator gardens, to seed banks, to carbon sinks, gardens can be designed to induce migration, rendering new strategies and tools for their conception. Moreover, because of the tremendous diversity in microclimates, plant materials, soil conditions, and levels of maintenance, gardens serve as exemplary laboratories for testing new design approaches that not only broaden their definition but also equally explore new human-environment relations. In this context, this essay explores the idea of gardens as migratory devices through three lenses: ecological assemblages, the politics of gardens, and migratory aesthetics.

Gardens as Ecological Assemblages

Among the most active designers engaging the notion of gardens and the role of human interventions with regard to control and maintenance of urban landscapes is Gilles Clément. Both a writer and landscape architect, Clément has developed three distinct, yet interconnected, thoughts on landscapes: the *Garden in Motion*, the *Planetary Garden*, and the *Third Landscape*. Collectively, these concepts propose a "human-centered commitment to landscape beyond the human, beyond the pastoral dyad of rural and urban."[07] Clément values the way plants *move* about the garden. Moving plants often incite concern or even fear—consider the warnings about plant species that "invade." Moreover, some plants,

Through projects like *Le jardin du tiers-Paysage*, Bordeaux, Clément has explored how the gardener can guide and enrich natural processes of spontaneous vegetation.

such as stands of trees, are valued for their rootedness when in fact maple forests are moving north with climate change. Most gardeners attempt to control plant movement, but for the past twenty years Clément has been realizing gardens that emphasize the movement of plant material over their fixed placement in specific locations. Treating his gardens like testing grounds, he prompts an appreciation of the subtle and sometimes disquieting narratives of survival that plants make visible in their struggle for air, light, water, and space.

For Clément specifically, the garden is a platform for staging the interplay between movement and control as well as a place for scientific inquiry and aesthetic exploration. "Flowers sprouting in a path present the gardener with a choice: to conserve the path or the flowers."[08] This seemingly inconsequential question hints at Clément's much bigger inquiry concerning the role of humanity in preserving biodiversity and planetary stewardship. Clément suggests, "Humanity depends entirely on the diversity it exploits but, in the course of evolution, it reaches a stage where the environment itself—hence diversity—becomes dependent on humanity."[09]

Here, the island as both a physical manifestation and symbolic representation has significantly influenced Clément's work. The notion of island is expressed in his design for *Parc Henri Matisse* in Lille. This park actually contains an artificial island—a 7-meter high plateau covering an area of 2,500 square meters—serving as an ecological sanctuary. Intentionally inaccessible to humans, its purpose is to provide an undisturbed habitat for (vulnerable) species to flourish, to promote open-ended processes, and to serve as a seed bank for the surrounding area. Named after the Derborence Forest in Switzerland—one of the very few remaining old-growth forests in Europe—the island is both a real space and an imaginary geography. This also resonates with French landscaper Sonia Keravel, who points out that this landscape "not only represents a biological system, it also represents a place that is held apart from the power system, a vacuum, an inaccessible therefore mysterious space over which no one has a hold."[10]

Parc Henri Matisse also functions as a scientific observatory to experiment with and document species movement and succession patterns over time. As suggested by Matthew Gandy, "the park as a whole can be conceived as a 'third object' produced dialectically from the antinomy between the island of disordered nature at its core and the more closely controlled features that surround it."[11] Conceptually, *Parc Henri Matisse* takes its cues from the *Sanctuarium* projects by Dutch artist Herman de Vries. For the 1997 Sculpture Project in Münster, De Vries conceived of an inaccessible space, 14 meters in diameter and enclosed by a 2.65-meter-high

144

Conceived as a "third landscape," Derborence Island is intended to evolve outside of direct human intervention, providing a refuge for urban ecosystems and biodiversity. *Parc Henri Matisse*, Lille.

brick wall. Four small openings allow observers to peek into the space. Filled only with soil, this is a place where pioneer plants have migrated, creating a design of chance patterns from nature that change remarkably over time. Rather than a static sculpture or planted space devised by the artist, *Sanctuarium* invites contemplation of the place of humans in the garden. It is spatially defined yet isolated from human intrusion. Even the designer and the maintenance workers are excluded. According to De Vries, the *Sancturaium* challenges us "to look and to reflect; it is also an act of resistance against the threat of the one-sided development of our technological-commercial culture."[12]

Inherent in the projects of Clément and De Vries, is the tension between social and ecological processes. The projects simultaneously engage the surrounding landscape and shut themselves off from it. Human agency is essential in shaping the spatial circumstances needed to frame and reveal "the independent agency of nature."[13] This draws people's attention to the subtle interplay of will and desire among humans and plants. Their work demands a certain engagement with the medium and the idea of landscape as "a portion of the earth's surface," an ever-changing, dynamic, social–ecological system, and with the role humans play in altering or suspending these processes.[14] At the same time, their work also points to new possibilities for landscape

design, as it forces designers to break down long-standing conceptions of gardens and landscapes as simply governed by human processes and needs.

Concepts such as Clément's *Garden in Motion* and De Vries's *Sanctuarium* provoke questions regarding how to construct future spatial, material, and socio-ecological assemblages. For how many different species do we design? What parts of the design are fixed and which are able to evolve? How do we shape new relationships among humans, technology, and the environment? Far from suggesting a more hands-off design attitude, this actually requires a more intimate relationship between the designer and the designed. And it also necessitates a more fundamental engagement with political, cultural, aesthetic, and environmental agendas associated with landscape design.

The Politics of Gardens

Gardens also enclose, include, and exclude. Whether in private gardens, community gardens, or farms, an enclosure such as a fence, hedge, or hedgerow often forms a significant component of bounding a space. In *The Story of Gardening: A Social History*, Martin Hoyles states, "enclosure is essential to gardening, and this raises fundamental questions, such as who is doing the enclosing, who owns the land, and who is being kept out."[15] This makes gardens inherently political,

145

Kees Lokman & Susan Herrington

Figure 3.1
Artemesia absinthium *"Wormwood"*
Year of Introduction: 1600's
Origin: Eurasia

Figure 3.2
Cirsium arvense *"Creeping Thistle"*
Year of Introduction: 1700's
Origin: Europe

Figure 3.3
Dipsacus fullonum *"Teasel"*
Year of Introduction: 1700's
Origin: Europe

Figure 3.4
Phragmites communis *"Common Reed"*
Year of Introduction: 1700's
Origin: Europe

Figure 3.5
Butomus umbellatus *"Flowering Rush"*
Year of Introduction: 1753
Origin: Eurasia

Figure 3.6
Centaurea maculosa *"Myrtle"*
Year of Introduction: 1700's
Origin: Eurasia

Figure 3.7
Hypericum perforatum *"Rosin Rose"*
Year of Introduction: 1793
Origin: Europe

Figure 3.8
Centaurea maculosa *"Spotted Knapweed"*
Year of Introduction: 1800's
Origin: Europe

Figure 3.9
Cynanchum nigrum *"Dog-strangling Vine"*
Year of Introduction: mid 1800's
Origin: Europe

Figure 3.10
Hemerocallis fulva *"Orange Daylily"*
Year of Introduction: 1800's
Origin: Europe

Figure 3.11
Lysimachia nummularia *"Goatweed"*
Year of Introduction: 1800's
Origin: Europe

Figure 3.12
Lythrum salicaria *"Purple loosestrife"*
Year of Introduction: 1800's
Origin: Eurasia

Figure 3.13
Phalaris arundinacea *"Reed canary grass"*
Year of Introduction: 1800
Origin: Europe

Figure 3.14
Angelica sylvestris *"Angelica"*
Year of Introduction: 1802
Origin: Europe

Figure 3.15
Berteroa incana *"Hoary Alyssum"*
Year of Introduction: 1885
Origin: Eurasia

Figure 3.16
Polygonum cuspidatum *"Japanese Knotweed"*
Year of Introduction: 1825
Origin: Asia

Figure 3.17
Carduus nutans *"Nodding Thistle"*
Year of Introduction: 1850
Origin: Eurasia

Figure 3.18
Chelidonium majus *"Swallow Wort"*
Year of Introduction: 1867's
Origin: Europe

Figure 3.19
Campanula rapunculoides *"Creeping Bellflower"*
Year of Introduction: 1863
Origin: Eurasia

Figure 3.20
Aegopodium podagraria *"Goatweed"*
Year of Introduction: 1885
Origin: Eurasia

Figure 3.21
Acinos arvensis *"Mother-of-thyme"*
Year of Introduction: 1913
Origin: Eurasia

Figure 3.22
Cisium arvense *"Eurasian Water Milfoil"*
Year of Introduction: 1960
Origin: Eurasia

particularly when the public affairs of a country are sanctioning the enclosing, as witnessed in the Enclosure Acts of the 18th century in Britain. By extension, migration—the act of moving from one place to another, whether voluntarily or by force—is also political and evokes questions of nativity and belonging. Human migration, global commerce, and scientific exploration allowed plants, animals, microorganisms, and other living things transport to new habitats and ecosystems. As a result, just as our cities host different cultures, so gardens and urban landscapes meld together an incredibly diverse and complex matrix of native and non-native species. As American botanist Peter Del Tredici points out, "Changes in urban vegetation over time clearly reflect constantly shifting human value judgments, socioeconomic cycles and evolving technological advances in transportation, communication, and construction."[16]

As a way of reconceptualizing how we can describe and productively integrate these constantly shifting mosaics of native and non-native plants both ecologically and politically, Del Tredici has introduced the term *cosmopolitan urban vegetation*. This matrix of plant species features a wide array of stress-tolerant plants that push aesthetic boundaries and are preadapted to extreme urban conditions (i.e. compacted and dry soils, pollution, salt, etc.). "Such an eclectic mix of species," according to Del Tredici, "acknowledges not only the long history of immigration and ecological abuse that characterize many urban areas but also the reality of climate change–induced environmental stresses that make the 'restoration' of past native ecosystems an ecological (and financial) fantasy."[17]

Early plant explorers traveling the world did not give conceptions of nativity and non-nativity in biotic material much consideration. Botanists assisting with the collection, transportation, and cultivation of plants as part of early scientific explorations similarly concerned themselves only with a plant's economic, scientific, or ornamental merit. As landscape scholar Kaye Wierzbicki suggests, "while debates about the most beautiful, healthy, strong, or useful plants were always at play in garden design, bioregional suitability was never a question except perhaps for purely practical matters of plant care."[18] Native and non-native assignments to plant material did not enter the landscape lexicon until the 20th century. A group of landscape architects and plant sociologists working in Germany prior to World War II promoted native species in German landscapes as a proxy for the Nordic race. Associating alien plants with the Jews, they castigated them as a threat to Nordic culture. This racist agenda

disguised as garden theory was quickly advanced by the National Socialists, who enshrined their "landscape rules" as governmental policy and hired landscape architects to redesigned the territory seized from Poland as an ideal German landscape.[19] Despite these fascist beginnings, the idea of native species and their use have shaped the moral underpinnings of garden theory in 21st-century North America. Non-native species are deemed morally suspect and invasive species are denounced as objects of fear and loathing.

A relevant example that challenges us to revisit our animosity towards non-native species is *The Garden of Displaced Roots*, a proposal developed by architect Neeraj Bhatia and the Open Workshop. The proposal draws its inspiration from the nearly 500 non-native plant species that exist in Canada, many of them introduced in the 19th century as ornamental additions to the garden. "Ironically, it is the success of these plants flourishing in non-native environments that now makes them a threat," Bhatia explains.[20] The installation highlights 22 of the earliest "invasive" plant species introduced to Canada. Contained in individual "rooms" as part of an overhanging tensile structure, the plants hover above the ground where visitors can observe them. As the plants grow throughout the season, their weight increases. This flexes the fabric armature and brings the plants closer to the ground, allowing visitors to interact with the species.

Although designed as a playful installation, the *Garden of Displaced Roots* discloses more serious notions of containment and quarantine. The tensile structure is at once interactive and symbolic of containment—a preventative measure to keep plants from spreading seeds, establishing roots, and invading the local ecosystem. At the same time, the formal enclosure created by the installation creates a space for the non-native plants to grow (quite literally) within the Canadian landscape. As such, the project presents a paradox: in order to integrate the plants with their surroundings, the installation applies principles of separation rather than seamless continuity. By elevating and highlighting these "unwanted" species, the installation repositions these plants both physically and conceptually as an inherent consequence of migration and an integral part of the historical transformations of the Canadian landscape. According to Bhatia, "By framing the tension between invasive and native species the project is in part a critique of culture through art and in part a critique of nature through garden design."[21]

Another way of exploring the nexus of migration, politics, and gardens is by looking at contemporary expressions of community gardening. In both extremely dense urban areas with limited open space and shrinking cities characterized by large swaths of vacant land, urban gardening is more often than not an expression of carving out spaces from city-owned land.[22] In this context the Guerrilla Grafters

147

Opposite: The Garden of Displaced Roots acts as a physical and visual tool to promote human/non-human interaction, and to problematize the notion of non-native species.

Kees Lokman & Susan Herrington

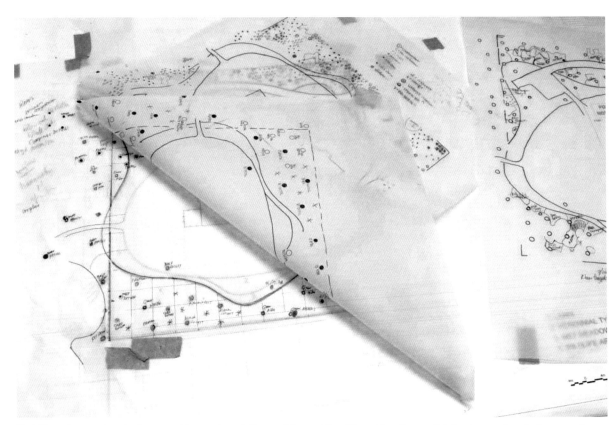

Oudolf's gardens are imagined as several layers of vegetation, each layer with a different function, spatial structure, and aesthetic expression.

symbolize a particular type of urban gardener who transgresses the borders of gardening, urbanism, politics, and environmental justice. The Guerrilla Grafters have been grafting fruit bearing branches (scions) onto ornamental street trees in the San Francisco Bay Area since 2011. To be sure, their tactics are guerrilla: these varieties of street trees were specifically selected by the city for their inability to produce fruit. In most private gardens the sweet and fleshy, seed-bearing products of a tree are welcomed. However, in the urban landscape the presence of fallen fruit, deemed litter, represents a liability, prompting cities to regulate their exclusion as a means of safeguarding against legal exposure. In other words, the performative nature of trees is bounded to the spatial and temporal codes of their location.

Municipal bylaws governing street trees and their conservation, ordinances determining tree maintenance and removal processes, and guidelines specifying species selection, soil mix, and tree installation have been instituted in conjunction with the planning process surrounding development and the protection of public health and safety. Not surprisingly, the City of San Francisco condemned the Guerrilla Grafters and categorized their guerrilla tactics as "a serious offense."[23] Despite these condemnations, the Guerrilla Grafters have continued their craft with temerity, judiciously transforming sterile streets and other publicly accessible urban areas into edible landscapes. Describing themselves as "a self-selected international cultural workforce," the grafters "aim to turn city streets into food forests, and unravel civilization one branch at a time."[24] The strategies deployed to enact this unraveling involve a combination of spontaneous interventions, face-to-face negotiations with individuals who have agreed to maintain the grafted trees, workshops, and other events—all documented on social media in order to raise awareness for their cause.

Migratory Aesthetics

The idea of gardens as migratory devices also resonate with James Corner's conception of the urban landscape as a *terra fluxus*. In contrast to *terra firma* (from the Latin, meaning solid earth), which is associated with the bounded conception of land from which surveyors and architects fashioned landscapes in England in the 18th century, *terra fluxus* facilitates temporal features, the "shifting processes coursing across the urban field."[25] Corner's conception of landscape as process challenges idealized versions of nature imported from English landscape gardens and romanticized by 20th-century environmentalists. The conventions of these idealized versions of nature adhere to a set of features that include

Moving from 2-D to 3-D, Oudolf's designs are carefully planted and maintained.

clumps of large deciduous trees, rolling hills of manicured grass, and flooded valleys. They present the image of what nature should look like in the practice of design but not necessarily how nature functions. Landscape architect and professor Udo Weilacher points out, "The pre-industrial clichés of picturesque and orderly woodlands are useless. The construction and maintenance of scenic woodland parks designed according to the common models of garden design [would result] in a grave loss of ecological efficiency."[26] Weilacher and others promote the inclusion of functional landscapes—fields and forests—into our conception of landscapes. This involves an aesthetic of agriculture and forestry based on cultural practices and ecological change over time, or what landscape architect Paolo Burgi calls *venustas et utilitas* (beauty and utility), and which includes farmers and foresters—"the involuntary landscape designers."[27]

But what exactly do gardens as migratory devices look like? Their aesthetics have been culled from an unlikely source—the perennial gardener—and are most poignantly exhibited in the work of Piet Oudolf. With no formal training in design or gardening, Oudolf gained his gardening knowledge from toiling in his own plant-propagation garden, Hummelo, in the Netherlands, where he has experimented firsthand with herbaceous perennials and grasses for

more than thirty years. While the history of gardeners working with grasses and herbaceous perennials finds its origins in the private border gardens of the Edwardian period, in the 1990s Oudolf scaled up this practice to public sites. Starting in 1995, Oudolf was "let loose" to replace lawns and floral displays with large blocks of grasses and perennial plantings, creating Dream Park in Enköping, Sweden.[28] From this set of practical and oneiric circumstances, a migratory aesthetic emerged. During the past two decades, Oudolf received commissions to create gardens in collaboration with leading architects and landscape architects. Several of his gardens are part of high-profile public spaces, including the High Line for James Corner Field Operations, the Lurie Garden for Gustafson Guthrie Nichol, and the Garden at the Serpentine Gallery for Peter Zumthor.

Oudolf's method eschews conventional approaches to design. His work shifts from an over-determinacy of location to the articulation of space through an accentuation of the dynamic nature of the plants themselves.[29] Layering is perhaps the most important component of this approach. From the initial design phase through the implementation and evolutionary stages of the project, Oudolf imagines and incorporates various vegetation layers within the garden. These layers progressively transform from two dimensions

149

Kees Lokman & Susan Herrington

Oudolf's own nursery and garden at Hummelo, The Netherlands, is a perfect example of a seemingly wild yet orderly framed planting design, introducing visitors to ecological aesthetics and raising environmental awareness.

(in the drawing overlays he uses to construct his designs) to three dimensions (in the vegetation layers he uses to create space and depth), and finally, into four dimensions (in the layered vegetation that changes over time).

Oudolf explains that his initial drawings typically incorporate three layers: "The first layer consists of structural plants, followed by a matrix of grasses, and then a layer of accent and filler plants. Lay all the sheets together and I'll have the makings of a highly intermingled perennial planting design."[30]

The combination of plant choice, plant choreography, and context (Oudolf's most compelling projects are the ones that juxtapose his lush planting against the backdrop of built form) amplify the dynamic nature of his designs. The gardens transform not only year to year but also season to season, with different varieties growing and blooming at different times. Oudolf carefully selects plants based on bloom times as well as on the texture of the plant when not in bloom. Unlike Del Tredici's cosmopolitan urban vegetation, Oudolf's planting designs require a good deal of maintenance, encouraging Oudolf himself to migrate back to most of his gardens each year.[31] Focused on *how* to plant, and on understanding the dynamics of plant communities, Oudolf is less concerned with using native vegetation for the sake of its preservation. Instead, he chooses plants for their compatibility, aesthetics, shape, texture, and expressions over time.[32]

In essence, a visit to Oudolf's migratory garden might look completely different from one week to the next. As a conduit for environmental understanding and awareness, the varied aesthetic experiences of Oudolf's landscapes play an important role in promoting a more dynamic and codependent relationship between nature and culture. As carefully framed and managed landscapes that incorporate ecological aesthetics, the gardens of Oudolf and his contemporaries are paving the way for more radical concepts, such as Clément's garden in motion and Del Tredici's cosmopolitan urban vegetation. These concepts fundamentally embrace notions of flux and resilience while providing a host of ecosystem services, including stormwater management, carbon storage, pollination, habitat, and more. Additionally, herbaceous perennials and grasses excel in recruiting other species, and perennials that require the division of their root systems will produce new plants for cultivation. The biomass generated by these types of plantings is notable for its sheer volume, with some plants reaching three meters in height during the course of a single growing season. In these projects, Oudolf provides a compelling spatial vision for the garden in the age of carbon-neutrality—an age which, as Paul Selmen, head of Department of Landscape at Sheffield University, has posited, "may acquire an attachment to new forms of landscape which hitherto might have been dismissed as untidy, hazardous and unmanicured."[33]

* * *

"If the defining feature of the 20th-century urban landscape was its freedom of definition—everything flowed into everything else," Michael Hebbert, professor of town planning at Bartlett, suggests, then the "emergent paradigm is based on spaces with definition and purpose."[34] Rather than a sprawling web of undifferentiated green spaces, we are now seeing open space management and design approaches based on spatial definition and heterogeneity. In this sense, the open space network of a city can be understood as a matrix of patches and corridors, which depend on connection and disconnection, openness and enclosure, managed and unmanaged zones.[35] The garden, while occupying only a small niche within this matrix, becomes a critical space—both physical and perceptual—in which to revisit and stage discussions about notions of migration, enclosure, politics, and aesthetics. It represents a tangible arena that challenges us to question and redefine relationships with one another and with natural systems and processes.[36] It is exactly the idea of active, hands-on involvement with living systems that makes gardens such powerful modes of exploration in ongoing conversations about the mediation of nature and culture. This also raises fundamental questions, such as how gardens are being enclosed, and what the political and ecological implications of this enclosure may be. What is the agency of nature, and how can it push back against a prevailing animosity toward non-native plants, animals, and perhaps even humans? What is the role and agency of the gardener—active facilitator of migratory processes, painter of aesthetic experiences, or a little bit of both? What is the preferred aesthetic of this human-nature collaboration? Although this essay does not provide answers to all of these questions, it presents gardens as fertile territories for future discussion and exploration for those interested in both the theory and practice of landscape architecture.

01. J. B. Jackson, *The Necessity for Ruins* (Amherst: University of Massachusetts Press, 1980).

02. Joan Nassauer, "Messy Ecosystems, Orderly Frames," *Landscape Journal* 14, no. 2 (1995): 169.

03. Ibid.

04. Brett Milligan, "Landscape Migration," *Places Journal*, June 2015, https://places journal.org/article/landscape-migration.

05. Ibid.

06. Maria Hellström Reimer, "Unsettling Eco-scapes: Aesthetic Performances for Sustainable Futures," *Journal of Landscape Architecture* 1 (2010): 24–37.

07. Jonathan Skinner, "Gardens of Resistance: Gilles Clément, New Poetics, and Future Landscapes," *Qui Parle: Critical Humanities and Social Sciences* 19, no. 2 (2011): 261.

08. Gilles Clément, *Gilles Clément: Une*

écologie humaniste, ed. Louisa Jones (Geneva: Aubanel, 2006): 19.

09. Ibid., 14. See also Gilles Clément, "L'alternative ambiente," *Carnets du Paysage*, vol. 19, *Ecologies à l'oeuvre* (Spring/Fall 2010), http://www.gillesclement.com.

10. Sonia Keravel, "'The Art of Transmission: Mediating Meaning in Contemporary French Landscape Design," *Journal of Landscape Architecture* 5, no. 1 (Spring 2010): 67.

11. Matthew Gandy, "Entropy by Design: Gilles Clément, Parc Henri Matisse and the Limits to Avant-garde Urbanism," *International Journal of Urban and Regional Research* 37, no. 1 (2013): 12.

12. Herman de Vries, "Sanctuarium," https://www.skulptur-projekte.de/skulptur-projektedownload/muenster/97/vries/k3_e.htm.

13. Gandy, "Entropy by Design," 15.

14. J. B. Jackson, "The Word Itself" in *Discovering the Vernacular Landscape*, ed. J. B. Jackson (New Haven: Yale University Press, 1984): 1–8.

15. Martin Hoyles, *The Story of Gardening: A Social History* (Newburyport, MA: Journeyman, 1991), 1.

16. Peter Del Tredici, "The Flora of the Future," *Places Journal*, April 2014, https://placesjournal.org/article/the-flora-of-the-future.

17. Peter Del Tredici and Michael Luegering, "A Cosmopolitan Urban Meadow for the Northeast," *Harvard Design Magazine* 37 (2014), http://www.harvarddesignmagazine.org/issues/37/a-cosmopolitan-urban-meadow-for-the-northeast.

18. Kaye Wierzbicki, "The Formal and the Foreign: Sarah Orne Jewett's Garden Fences and the Meaning of Enclosure," *Nineteenth-Century Literature* 69, no. 1 (2014): 75.

19. Gert Groening and Joachim Wolschke-Bulmahn, "Some Notes on the Mania for Native Plants in Germany," *Landscape Journal* 11, no. 2 (Fall 1992): 116–26.

20. Neeraj Bhatia, "The Subjects of Performance," *ARPA Journal* Issue 3 (July 2015), http://www.arpajournal.net/the-subjects-of-performance.

21. Ibid.

22. Antony Giddens, *The Constitution of Society: Outline of the Theory of Structuration* (Berkeley: University of California Press, 1984).

23. Amy Crawford, "Renegade Arborists Creating Forbidden Fruit in San Francisco," *San Francisco Examiner*, January 4, 2012, http://archives.sfexaminer.com/sanfrancisco/renegade-arborists-creating-forbidden-fruit-in-san-francisco/Content?oid=2189270.

24. http://www.guerrillagrafters.org.

25. Kenneth Robert Olwig, *Landscape, Nature, and the Body Politic: From Britain's Renaissance to America's New World* (Madison: University of Wisconsin Press, 2002), 117; and James Corner, "Terra Fluxus," in *The Landscape Urbanism Reader*, ed. Charles Waldheim (New York: Princeton Architectural Press, 2006), 30.

26. Udo Weilacher, "Ferme Ornée Mechtenberg: Field Experiments between Postindustrial Wilderness and Usefulness," in *Feldstudien: Zur neuen Ästhetik urbaner Landwirtschaft (Field Studies: The New Aesthetics of Urban Agriculture)*, ed. Regionalverband Ruhr (Basel: Birkhäuser, 2010), 88–89.

27. Paolo Burgi, "Mechtenberg—Venustas et Utilitas," *La China Magazine* 9 (2010): 97.

28. Piet Oudolf and Noel Kingsbury, *Hummelo: A Journey through a Plantsman's Life* (New York: Monacelli, 2015), 157.

29. Ibid., 342.

30. Piet Oudolf, quoted in Tony Spencer, "Bringing Hummelo Home," *The New Perennialist: Explorations in Naturalistic Planting Design*, http://www.thenewperennialist.com/bringing-hummelo-home.

31. Oudolf, *Hummelo*, 331.

32. Piet Oudolf and Noël Kingsbury, *Designing with Plants* (Portland, OR: Timber Press, 1999), 16–17.

33. Paul Selman, "Learning to Love the Landscapes of Carbon-Neutrality," *Landscape Research* 35 (2010): 161.

34. Michael Hebbert, "Re-enclosure of the Urban Picturesque: Green-Space Transformations in Postmodern Urbanism," *Town Planning Review* 79, no. 1 (2008): 47.

35. Richard T. T. Forman, "Some General Principles of Landscape and Regional Ecology," *Landscape Ecology* 10, no. 3 (1995): 133–42.

36. See Hilda Kurtz, "Differentiating Multiple Meanings of Garden and Community," *Urban Geography* 22, no. 7 (2001): 656–70.

Image Credits

Kees Lokman & Susan Herrington

Designing Cities
with Mesocosms

Alexander J. Felson

The effective translation of ecological knowledge into design strategies is a core component of urban sustainability. With the growing interest in creating cities that are resilient and provide social and ecological advantages, designers and ecologists benefit from close collaboration and the sharing of one another's expertise.[01] Of particular value is the potential shared use of mesocosms as instruments for and ingredients in the design of urban ecosystems. These medium-scale, outdoor bounded experiments constitute a powerful tool for examining ecosystem dynamics and identifying drivers and mechanistic relationships in an otherwise complex and messy system.[02] Because mesocosms can be designed to be useful under a range of environments, they can also take advantage of ecological reference conditions and ecological engineering.

Like the smaller "microcosm," the mesocosm reduces variables and facilitates experimental replication.[03] Unlike microcosms, however, mesocosms incorporate more biologically complex systems and can capture richer community- and ecosystem-level responses.[04] Hence, mesocosms are effective for studying larger landscape dynamics and extrapolating insights from microcosms into more natural systems. Granted, mesocosms are more constrained and therefore often less robust or contextual than many large field experiments—such as whole lake studies—used to analyze ecological patterns and processes in situ.[05] As manipulated environments, mesocosms are sometimes within larger natural systems, sometimes embedded within highly managed environments. Their artificiality and reduced variables distinguish them from other types of larger field experiments, often designed at scales in which biological processes are more intact.[06] Large field experiments may include manipulations to reduce variables but the complexity of the system under consideration can make it difficult to set up effective research methods.[07] As a result, given the noise and experimental challenges, the validity of these studies in effectively teasing out cause-and-effect drivers is often challenged.[08] As mid-scale experiments, mesocosms provide a bridge between the lab and the field, enabling ecologists to develop conceptual frameworks and theories that simplify ecosystems, while allowing for some interpretation, differentiation, and organization of the interconnected and overlapping ecological patterns and processes.[09]

Ecologists use mesocosm experiments to assess the impact of discrete variables on a limited number of measured responses. They focus on ecosystem processes such as nutrient cycling, primary production, trophic systems, biomass, species traits, and niche development, investigating how these activities regulate the flux of energy and matter through an ecosystem.[10] In all cases, ecologists focus on the interactions among organisms and between organisms and their abiotic environments. They also study diversity, population dynamics, species distribution, and ecosystem dynamics, as well as behaviors among organisms and communities, such as predation, competition, and cooperation.[11] In order to study these complex systems at different organizational levels (for example, community, population, and ecosystem), ecologists have treated and manipulated aquatic islands, isolated tide pools, and vegetative patches as mesocosms.[12]

Ecological Debates around Mesocosms

The use of mesocosms began in the 1950s and continued to be discussed and debated through the 1990s.[13] Since that time, controlled, manipulative experiments that could not have been undertaken in more natural environments have multiplied. For four decades, the University of Rhode Island Marine Ecosystems Research Laboratory has hosted one such example. Tanks drawing water from the nearby river serve as a mesocosm to study pollution and experimental marine ecology. While mesocosms have been critical in teasing out ecological patterns and processes where testing would otherwise be difficult, debates around the outcomes and implications of studies employing mesocosms are not without precedent.[14] One study of island biogeography that is foundational for conservation biology drew a particularly heated debate.[15]

The mesocosm study took place on Biscayne Bay in South Florida, where mangrove islands were denuded to compare natural conditions to highly disturbed ones. The spatially explicit theory that developed out of this research was critical in clarifying rules governing species extinction and re-colonization in patches—that is, species extinction within isolated areas or other distinct conditions, such as mountain tops, fragmented forests, or remnant habitats marooned by human land development. The theory states that immigration and extinction determine the number of species one would find on such an island and that the distance effect, or the distance of an island from a source of species colonizers, affects immigration and emigration. Another central principle of this theory is the so-called area effect. This principle holds that the rate of species extinction in an isolated habitat patch is inversely related to the patch size.[16] Habitat fragmentation is known to produce edge effects, whereby the ratio of edge habitat to interior habitat increases as fragment size decreases.[17] Fragmentation and habitat destruction can also lead to increased distances between suitable habitat patches. For organisms, this translates into increased dispersal distances and greater isolation. These ecological theories are increasingly being applied to coupled human natural systems.[18]

The heated debate that was spawned by island biogeography, known as SLOSS, involved research into which reserves were more effective for conserving biodiversity:

The Mississippi River Basin Model mesocosm bridging ecology and engineering. The 200-acre mesocosm built along the Mississippi River flood zone (1943–1946) was designed as a tool for analyzing and addressing flood risks with engineering solutions.

the "single large" reserves or "several small" reserves of equal overall size.[19] Although recommendations to preserve single large reserves were common, the empirical challenge to these initial assumptions illustrated that the theory of island biogeography was neutral on this topic.[20] After considerable debate and numerous studies, researchers argued that the application of island biogeography to the distribution of species in space and time is highly dependent on the site context. Small, dispersed sites commonly contain at least as many species collectively as large sites of equal overall area, and the gradient of colonizing abilities among species in the available gene pool determines at what size the smaller units break down in terms of their ecological functions.[21] Ultimately, there are no simple answers as to how these systems will function: survival depends on the particular species present on the islands and the gradient of colonizing abilities among species in the available pool.[22]

These evaluations have significant implications for habitat management, not only within reserve design but especially within a highly fragmented landscape in large land development projects or nature reserves.[23] Even after years of debate, however, the recommendations remain the same: minimize habitat fragmentation and, where unavoidable, establish corridors, making sure that there are connections for species dispersal and patch recolonization.[24]

Although designers have embraced concepts around habitat patches and corridors, many of their assumed practices are poorly substantiated by empirical studies of real populations.[25] Many designers focus narrowly on individual sites, based on the project at hand. Biodiversity and species richness are the most common goals. Others have argued for focusing more broadly on genetic and habitat diversity. Eugene Odum, biologist from the University of Georgia and one of the fathers of ecosystem ecology, summarized this point in his set of axioms, stating, "An expanded approach to biodiversity should include genetic and landscape diversity, not just species diversity. The focus on preserving biodiversity must be at the landscape level, because the variety of species in any region depends on the size, variety, and dynamics of patches (ecosystems) and corridors."[26] This argument challenges the design approach to biodiversity that commonly uses a piecemeal, site-by-site basis, emphasizing the need for landscape-scale design considerations and monitoring.

Landscape ecology is an area where the translation of ecological theory to practice is occurring most effectively.[27] A landscape ecology grassland mesocosm experiment was developed to study the impacts of habitat loss and fragmentation on the persistence of native insect species, communities, and ecosystems.[28] Focusing on testing a variety of corridor configurations through the manipulation of size, connectivity, spatial distribution, shape, and boundary contrast, the research measured insect species composition before and after the experimental manipulations and found that the fragment size influenced species loss: smaller fragments lost species at a higher rate than larger fragments. According to the experiment, corridors linked to medium-sized fragments were successful in reducing rates of species loss and in enhancing recolonization.[29] This research is very useful in suggesting sizing of grassland patches for insects. Researchers debate whether these results can be extrapolated to larger organisms at broad spatial scales.[30] Given the limitations to the application of research results, and thus, the piecemeal nature of ecological information that designers are able to employ, there is value in facilitating collaborative working relationships using tools like mesocosms to communicate and coordinate partnerships for learning.

Mesocosms and Urban Design

For the growing discipline of urban ecology, researchers are employing a variety of approaches, including the use of experiments, models, and surveys to decipher urban ecosystem dynamics.[31] Understanding and predicting the ecological performance of urban ecosystems requires the use of multiple complementary approaches often including mesocosm experiments. Although critics of mesocosms argue that, as simplifications of biological systems, these systems may not accurately reflect conditions in situ,[32] they correspond well to scales of urban design and provide a means of linking ecological research with projective urban design proposals, building on the approach known as *designed experiments* and serving as an applied ecological design tool.[33] In this projective role of shaping urban ecosystems, mesocosms have much to offer.[34]

For urban designers, mesocosms can serve as instruments for testing and retooling urban land parcels. For example, parks, yards, and architecture may allow the study of ecosystem dynamics in simplified systems as repetitive and bounded experimental units.[35] For ecologists, mesocosms can provide a venue in which to invent viable biological communities that can fit within the constraints and altered condition of urban environments as designed ecosystems. Embedding mesocosms as "ecological ingredients" within urban design offers distinct advantages, which can be summarized as follows:

01. More complex than laboratory experiments, mesocosms still have reduced variables and therefore are more "neat," or less "messy," than other experimental environments such as field studies.[36]

02. Although they simplify the underlying ecology, mesocosms still constitute functioning ecosystems that can be used for establishing experiments to test the design, construction, and management of urban ecosystems.

03. The scale and replicability of mesocosms, as well as the architecture of these experiments, reflect an urban design aesthetic and provide a new approach for designers to integrate ecological strategies into urban design.

04. Mesocosms have explanatory value: they can teach designers about ecology and ecological functions.

05. Mesocosms provide an iterative learning tool for designers and ecologists to collaborate.

06. Mesocosms provide opportunities for adaptive climate change research.[37]

The complex nature of ecosystems and species dynamics creates challenges for designers actively seeking to translate ecological knowledge into practice. These translations occur in many ways, from formal strategies building on ecologically informed approaches to metaphorical strategies. Often, important aspects of ecological knowledge are reframed or prioritized differently in ways that sacrifice critical ecological factors.[38] Given these challenges, mesocosms provide designers with simplified instruments for selectively distilling ecological information and knowledge into spatially explicit choices that can inform siting, design layout, and construction of the built environment.

Another way in which mesocosms can inform designers and ecologists is by serving as "boundary objects." Mesocosms can serve as such because they bridge theoretical differences and distinct priorities and facilitate the communication of diverse stakeholder viewpoints.[39] As defined by Isto Huvila, professor of information studies at Uppsala University, and his colleagues in their paper, "Boundary Objects in Information Science Research," boundary objects are "abstract or physical artefacts that reside in the interfaces between organisations or groups of people."[40] The concept has been used in a variety of research communities and management fields as a framework, tool, or model to negotiate meaning among stakeholders. Boundary objects establish a working "tool" that groups of people can interpret differently, even as the system retains enough immutable content to maintain integrity and serve as an integrator of distinct knowledge types.[41] By fostering cooperation and mutual understanding, boundary objects can inform designers how to construct urban ecosystems and at the same time help ecologists set up innovative experiments in cities. As research

Researchers fumigating several small mangrove islands in Biscayne Bay, Florida, clearing the arthropod communities and studying the recolonization of species on the islands, which occurred within a year. Researchers discovered that islands closer to the mainland recovered faster, as predicted by the Theory of Island Biogeography.

tools, then, mesocosms provide tremendous value for ecologists working in urbanized systems where artificial and novel ecosystems are increasingly being explored.[42]

Examples of Mesocosm Field Experiments: Precedents for Future Urban Designs

Mesocosms are useful ecological building blocks that can translate knowledge from ecologists into units that can be inserted into urban areas. Designers can embed ecologist-developed mesocosm experiments within their designs as models of ecological systems. Currently, designers are actively exploring ecological approaches at a range of scales from city planning to neighborhood development and park design. These explorations include green infrastructure networks, constructed ecosystems designed for public health and well-being, and symbiotic industrial ecologies for city systems. Urbanized landscapes designed as public spaces are often well-bounded and repeated units and/or systems that, like mesocosms, can be constructed and managed similarly

to field experiments, as discrete patches. These efforts on the part of designers are intended to perform ecosystem functions. Designed as mesocosms, they could position ecologists in a crucial role of quantifying ecosystem processes and informing the built environment. This will also allow city managers to quantify or establish metrics by designs that can be evaluated through ecological research and data. This approach addresses a critical challenge in the design world of establishing the value of quality designs in terms of clear value metrics that go beyond a subjective position.

The mesocosms incorporated into urban design can also inform an urban aesthetic. As Joan Nassauer, professor of landscape architecture at the University of Michigan, writes in "Messy Ecosystems: Orderly Frames," ecological functions are not inherently recognizable and may not be valued; nevertheless, she notes: "Landscape language that communicates human intention . . . offers a powerful vocabulary for design to improve ecological quality."[43] The proposal to use mesocosms as boundary objects builds on Nassauer's

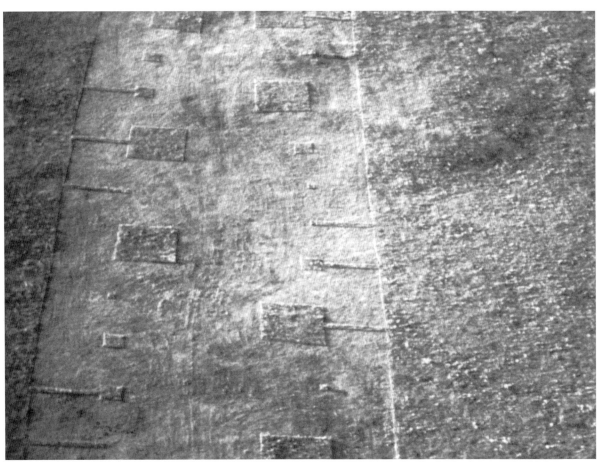

Aerial photograph illustrating a roughly two-hectare mesocosm field experiment near Boulder, Colorado. Focusing on fragment size and connectivity using corridors and patches, three sizes of unmown grassland plots are shown (small-1 m^2, medium-10 m^2, and large-100 m^2) exhibiting the gradient of connectivity treatments (control, corridor, and isolated).

perspective on the value inherent in establishing a recognizable landscape language for both remnant ecological landscapes and novel ecosystems. Ecologists can even develop ecological typologies using urban mesocosms that designers could then modify and deploy.[44]

Case Studies

Cities offer an opportunity to envision mesocosms not simply as tools for research but as instruments and ingredients for designing robust and resilient ecosystems capable of withstanding environmental change and unanticipated events.[45] In the engineered environments of cities, establishing viable urban ecosystems will require coupling ecological processes with design configurations at scales that are appropriate not only to ecosystem performance but also to the improvement of public spaces and the enhancement of human well-being.[46] It is therefore useful to examine in greater detail a series of mesocosm projects in which ecologists, working with designers, have developed mesocosms as functional urban design strategies.

Tuxedo, New York

In Tuxedo, New York, ecological research informed the redesign of a large-scale master plan for a 1,235-acre suburban housing development. The goal of the project, developed from 2007 to 2008, was to reposition proposed houses away from major amphibian migration paths and to insert green infrastructure, using rain gardens in place of lawns, to minimize overland storm flow and ensure groundwater recharge. The team made an argument to the developer that through research, they could improve wildlife habitat protection, reduce costs associated with the stormwater flows that the original development would have created, and even help negotiate the retention of housing units targeted for removal by the planning board. The developer supported the rationale and chose to fund the ecological research.[47] The redesign was achieved by employing an ecologist/designer as part of the masterplanning team to study amphibian migration and species responses to habitat focusing on the site's vernal ponds, and to translate research results into the planning process.

Alexander J. Felson

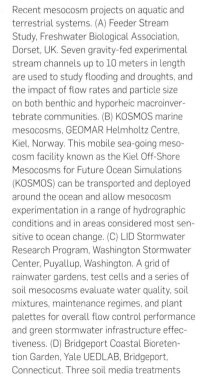

Recent mesocosm projects on aquatic and terrestrial systems. (A) Feeder Stream Study, Freshwater Biological Association, Dorset, UK. Seven gravity-fed experimental stream channels up to 10 meters in length are used to study flooding and droughts, and the impact of flow rates and particle size on both benthic and hyporheic macroinvertebrate communities. (B) KOSMOS marine mesocosms, GEOMAR Helmholtz Centre, Kiel, Norway. This mobile sea-going mesocosm facility known as the Kiel Off-Shore Mesocosms for Future Ocean Simulations (KOSMOS) can be transported and deployed around the ocean and allow mesocosm experimentation in a range of hydrographic conditions and in areas considered most sensitive to ocean change. (C) LID Stormwater Research Program, Washington Stormwater Center, Puyallup, Washington. A grid of rainwater gardens, test cells and a series of soil mesocosms evaluate water quality, soil mixtures, maintenance regimes, and plant palettes for overall flow control performance and green stormwater infrastructure effectiveness. (D) Bridgeport Coastal Bioretention Garden, Yale UEDLAB, Bridgeport, Connecticut. Three soil media treatments

and two planting palettes prevent flooding and serve as recreational space for the adjacent historic Seaside Village community while also serving as a test site for coastal resiliency strategies due to the impending risks of storm surge and sea level rise tied to the location. Future expansions have been proposed to adapt Seaside Village to future storm events. (E) Virginia Coast Reserve Long Term Ecological Research Mesocosm Study, Anheuser-Busch Coastal Research Center, Oyster, Virginia. A network of experimental mesocosms established by the National Science Foundation (NSF) to long-term monitor variations in the ecosystem as well as manipulate the ecosystems for modeling experimental conditions. (F) Pond mesocosm experiments, Rutgers University and AECOM, Tuxedo, New York. Mesocosms were used across eight ponds. Within each enclosure, the initial density of predator salamanders was varied while keeping prey species densities constant. The density range of *A. opacum* was intended to mimic population fluxes across annual breeding events. Each pond included 12 enclosures with three replicates (low, medium, high, and absent) predator salamander densities. (G) The MillionTreesNYC

Afforestation Study, Yale UEDLAB and Bradford Lab and AECOM, New York. The study fits under the PlaNYC2030 Initiative for air pollution abatement, carbon dioxide sequestration, and control of storm-water runoff. The design team worked with the client, the New York City Department of Parks and Recreation (NYCDPR), and a voluntary science advisory board to establish hypothesis-driven research and an experimental design to test the performance and persistence of a constructed native urban forest. (H) and (I) BioCON Elevated CO2 Experiment, Cedar Creek Ecosystem Science Reserve, University of Minnesota, East Bethel, Minnesota. This experiment was set up in 1997 and consists of 371 2-meter by 2-meter plots, arranged into six circular areas or "rings" (20 meters in diameter). Sixteen species of herbaceous perennial prairie species, native or naturalized to the area, were planted. BioCON is a split-plot arrangement of treatments in a completely randomized design with manipulated biodiversity, nitrogen, carbon dioxide, and water. These manipulated conditions allow the examination of how each factor affects ecosystem processes independently and in combination.

The team proposed using drift fences and pitfall traps to provide specificity about the direction of amphibian migration, as well as setting up mesocosms across eight ponds, in order to compare the impact on survival and growth rate of a group of amphibians of predator density within ponds versus habitat quality across ponds. The results were used to assess the effectiveness of the consultants' pond ranking practices and further inform decisions about siting the development.

The research clarified site-specific migration patterns and empirically delineated the most sensitive habitat areas. The inclusion of these findings in the revised master plan helped the developer navigate the planning approval process and avoid future postponements, while reducing development impacts on the resident ecological community. In addition, the research sites became boundary objects in discussions over the conservation or development value of various land parcels between the owner and the local municipality.

The Tuxedo study served as a platform for experiential and collective learning for everyone involved. The developer learned about watersheds and the hydrologic integrity necessary for ecosystem health. The design team learned how to develop empirically based site plans. Engaging directly with the research team, the local planning board learned how to incorporate results into their negotiations with the developer. The ecologist learned how to insert applied research into the land planning process. Tuxedo's designed experiment illustrates the value of mesocosms as a tool to both create educational opportunities across sectors and move land planning toward more informed ecological solutions.[48]

New York City, New York

The Reforestation Plan for New York City and the subsequent NYC Afforestation Project or NYC-AP (part of the sustainability-driven agenda PlaNYC2030), brought together landscape architects, ecologists, park managers, and landscape contractors, to establish a research based afforestation project in Kissena Corridor Park in Queens, New York. The team incorporated basic and applied research into the design of the urban forest to explore the impact of differences in vegetative structure, species richness, and soil amendment on plant performance and survival.[49] The research has facilitated an investigation of the mechanisms influencing the performance and resilience of a constructed native urban forest, including the impact of urban biological influences.[50] The researchers assumed that urban soils are low in fertility, thus organic compost amendments would promote native plant growth, while also impacting recruiting species. Thus amendments could function as a trade-off between promoting both the desired species and the undesired ones. Based on more natural systems, another assumption was also that biodiversity would promote ecosystem

functioning. The limited knowledge of urban forest performance and ecosystem services such as storm-water management, air-quality improvements or carbon sequestration meant that establishing a rigorous mesocosm experiment to test these assumptions was an essential next step for informing urban forest practices. A third assumption was that by increasing understory complexity with shrub plantings, the planted conditions would reduce the areas where unwanted species might invade.

During the project design and implementation, ecologists, designers, and the Department of Parks and Recreation managers worked collaboratively to develop experiments intended to explore the basic ecological questions described above. The team also promoted an adaptive management approach to update underlying assumptions informing urban land management, and to expand the application of ecological knowledge to improve the resiliency and health of New York City park landscapes. These experiments helped urban ecologists to situate hypothesis-driven research on sites that have been historically inaccessible to ecological experiments. In this way, the mesocosm created a boundary object for experimenting with adaptive management tools alternative to the standard operating procedure.[51] Recognizing and accounting for specific trade-offs enabled project participants to advance the integration of experimental research directly into management decisions, using mesocosms, through scientific, local, and managerial knowledge.[52] The designed experiments approach provided a framework for the collaboration of designers and ecologists where each group was able to inform and complement each other's roles while employing their own respective expertise.[53]

Bridgeport, Connecticut

The experiment centered on the creation of a series of six hydrologically connected swales that evenly redistributed water drained from an existing, intermittently flooded public parking lot. Organic matter and vegetation were manipulated across the swales, with controls, to investigate their effects on drainage and water retention.[54] The swales were designed to function as aquatic habitat for local wildlife and to accommodate potential sea level rise for coastal adaptation.

As part of the design experiment, the UEDLAB team hosted multiple community planting days and educational programs directed at highlighting the fragility of the local landscape. The team reinforced the need for long-term care and local involvement in environmental issues facing the community. The project exemplifies the value of mesocosms for local communities, particularly those with limited resources. The multifaceted nature of this project in particular illustrates the value of mesocosms as boundary objects, providing equitable access to opportunities for self-expression

161

and realization, and for environmental stewardship, education, and social value through outreach around sustainability.

New Directions for Urban Ecology

Mesocosms can play an important role as instruments for urban ecology and as ingredients in urban design for the future. There is a need for integrating design and ecology in a hybrid approach, since designers are seeking new ways of translating ecological knowledge into design practice and urban ecologists are concurrently considering new outlets for ecological knowledge that can shape human environments to face complex environmental problems. As one step forward, mesocosms can be used as boundary objects, to frame messy systems in orderly ways. Building on Nassauer's insights, the effective translation of ecological knowledge into design practice requires recognizing when and how to choreograph messy and neat conditions into legible landscapes, building on ecologists' knowledge and research interests in ecosystem dynamics. Recognizing the highly manipulated nature of urban systems, urban ecology and ecological urban design can benefit from the artificial nature of mesocosms and from the theoretical frameworks developed around research areas such as island biogeography. Simplified ecosystems are easier to work with than inherently complex, natural ecosystems: developing mesocosms collaboratively will help inform resilient urban ecosystems and services.

01. Alexander J. Felson, Mark A. Bradford, and Emily Oldfield, "Involving Ecologists in Shaping Large-Scale Green Infrastructure Projects," *Bioscience* 63, no. 11 (2013): cover and 881–890. Diane E. Pataki, "Grand Challenges in Urban Ecology," *Frontiers in Ecology and the Evolution* 3 (2015): 57. Chris Tanner et al., "Urban Ecology: Advancing Science and Society," *Frontiers in Ecology and the Environment* 12 (2014): 574–581. F. Stuart Chapin III et al., "Earth Stewardship: Science for Action to Sustain the Human-Earth System," *Ecosphere* 2, no. 8 (2011): 89.

02. Eugene P. Odum, "The Mesocosm," *Bioscience* 34 (1984): 558–562; and Damien A. Fordham, "Mesocosms Reveal Ecological Surprises from Climate Change," *PLoS Biology* 13, no. 12 (2015): 1–7.

03. John H. Lawton, "The Ecotron Facility at Silwood Park: The Value of 'Big Bottle' Experiments," *Ecology* 77, no. 3 (1996): 665–69. Tim G. Benton, "Microcosm Experiments Can Inform Global Ecological Problems," *Trends in Ecology & Evolution* 22 (2007): 516–21.

04. Stephen R. Carpenter, "Microcosm Experiments Have Limited Relevance for Community and Ecosystem Ecology," *Ecology* 77, no. 3 (1996): 677–80. Lester L. Eberhardt and J. M. Thomas, "Designing Environmental Field Studies," *Ecological Monographs* 61, no. 1 (1991): 53–73.

05. Carl J. Walters and Crawford S. Holling, "Large-Scale Management Experiments and Learning by Doing," *Ecology* 71, no. 6 (1990): 2060–2068. David B. Lindenmayer, *Large-Scale Landscape Experiments: Lessons from Tumut* (Cambridge University Press, 2009), 39–95.

06. Damian A. Fordham, "Mesocosms Reveal Ecological Surprises from Climate Change," *PLoS Biol* 13, no. 12 (2015): 1–7.

07. Osvaldo E. Sala et al., "Global Biodiversity Scenarios for the Year 2100." *Science* 287 (2000): 1770–74. Stuart H. Hurlbert, "Pseudoreplication and the Design of Ecological Field Experiments," *Ecological Monographs* 54, no. 2 (1984): 187–211.

08. Janet Lubchenco and Leslie A. Real, "Manipulative Experiments as Tests of Ecological Theory," in *Foundations of Ecology*, ed. Leslie Real and James Brown (University of Chicago Press, 1991), 715–33.

09. Lubchenco and Real, "Manipulative Experiments." See also James P. Evans, "Resilience, Ecology and Adaptation in the Experimental City," *Transactions of the Institute of British Geographers* 36, no. 2 (2011): 223–37; and Lindenmayer, *Large-Scale Landscape Experiments*, 139–65.

10. Robert E. Ricklefs, *The Economy of Nature*, 6th ed. (W.H. Freeman, 2008), 1–19.

11. See Portland State University's eco-complexity project, http://ecoplexity.org/?q=experimentation.

12. Stephen R. Carpenter et al., "Trophic Cascades, Nutrients, And Lake Productivity: Whole-Lake Experiments," *Ecological Monographs* 71 (2001): 163–186.

13. David W. Schindler, "Replication versus Realism: The Necessity for Ecosystem-scale Experiments, Replicated or Not," *Ecosystems* 1 (1998): 323–334.

14. Schindler, "Replication versus realism," 323–34. David K. Skelly and Joseph M. Kiesecker, "Venue and Outcome in Ecological Experiments: Manipulations of Larval Anurans," *Oikos* 94 (2001): 198–208.

15. Robert H. MacArthur and Edward O. Wilson, *The Theory of Island Biogeography* (Princeton: Princeton University Press, 1967).

16. Edward O. Wilson and Daniel S. Simberloff, "Experimental Zoogeography of Islands: Defaunation and Monitoring Techniques," *Ecology* 50, no. 2 (1969): 267–78.

17. Jodi A. Hilty, William Z. Lidicker Jr., and Adina M. Merenlender, *Corridor Ecology: The Science and Practice of Linking Landscapes for Biodiversity Conservation* (Washington: Island Press, 2006).

18. Jianguo Liu et al., "Complexity of Coupled Human and Natural Systems," *Science* 14 (2007): 1513–16.

19. Jared M. Diamond, "The Island Dilemma: Lessons of Modern Biogeographic Studies for the Design of Natural Reserves," *Biological Conservation* 7, no. 2 (1975): 129–46. Michael E. Soule and Daniel Simberloff, "What Do Genetics and Ecology Tell Us about the Design of Nature Reserves?," *Biological Conservation* 35, no. 1 (1986): 19–40.

20. Edward O. Wilson and Edwin O. Willis, "Applied Biogeography," in *Ecology and Evolution of Communities*, ed. Martin L. Cody and Jared M. Diamond (Cambridge, MA: Harvard University Press, 1975): 522–34. Daniel S. Simberloff and Lawrence G. Abele, "Island Biogeography Theory and Conservation Practice," *Science* 191 (1976): 285–86.

21. Michael E. Soule and Daniel Simberloff, "What Do Genetics and Ecology Tell Us," *Biological Conservation* 35 (1986): 19–40.

22. Diamond, "The Island Dilemma," 146.

23. Daniel Simberloff and Lawrence G. Abele, "Refuge Design and Island Biogeographic Theory: Effects of Fragmentation," *American Naturalist* 120, no. 1 (1982): 41–50.

24. Michael E. Soulé, "Land Use Planning and Wildlife Maintenance: Guidelines for Conserving Wildlife in an Urban Landscape," *Journal of the American Planning Association* 57, no. 3 (1991): 313–23.

25. Reed F. Noss, "From Plant-Communities to Landscapes in Conservation Inventories: A Look at the Nature Conservancy (USA)," *Biological Conservation* 41 (1987): 11–37. Daniel Simberloff and James Cox, "Consequences and Costs of Conservation Corridors," *Conservation Biology* 1 (1987): 63–71. Kerrie A. Wilson et al.,"Conserving Biodiversity Efficiently: What to Do, Where, and When," *PLoS Biol* 5, no. 9 (2007): 223.

26. Eugene P. Odum, "Great Ideas for Ecology in the 1990s," *Bioscience* 42, no. 7 (1992): 542–45.

27. André Botequilha-Leitão and Jack Ahern, "Applying Landscape Ecological Concepts and Metrics in Sustainable Landscape Planning," *Landscape and Urban Planning* 59 (2002): 65–93.

28. Sharon K. Collinge, "Spatial Arrangement of Patches and Corridors: Clues from Ecological Field Experiments," *Landscape and Urban Planning* 42 (1998): 157–68.

29. Ibid.

30. David Lindenmayer et al., "A Checklist for Ecological Management of Landscapes for Conservation," *Ecology Letters* 11 (2008): 78–91.

31. Colby J Tanner et al., "Urban Ecology: Advancing Science and Society," *Frontiers in Ecology and Environment* 12, no. 10 (2014): 574–81. Mary L. Cadenasso and Steward T. A. Pickett,"Urban Principles for Ecological Landscape Design and Management: Scientific Fundamentals," *Cities and the Environment* 1, no. 4 (2008): 1–16.

32. Skelly and Kiesecker, "Venue and Outcome in Ecological Experiments," 198–208.

33. Alexander J. Felson et al., "Mapping the Design Process for Urban Ecology Researchers," *Bioscience* 63, no. 11 (2013): 854–64.

34. Alexander J. Felson, Mark A. Bradford, Timothy M. Terway,"Promoting Earth Stewardship through Designed Experiments," *Earth Stewardship Special Issue. Frontiers of Ecology and the Environment* 11, no. 7 (2013).

35. James P. Evans. "Resilience, Ecology and Adaptation in the Experimental City," *Transactions of the Institute of British Geographers* 36 (2011): 223–37.

36. Joan I. Nassauer, "Messy Ecosystems, Orderly Frames," *Landscape Journal* 14 (1995): 161–70.

37. Rebecca I. Stewart et al., "Mesocosm Experiments as a Tool for Ecological Climate-Change Research." *Adv. Ecol. Res.* 1, no. 48 (2013): 71–181. "Mesocosms Reveal Ecological Surprises from Climate Change," *PLoS Biol* 13, no. 12 (2015): 1–7.

38. Richard T. T. Forman, "The Missing Catalyst: Design and Planning with Ecology Roots," in *Ecology and Design: Frameworks for Learning*, ed. Bart R. Johnson and Kristina Hill (Washington: Island Press, 2002). Laura R. Musacchio,"The Scientific Basis for the Design of Landscape Sustainability: A Conceptual Framework for Translational Landscape Research and Practice of Designed Landscapes and the Six Es of Landscape Sustainability," *Landscape Ecology* 24 (2009): 993–1013.

39. Jennifer L. Shirk et al., "Public Participation in Scientific Research: A Framework for Deliberate Design," *Ecology and Society* 17 (2012): 29. Helena Karsten et al., "Crossing Boundaries and Conscripting Participation: Representing and Integrating Knowledge in a Paper Machinery Project," *European Journal of Information Systems* 10, no. 2 (2001): 89–98 (paper delivered at the Association for Information Science and Technology, Seattle, WA, October 31–November 5, 2014).

40. Huvila, "Boundary Objects."

41. Beatrice Crona and John Parker, "Learning in Support of Governance: Theories, Methods, and a Framework to Assess How Bridging Organizations Contribute to Adaptive Resource Governance," *Ecology and Society* 17, no. 1 (2012): 32.

42. Diane E. Pataki et al.,"Coupling Biogeochemical Cycles in Urban Environments: Ecosystem Services, Green Solutions, and Misconceptions,'" *Frontiers in Ecology* 9 (2011): 27–36.

43. Nassauer, "Messy Ecosystems," 161.

44. Joan I. Nassauer, Zhifang Wang, and Erik Dayrell, "What Will the Neighbors Think? Cultural Norms and Ecological Design," *Landscape and Urban Planning* 92 (2009): 282–92.

45. Laura A. Ogden, "Integrating Designed Experiments into Urban Planning," *Bioscience* 63, no. 11 (2013): 845–51.

46. Diane E. Pataki et al., "Coupling Biogeochemical Cycles in Urban Environments." Marina Alberti et al.,"Integrating Humans into Ecology: Opportunities and Challenges for Studying Urban Ecosystems," *Urban Ecology* (2008): 143–58. Jack Ahern, "Integration of Landscape Ecology and Landscape Architecture: An Evolution and Reciprocal Process," in *Issues and Perspectives in Landscape Ecology*, ed. John A. Wiens and Michael R. Moss (Cambridge: Cambridge University, 1999), 311–19.

47. Alexander J. Felson, "The Role of Designers in Creating Wildlife Habitat in the Built Environment," in *Designing Wildlife Habitat*, ed. John Beardsley (Cambridge, MA: Harvard Press, 2013), 215–40.

48. F. Stuart Chapin et al., "Earth Stewardship: Science for Action to Sustain the Human-Earth System," *Ecosphere* 2 (2011): 1–20.

49. Emily E. Oldfield et al., "Positive Effects of Afforestation Efforts on The Health of Urban Soils," *Forest Ecology and Management* 313 (2014): 266–73. E. Oldfield et al., "Growing the Urban Forest: Tree Performance in Response to Biotic and Abiotic Land Management," *Restoration Ecology* 23, no. 5 (2015): 707–18.

50. Alexander. J. Felson et al., "Constructing Native Urban Forests as Experiments to Evaluate Resilience," *Scenario Journal* 4, special issue, "Building the Urban Forest," ed. Stephanie Carlisle, Nicholas Pevzner, and Max Piana (2014).

51. Lance H. Gunderson, "Resilience, Flexibility and Adaptive Management: Antidotes for Spurious Certitude?," *Conservation Ecology* 3, no. 1 (1999): 7.

52. Oldfield et al., "Growing the urban forest," 707–18.

53. Alexander J. Felson et al., "Mapping the Design Process for Urban Ecology Researchers," *Bioscience* 63, no. 11 (2013): 854–64.

54. Allen Arthur, "Sooner or Later at Seaside," *Landscape Architecture* (November 2013): 188–97.

Image Credits

156: Public domain.

158: Courtesy of Edward O. Wilson and Daniel S. Simberloff.

159: Courtesy of Sharon Collinge.

160: (B) Courtesy of Maike Nicolai; (C) Courtesy of MiG|SvR; (D) Courtesy of the author; (E) Courtesy of LTER Network Office; (F) Courtesy of the author; (G) Courtesy of the author; (H) Courtesy of the National Science Foundation; (I) Courtesy of the National Science Foundation.

Beyond the Limits of the City: Urbanizing Territories

**Milica Topalovic
with images by
Bas Princen**

How might we investigate the problematic of planetary urbanization from the viewpoint of architecture and urbanism? How might we conceptualize architecture and urbanism as disciplines whose boundaries extend beyond the limits of "the city"?

Nowadays, urban researchers tend to focus on cities and at the expense of wider productive territories. That cities now house more than half of the world's population is a well-established cliché, provoking both foreboding over the dawn of an "urban age" and celebrations of the "triumph of the city" over the countryside.[01] But what if we reverse this perspective: what if we adopt a territorial approach instead of the city-centric view? Since cities cover only two percent of the world's surface, what if we were to also focus attention on the remaining 98 percent?[02] As cities grow and transform, territories are undeniably pulled into the same vortex of urbanization. This suggests that revisiting the relationship between cities and wider urbanizing territories from this perspective might prove interesting. Understanding the dynamic of urbanizing territories—of productive landscapes, natural areas, countrysides, and hinterlands—might even prove central to understanding cities and urban sustainability.

The concept of the *hinterland* is particularly useful from the viewpoint of planetary urbanization. While not synonymous with territory, hinterland does signify a particular territoriality of economical incorporation of land and resources to a given center.[03] Throughout history cities have functioned as centers of political and economic power from which the agricultural and resource-rich hinterlands have been controlled. From the nineteenth century onward, however, new technologies, transportation modes, and the opening of new trade routes have lengthened the distances between cities and their productive hinterlands and introduced remarkable complexities into their relations. This process of "disintegration" of the more contiguous "erstwhile hinterlands"[04] that characterized preindustrial cities led to the formation of increasingly dispersed and globalized hinterlands since the second half of century. This formation takes place along logistical chains of production, processing, transportation, and consumption of raw materials and goods that today span the globe and continue to evolve, catalyzed by successive technological revolutions.

[…]

Since 2011, the Architecture of Territory group at the Future Cities Laboratory of the Eidgenössische Technische Hochschule (ETH) has studied the contemporary city's relationship with its hinterlands. It has done so by examining the case of Singapore. At first glance, Singapore appears paradoxical. With nearly six million residents inhabiting a dense urban form, it has hardly any productive land or countryside of which to speak. A self-declared "city without a hinterland,"

Singapore relies on production grounds and resources that lie beyond its national borders—in territories near and far, in both cross-border and transnational settings. Singapore's hinterlands are as vital as they are free from its direct jurisdiction and governance. The radical openness adopted by the city-state toward global flows of goods, people, and capital is both a risky necessity and an economic opportunity. And yet somehow, neither its urban development nor economic growth seems threatened by this. To the contrary, the "Singapore model" of urban development is widely considered to be highly successful, achieving the status of a leading urban brand for cities around the world and a prototype for Asian urbanization. How are we to understand this apparent paradox?

Analysis of this island city-state reveals dispersed and globalized city-hinterland relations characteristic of the modern, industrial order. Does the Singapore case also present a promise of radical globalization for cities? Should cities be envisioned as globalized "islands," whose productive hinterlands are dynamically shaped and continually reterritorialized across the planet under global market forces? Or does the case reveal evidence to support the persistence of the compact and contiguous regional hinterlands of previous eras? To help resolve this dilemma for the benefit of all contemporary cities, Singapore has great illustrative value. As an island and a city-state, it is uniquely—if not ideally—suited to the study the hinterland. It presents a special situation in which city and hinterland can be separated in terms of their physical, political, and economic geographies and where the flow of resources can be monitored as they cross national borders, moving from one state to the other.

These flows are quite literal. They can be traced across maritime space devoted to shipping, which might be considered one of Singapore's most vital hinterlands. Ninety percent of the world's traded goods pass through the Singapore Strait each year, making it one of the most densely occupied sea surfaces on Earth. Singapore is a city with a view to these otherwise largely invisible territories of the global circulation of goods.

Since its independence from Malaysia in 1965, Singapore has been the destination par excellence of population and capital flows as well as a veritable laboratory of socioeconomic experimentation and territorial engineering, under the political umbrella of the so-called hard, or developmental, state. It has been hailed as the foremost example of imaginative state entrepreneurship, planning, and foresight—a realizable ideal and urban model for other Asian cities—while at the same time being repeatedly dismissed on account of its authoritarian political regime.[05]

Singapore's population density is presently estimated at nearly 8,000 people per square kilometer, almost ten times the density of the Canton of Zurich.[06] At the same time,

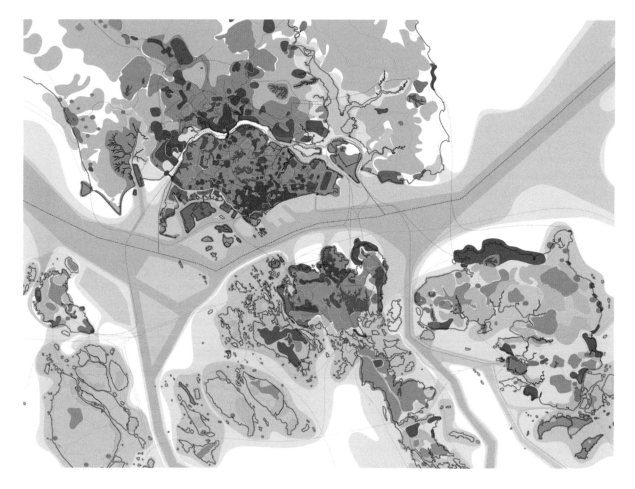

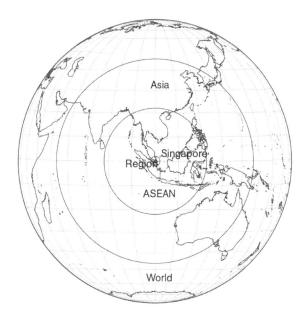

economic disparity along Singapore's border is extreme, creating a state of compression: in terms of the number of passenger border crossings, Singapore, with only eight, appears even less accessible than West Berlin, which had 14 border checkpoints before the Fall of the Wall. [07]

Within the three-country archipelago of Singapore, Malaysia, and Indonesia, the national maritime borders and the wider border zone encircling Singapore island are defining features of metropolis-hinterland geographies, separating the metropolitan core from the wider periphery, and performing as elaborate regulatory membranes between the two. Singapore's territorial waters represent a complex urban space, regulated three-dimensionally above and below the surface by the demands of national security, shipping logistics, and the petrochemical industry. The combined regimes of maritime border crossings, coastal industries, military uses, and other regulatory measures have formed a wide, technical space, a nonpublic border zone that extends from sea to land, incorporating much of the island's coast. Through extensive land reclamation, new "prosthetic limbs" augment the old island in the littoral zone; here, the insular character of industrial and logistics areas helps reinforce the national border.

166

Beyond the island's technical perimeter extends the "borderless" space of global shipping. Through various regimes of exception—notably, the free-trade zones in the port and airport areas—large stretches of the island's coastline are incorporated in a globalized space, off limits to public circulation. Public contact with the coast and the sea is limited to a number of controlled gaps that, according to our survey, comprise only 7.5 percent of Singapore's coastline.[08]

The consequence of urbanization on the island city is thus, unexpectedly, a loss of *islandness*. Once a constituent part of an open maritime region, the sea encircling Singapore is increasingly industrialized, urbanized, and fragmented. In Indonesian archipelagic cultures, the concept of *tanahair* (sealand) represents a space of unbroken continuity. In Singapore today, public perception of the island limited by water reinforces the paradigm of Singapore as an island city-state—that is, as an intensely networked and globalized city,

Above: Sand Hinterland: Sand mining for construction on the Indonesian island of Batam, the industrial periphery of Singapore. Opposite page, top: Cross-border metropolitan region Singapore-Johor-Riau Archipelago: Territories of Urbanisation. Bottom: Scales of (Singapore's) socio-metabolist hinterlands.

disconnected or even liberated from its immediate context. Marginalized without much public access, the island's coast and the sea are gradually becoming the frontiers of public interest and imagination.[09]

Singapore's "spatial and geographic reorientation" away from its regional context and toward the "entire 'world'" which now "became imaginable as Singapore's 'market'"[10] is also illustrative of the mainstream political and economic ideologies shaping urban governance elsewhere throughout the world. In this view, the significance of city-hinterland linkages is often downplayed in light of the assumption that contemporary cities rely less and less on their immediate surroundings for supplies and subsistence. Instead, cities are frequently seen as being progressively emancipated from the constraints of geography, operating in a global web of dependencies, flows, and exchanges. Singapore is among the most acute examples of cities where political imaginations and narratives continue to ignore any geographic restrictions. Generations of urban policy-makers have strongly identified with the paradigm of a "global city" whose "hinterland is the world."[11] Reinforcing this orientation is the political history of the region and the unstable relationship of Singapore

167

Milica Topalovic

with Indonesia and Malaysia, both pre- and post-independence. This instability continues to fuel a specific denial in Singapore of its immediate regional context and of the importance of that context for the city.

Singapore's self-perception as a "global city" and one "without a hinterland" is patently wrong. Even a quick examination of urbanization processes reveals that Singapore is not a contained urban island but rather part of an urbanizing region that extends to the Malaysian Johor State in the north and the Indonesian Riau Archipelago in the south. There, one finds booming cities and settlements including Johor Bahru and Batam, each with more than one and a half million residents. This immediate regional space, also known as Sijori (for Singapore-Johor-Riau Archipelago), has developed at Singapore's doorstep—or in its shadow, as it were. It now counts more than eight million legal residents and a significant migrant population. Following the enactment of a political-economic partnership agreement among the three governments, the Sijori Growth Triangle urbanized in the late 1980s, accommodating the expansion of Singapore's economy over its borders. The main impetus for urban growth in Indonesia and Malaysia was industrial production, especially by the multinational electronics industry. This production was facilitated by Singapore and attracted work migration from other parts of the countries into shanty towns and dormitory cities now in the process or urban consolidation.

The region's population is projected to double during the next 15 years to reach at least 16.8 million.[12] It is fascinating to note that, as the region's population grows, the diagram of its city-hinterland relationship (presently hinged on Singapore) is likely to be radically transformed; whereas Singapore's working population is projected to shrink, that of adjacent cities in Malaysia and Indonesia is expected to grow vigorously. By 2030 Singapore will likely hand over a share of its central functions to its neighbors, gradually relinquishing its role as the dominant city in the region to become part of a constellation of more equal cities.

* * *

169

The perception of all remote territories, from nature's wilderness to the rural countryside, has historically been initiated from an urban perspective: the periphery has always been imagined from the viewpoint of the center. This leads us to wonder, how might we actually study a hinterland?

Observation of a city's hinterland can really only begin when the city itself is eclipsed. Only when the center of

Labor Hinterland: Shipyards and other multinational manufacturing sites in the Indonesian Riau Archipelago work as extension of Singapore's port and industries.

Milica Topalovic

gravity and its blinding sources of light become temporarily obscured can the phenomena unfolding in its shadow be adequately perceived and analyzed.

Through ethnographic fieldwork experience conducted over the years, we developed the method of the eclipse. In practice, we spent relatively little time studying Singapore itself and a significant amount in ethnographic expeditions by land and sea in the region beyond Singapore's border. We approached the hinterland problematic in two ways related to two different conceptions of scale. First, we examined Singapore's discontinuous hinterlands, from local to planetary, by following the flows of five key resources: sand, food, water, labor, and oil. We called this the *sociometabolist hinterland* analysis, to emphasize the qualitative (rather than quantitative) urban transformations and relationships. Second, we studied the *geographical hinterland*, at the scale of the trinational region. In this view, the hinterland is understood as contiguous territories in Indonesia and Malaysia, directly exposed to the gravitational force of the city-state.

In these two ways of looking at a city and its hinterlands there lies also a deeper philosophical dilemma on the nature of cities, described by the French geographer Jean Gottmann:

> To understand the evolution of contemporary ways of the world, networks of cities are fundamental. Too often however, a city is considered only in the framework of the surrounding region. The question has arisen, worrying geographers, historians, sociologists, and politicians, whether a city lives, works, lasts, and falls mainly as the center of a region, determined by local circumstances, or chiefly as a partner in a constellation of far-flung cities. This is not in fact a new problem born in our time. It is an ancient problem which has been with mankind since the dawn of history.[13]

Gottmann goes on to describe debates between Plato and Aristotle as to what might be the best geographical framework to obtain happier political life:

> Small scale, austerity, isolation, restricted maritime and trading activities, such is Plato's recipe for a righteous and stable society. This doctrine of political geography has often been offered as great wisdom to this day . . . The Platonic model of the small, equal, self-sufficient and self-absorbed territorial units may be opposed to the Alexandrine model [after Alexander the Great, Aristotle's disciple] of a vast, expanding, pluralistic political and cultural system, bound together and lubricated by the active exchanges and linkages of a network of large trading cities.[14]

Between the Platonic and Alexandrine models, Singapore seems to belong decidedly to the latter: highly networked and global and entirely not self-sufficient. In the corresponding analysis of Singapore's discontinuous sociometabolist hinterlands, we have shown that most of the studied resource flows (except water) are supplied from foreign sources and arrive from across long distances.

Food: Although a leading supplier of agro-technologies, Singapore itself does not produce its own food anymore. Food is supplied to Singapore from all over the world. The cross-border region plays a relatively modest role in supplying fresh produce. The emphasis here is on agro-commodities, especially palm oil. Vast palm plantations cover the landscapes of Johor.

Water: Singapore doesn't have natural water sources. Around 40 percent of its supply arrives from Malaysia. The rest comes from the local desalination and water treatment infrastructures, and also from the meticulous engineering of the island's surface to increase rainwater catchment and storage capacity.

Labor: Singapore has always been dependent on foreign labor migration. Although it imports 30,000 foreign workers each year from all over the world, the critical part of its labor pool is not located at home but is spread throughout the cross-border region and the countries of the ASEAN (Association of Southeast Asian Nations). Among the many examples of cross-border value chains anchored in Singapore are industrial parks for electronics manufacturing, which are located across the border on Batam Island, Indonesia.

Oil: The main pillar of Singapore's economy is the oil trade, with a large part of crude oil and petroleum products arriving in Singapore en route from the Middle East to the Southeast Asian countries and China. The state boosts the oil industry by providing gargantuan storage and processing facilities. Since less than 1 percent of imported petroleum is consumed domestically, Singapore's elaborate infrastructures are dedicated almost exclusively to production and trade.

Sand: Finally, Singapore is one of the world's largest importers of sand for construction and land reclamation. Its topography is profoundly artificial. Around one-quarter of its land area—more than 150 square kilometers—has been reclaimed from the sea. With local and regional sand sources depleted since the 1990s, Singapore's sand hinterland continues to expand together with its land surface—now stretching as far as China and Myanmar.

To compare these five resource hinterlands, we developed an analytical vocabulary capturing the key characteristics of the hinterland territories. These analytical concepts included:

Hinterland Scale and Territorial Development: The hinterland territory expands and disintegrates over time as the city grows. Enabled by modern infrastructures and transportation

170

Oil Hinterland: Artificial underground caverns for storing crude oil on Jurong Island in Singapore.

means, the more contiguous hinterlands characteristic of the 19th- and early 20th-century city expanded, globalized, and disintegrated in the latter part of the 20th century.[15]

Resource Metabolism: Although metabolism as a concept in urban sociology goes back to writings of Karl Marx and Friedrich Engels in the second half of the 19th century, urban metabolism as a model of analysis of material and energy flows in cities has been in wide use only since the mid-1960s.[16] In our analysis, we examined and presented each resource as a particular balance of import, export, consumption, and waste.[17]

Territories of Extraction: Each resource hinterland involves more or less identifiable territories of extraction. We investigated the resource origins and tried to represent, where possible, the geographies and urbanisms of extraction in the form of maps and plan drawings.

Infrastructures of Resource Flows: These flows involve physical infrastructures as well as the formal and informal regulatory regimes that cut across borders. The absence of clear regulation applying to resource extraction and trade in the transnational space and the ensuing geopolitical

dynamics surrounding the resource flows represents one of the most surprising insights on the hinterland territories gleaned from our study.

Organization: We discussed the organization of the protagonists of resource extraction, trade, and accumulation, where the focus was placed on identifying, in the transnational hinterland space, the presence and mechanisms of influence exertion of state, private, and transnational entities.

Urbanisms of Accumulation: Resource flows fuel the production of urban space with its sociocultural and monetary values. From sand depots to underground storage for crude oil, we studied the distinctive urbanisms and politics of resource accumulation in the city, by focusing on sites, urban structures, and networks of resource "stocks" and "flows."[18]

The second part of the investigation, the study of the *geographical hinterland*, examined urbanization processes as they extend in the three-country archipelago centered in Singapore. It resulted in a thesis on the cross-border metropolitan region, described in terms of characteristic territories of urbanization. The methodology of mapping the urbanization patterns in the region that we used involved a complex

171

Milica Topalovic

Maritime borderzone: Industrial archipelago in the southwestern edge of Singapore, comprising military sites, petrochemical industry, container port and waste disposal areas.

procedure of collecting and assembling 150 layers of map-information, each layer serving to indicate a specific urban performance, such as centrality, productive function, residential fabric, and so on. Importantly, this mapping method was qualitative, grounded in a phenomenological approach to the territory, and resulting in an in-depth knowledge of urban spaces and places based on direct experience. The thesis proposes six distinct territories of urbanization in the region:

Trinational Metropolis comprises the area of urban centers and residential fabric served by social and technical infrastructures.

Cross-Border Territories are understood as the specific character of urbanization, produced through global capital investment and real estate speculation. They encompass a broad spectrum of urban programs, from housing and tourism to education and healthcare, with investment flows often originating in China and the Middle East.

Strategic Reserved Lands are unbuilt areas, yet their forms and functions are irreducible from the urban system. They include military zones and water storage areas, as well as land banks set aside for future urban expansion.

Industrial Primary Production covers the fringes of the metropolitan region, comprising mainly landscapes of the palm oil industry in Johor and mining in the Riau Archipelago.

Urbanized Sea and Air describes a territory of urbanization related through the functions of shipping, petrochemical industries, and air transportation. It extends from the sea to the land and consumes large sections of the coast on all three of the region's sides.

Quiet Archipelago covers mainly remote "rural" areas and small islands in the Riau Archipelago, still based on traditional economies, especially fishing. While some parts of the archipelago are under pressure to industrialize, most areas are shrinking and losing population to cities.

The thesis map of the cross-border metropolitan region does not simply represent the existing reality, it actively constructs reality. In this sense the map is also a plan, and a design: it can be understood as both analysis and as project. It is a tool to generate knowledge, to shift terms of debate, and to create awareness of urban potentials that could be pursued at the metropolitan scale and in the trinational context.

Urbanised Sea: Anchorage zone for container ships, crude carriers and other vessels along Singapore's east coast.

[…]

Which leads us to wonder, in the end, what the city's relationship to its hinterland actually is. How is the urbanization of cities reflected in the hinterland? Should the productive hinterlands be imagined as parts of cities, or vice versa? Is there a limit to a city's hinterland? Could hinterlands be planned and designed?

Based on the case of Singapore, the hinterland project offers a couple of insights. Through the investigation of geographical hinterlands, the project arrives at an understanding of Singapore as a city tightly linked to its neighboring region. It questions the persisting political imagination of Singapore as an island developed according to the paradigm of a global city-state, which has shaped its urban development and form since its independence. Instead, it articulates a counter-paradigm that posits Singapore as an open and connected cross-border metropolis. Similar unused metropolitan potentials for developing cities in their geographic regions are likely to be discovered in other cities, too.

The experience of Singapore's hinterlands leads us to argue for what several authors have termed the new "ethics of visibility,"[19] which should permeate hinterland territories through photography, art, maps, and other forms of representation. Architecture and the visual arts have an important role to play in researching, describing, and making visible to the urban dweller the ongoing industrial reorganization of territories exposed to the influence of large cities, regardless of distance. The hinterlands can no longer be seen as remote, residual, or anachronistic: they are crucial territories of global capitalism and of urbanization processes. A new ethics of visibility that extends from cities to the hinterlands is required.[20]

The investigation of resource extraction and flows leads us to question the appropriate scales of urban governance. Without doubt, new forms of large-scale acting and of governance that apply to transnational dimensions of urbanization processes are necessary. Thinking of the sustainability of cities only as a function of the center is exposed through this research as simplistic, almost a trivialization of the issues at hand. Large-scale metabolic flows are mobilized, and remote areas of the planet are industrialized and urbanized, in order to support cities. They need to be brought into the

173

Milica Topalovic

Hinterland as territory of
urbanization: Land reclamation
for a new commercial centre in
Batam City, Indonesia.

discussion of governance that extends well beyond the limits of the city.

Finally, we ask, what is the right scale of a city's hinterland? Should it be regional or global? Should the city's "orbits" follow the Platonic model of small, self-sufficient territorial units, or the Alexandrine model of vast, expanding urban networks? According to Gottmann himself, there is no single answer: "It is generally true of cities that each of them works as a hinge between the region of which it is the center and the outside world, between the local and the external orbits."[21] We believe that a city's relation with its hinterland is inevitably both Platonic and Alexandrine, both regional and global. We need to learn how to strike a balance.

This essay is an edited excerpt of Milica Topalovic, "Architecture of Territory—Beyond the Limits of the City: Research and Design of Urbanizing Territories," lecture, presented at ETH Zurich on November 30, 2015. For a full transcript of the lecture, see http://topalovic.arch.ethz.ch/materials/architecture-of-territory.

01. See Rem Koolhaas, "OMA: On Progress," lecture, presented at the Barbican Art Gallery, London, November 10, 2011, http://www.youtube.com/watch?v=CNPRWgfVPKs; Neil Brenner and Christian Schmid, "The 'Urban Age' in Question," *International Journal for Urban and Regional Research* 38, no. 3 (2014): 731–55; and Edward Glaeser, *Triumph of the City: How Our Greatest Invention Makes Us Richer, Smarter, Greener, Healthier, and Happier* (New York: Penguin, 2011).

02. Koolhaas, "OMA: On Progress."

03. For a comprehensive discussion of the hinterland concept, see for example William Cronon, *Nature's Metropolis: Chicago and the Great West* (New York: W. W. Norton & Company, 1991).

04. See Neil Brenner and Christian Schmid, "Planetary Urbanization," in *Urban Constellations*, ed. M. Gandy (Berlin: Jovis Verlag, 2011), 10–13.

05. The term *hard* or *developmental state* was first introduced to describe state-led macroeconomic planning in Singapore as well as other East Asian countries including Japan, China, Thailand, and South Korea, since the 1960s. It was later applied to other countries outside East Asia. It refers to a capitalist model in which the state displays both entrepreneurial and authoritarian characteristics, exerting more political autonomy and more control over the economy than in traditional capitalist states. Slovenian philosopher Slavoj Žižek, following Peter Sloterdijk, credited Singaporean leader Lee Kwan Yew with conceiving and putting into practice this "capitalism with Asian values," now spreading throughout Asia and around the globe. See Slavoj Žižek, "Berlusconi in Tehran," *London Review Of Books* 31 no. 14 (July 23, 2009): 3–7, http://www.lrb.co.uk/v31/n14/slavoj-zizek/berlusconi-in-tehran. On the particular features of Singapore's authoritarianism, see Beng Huat Chua, "Singapore as Model: Planning Innovations, Knowledge Experts," in *Worlding Cities: Asian Experiments and the Art of Being Global*, ed. Ananya Roy and Aihwa Ong (Chichester, UK: Wiley-Blackwell, 2011).

06. See "Country Comparison > Population Density," Index Mundi, January 1, 2014, http://www.indexmundi.com/g/r.aspx?v=21000; and "Swiss Federal Statistical Office > Regional Data > Cantons > Zurich > Key Figures," 2014 http://www.bfs.admin.ch/bfs/portal/en/index/regionen/kantone/zh/key.html.

07. The idea of comparing Singapore and West Berlin in terms of accessibility comes from ETH Professor Kees Christiaanse, who generously offered it in a conversation with the author and two students, Magnus Nickl and Verena Stecher, at the ETH Future Cities Laboratory in Singapore in early 2013.

08. Magnus Nickl and Verena Stecher, "Sealand," masters thesis at the ETH Zurich DARCH Assistant Professorship of Architecture and Territorial Planning, Asst. Prof. Milica Topalovic, ETH FCL Singapore and ETH DARCH Zurich, 2014.

09. Milica Topalovic, "Constructed Land: Singapore in the Century of Flattening," in *Constructed Land: Singapore, 1924–2012*, ed. Uta Hassler and Milica Topalovic (Zurich and Singapore: ETH Zurich D-ARCH and Singapore-ETH Centre, 2014), 56-57. For more, visit http://topalovic.arch.ethz.ch/materials/constructed-land.

10. Chua, "Singapore as Model," 30.

11. Chua, "Singapore as Model," 30–31.

12. Aris Ananta, "The Population of the SIJORI Cross-Border Region," in *The SIJORI Cross-Border Region: Transnational Politics, Economics, and Culture*, ed. Francis E. Hutchinson and Terence Chong (Singapore: The ISEAS—Yusof Ishak Institute, 2016), 49.

13. Jean Gottmann, *Orbits: The Ancient Mediterranean Tradition of Urban Networks* (London: Leopard's Head Press, 1984), 3.

14. Ibid., 9–10.

15. Brenner and Schmid, "Planetary Urbanization."

16. Abel Wolman, "The Metabolism of Cities," *Scientific American* 213, no. 3 (1965): 179–90.

17. See Milica Topalović, Martin Knüsel, Marcel Jäggi, and Stefanie Krautzig, eds. *Hinterland – Singapore, Johor, Riau; Studio Report*, ETH Zurich DARCH Assistant Professorship of Architecture and Territorial Planning, Asst. Prof. Milica Topalovic, (Zurich and Singapore: ETH Zurich D-ARCH and Singapore-ETH Centre, 2013). The model of material flow analysis was outlined by Peter Baccini and Paul H. Brunner in: Baccini, P., Brunner, P.H. "Metabolism of the Anthroposphere," (Berlin and Heidelberg: Springer, 1991).

18. On the metabolism of sand, see *Constructed Land: Singapore, 1924–2012*, ed. Hassler and Topalovic.

19. Bill Roberts, "Production in View: Allan Sekula's Fish Story and the Thawing of Postmodernism," *Tate Papers*, Issue 18 (2012), http://www.tate.org.uk/research/publications/tate-papers/production-view-allan-sekulas-fish-story-and-thawing-postmodernism.

20. For more on this topic, see Milica Topalovic, "Palm Oil: A New Ethics of Visibility for the Production Landscape," in *Designing the Rural: A Global Countryside in Flux*, Architectural Design series, ed. Christiane Lange, John Lin and Joshua Bolchover (New York: John Wiley & Sons Inc., 2016), 42–47.

21. Gottmann, "Orbits," 14.

Image Credits

166: Courtesy of the author. Research and concept: ETH Architecture of Territory. Map development: Karoline Kostka, 2015–16.

167–169, 171–174: Courtesy of Bas Princen.

175

Milica Topalovic

The World in the Architectural Imaginary

Hashim Sarkis

Many architects conceived of the world as a project before the advent of globalization. Although these ecumenical aspirations may not resemble what globalization has produced in terms of physical environment, they do however stress the spatiality of the world and the need for a formal imagination to make it legible. Today we hear that globalization manifests itself in cities, not in the world. Even if the emerging settlement patterns across the world supersede the metropolitan model, we still persist in describing the inhabited world based on categories that no longer correspond to the conditions at hand. "The World According to Architecture," an exhibition initiated by the Harvard University Graduate School of Design New Geographies Lab and subsequently shown at the Massachusetts Institute of Technology (MIT), demonstrates ways in which the world has proven a rich domain for the modern architectural imaginary. It also invites us to reclaim the scale and challenges of the city-world (as opposed to the world city) as a vital architectural project.

The World between Four Lines

Within these projects in "world-making," an experience of horizontality recurs. Four types of lines weave together to generate this effect:

01. the horizon line: the limit of our experience; the frontier of possibilities
02. the ground line: the certainty of continuity; the friction against mobility
03. the skyline: the negative of the horizon; the seam of Bowles's shelter
04. the raised line: the constructed ground from which the relationship among the different lines could be reconstrued; the thickness of the inhabited world; the sum total of all verticality

Many of the projects presented here rely on activating one or more of these horizontals: exposing the horizon, enhancing the feeling of continuity on the ground, lifting the viewer up high enough to see the limits of the inhabited world, or creating a clearing to understand where one is in the world. The differences between these designed worlds could be measured in terms of the differences in the composition of these four lines.

The lines impose a certain set of metrics on the architecture of the world, exemplified in the following dimensions:

4.66 kilometers: the horizon line for an eye placed at ground level
1.61 meters: the interior inscription of the horizon; the horizontal symmetry of Mies van der Rohe's Barcelona Pavilion

200 meters: the skyline; the measure of geography, starting at the 200-meter level of Le Corbusier´s towers
9–20 meters: the raised ground that opens the city to the space beyond the city; the ground from the Smithson's *Haupstadt* and Golden Lane to Leonidov's Columbus Monument

The World at Different Scales

"I could be bounded in a nutshell, and count myself a king of infinite space," believed Hamlet. Many of these projects use architecture as Hamlet's nutshell, to project entire worlds from the confines of an architectural project.

The scalar juxtaposition among the different projects, from the space of the interior to outer space, helps us compare different architectural tools and potentials. The instruments used in these projects vary from one scale to another, the scale usually alluding to what the space of an architect's operation is but also what is possible at a particular moment in time. Some architects choose one scale, while others choose many. Whereas, for example, Arturo Soria y Mata works primarily with new infrastructure and spreads it across continents, R. Buckminster Fuller makes his world with buildings, satellites, and maps, orchestrating different scales toward one experience of the world.

The World through Different Strategies

Employing evidence, as well as signs and symbols, the architecture of the world is attained through references and referents that connect architecture (or some aspect of it) to the world (or some part of it). The examples here vary in strategy depending upon the scale of intervention, cultural context, and forms and imagery employed. To explain these strategies, we have divided the projects into five categories: microcosm, partial worlds, parallel worlds, making visible, and making invisible. Although more than one strategy may apply to a single project, each is presented separately in order to highlight certain differences.

The World According to Architecture

The following pages present a fragment of a broader visualization of the 25 projects exhibited in "The World According to Architecture." The authors would like to thank the researchers and students who participated in the New Geographies Lab, as well as Daniel Daou, Samuel Ghantous, Rania Ghosn, Daniel Ibañez, Rola Idris, El Hadi Jazairy, Nikos Katsikis, Jarrad Morgan, Pablo Pérez-Ramos, Chris Roach, Pablo Roquero, and Difei Xu, for their contributions to the project. We would also like to thank the students who participated in the MIT workshop "Constructing Vision: The Eye, Architecture, the World" and who have continued to explore the themes and categories of this research.

The World According to Architecture

Gabriel Kozlowski, Roi Salgueiro Barrio
& Hashim Sarkis

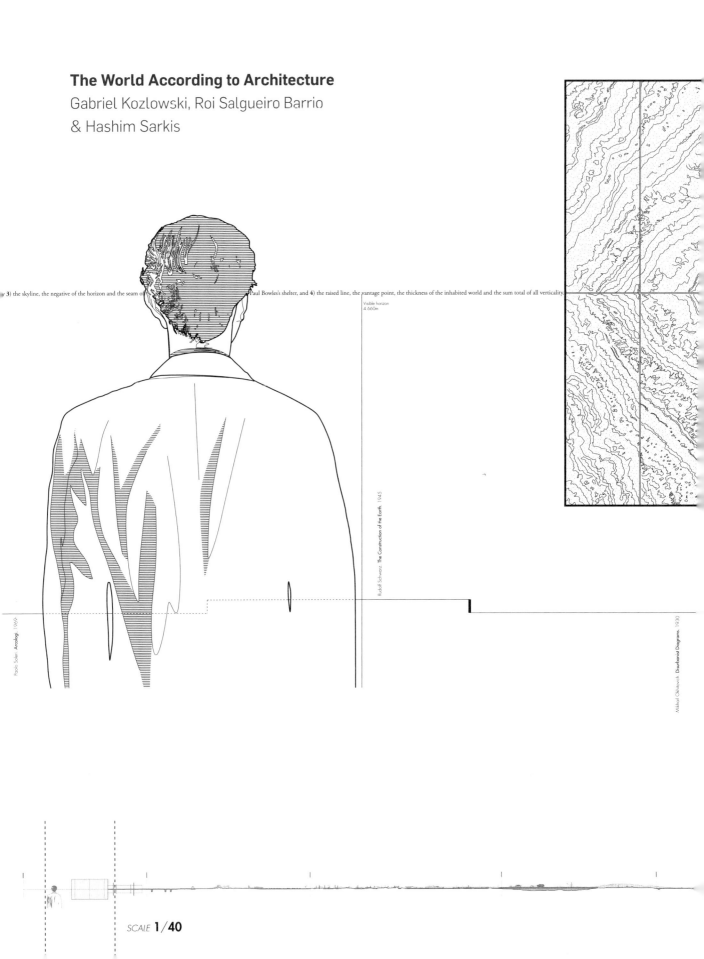

3) the skyline, the negative of the horizon and the seam of [...] Paul Bowles's shelter, and 4) the raised line, the vantage point, the thickness of the inhabited world and the sum total of all verticality.

Visible horizon
4.660m

Rudolf Schwarz: The Construction of the Earth, 1945.

Paolo Soleri: Arcology, 1969.

Mikhail Okhitovich: Disurbanist Diagrams, 1930.

SCALE **1/40**

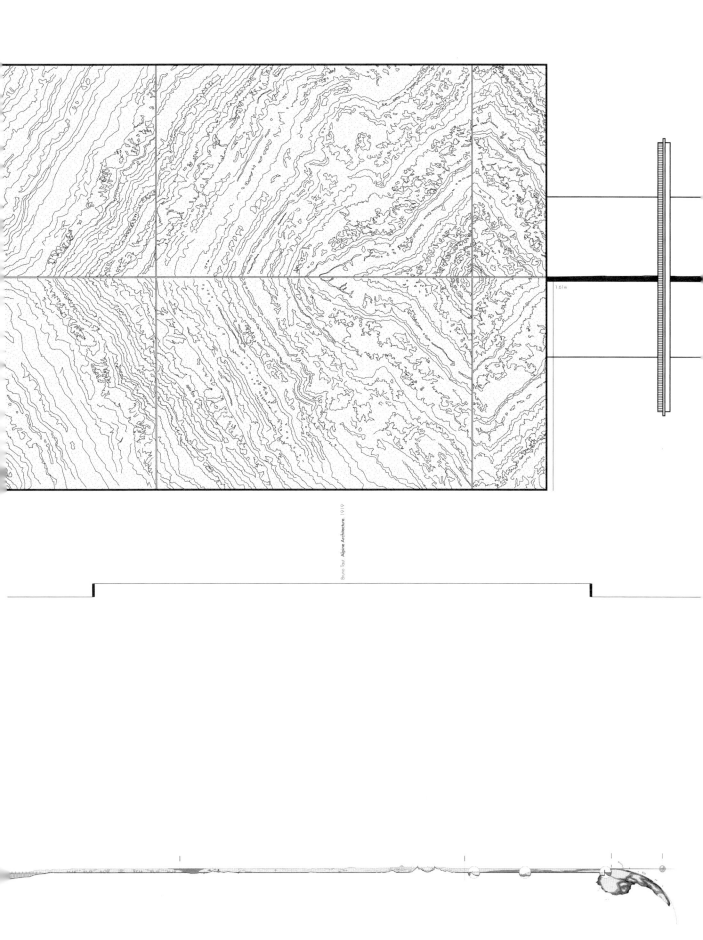

Bruno Taut, Alpine Architecture, 1919

1.61m

14

| Yves Klein with Walter Rühnau and
Claude Parent. Air-Architecture. 1958-1962

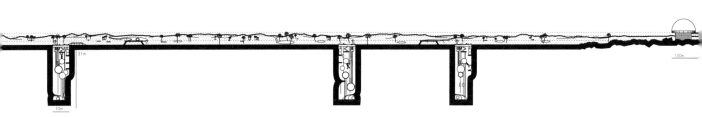

14

| Yves Klein with Walter Rühnau and Claude Parent. Air-Architecture. 1958-196[...]

Klein's first projects for Air-Architecture explored the possibility of air-conditioning limited spaces. The work took on an increasing planetary scale, informed by the parallel explorations of other members of the Zero Collective, in drawings produced by Claude Parent's office. In these drawings, Air-Architecture reenacted Le Corbusier's notion of the urban void as social space, but it was now extended to the whole earth. The proposal is conceived for a society liberated from any relation to work. The only exposed elements of human habitation on the surface of the earth are transport and air-conditioning infrastructures. Dwellings and any other functions are relegated to the underworld. The proposal eschews construction in order to recover the ground, horizon, and skyline.

ARCHIVE

Claude Parent personal archive / Foundation Yves Klein, Paris.

BIBLIOGRAPHY

Cabañas, Kaira M. 2008. "Yves Klein's Performative Realism." *Grey Room*, n.31. Print.

Musèe des Arts Decoratifs. 1960. *Antagonismes*. Paris: Missotte.

Noever, Peter and François Perrin (Ed.). 2004. "Travelling through the Void." *Air-Architecture: Yves Klein*. Ostfildern-Ruit: Hatje Cantz.

Ottman, Klaus. (Ed) 2007. *Overcoming the Problematics of Art. The Writings of Yves Klein*. Putnam, CO: Spring Publications.

Parent, Claude, Yves Klein et al. 2012. *The Memorial. An Architectural Project*. London: Cornerhouse.

Piene. Otto (Ed.). 1973. *ZERO*. Köhln: Dumont Schaunberg. Print.

SCALE **1/3.000**

8

‖ Ivan Leonidov. Club of a New Social Type. 1928

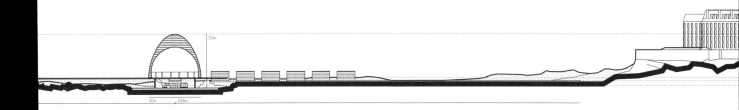

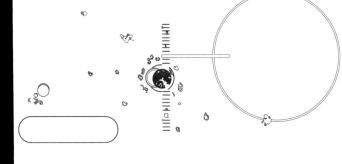

8

‖ Ivan Leonidov. Club of a New Social Type. 1928

Conceived for a new society, the Social Club includes educational activities, a museum and a planetarium. The activities are overseen from a central building that receives information from the exterior world through radio and an imagined television system. This information is retransmitted within the Club. The Club occupies an undefined, universal space. As a new typology, it is meant to be replicated. The project is rendered in black to strengthen its relation to cosmic space. In addition, the organization of buildings and programs follows the logic of planetary orbits.

Archive

A. V. Shchusev State Research Museum of Architecture in Moscow. See: Gozak and Cooke, 1988, p.34.

Bibliography

Khan-Magomedov, Vieri Quilici, and Massimo Scolari. 1975. *Ivan Leonidov.* Milano: F. Angeli.

De Magistris, Alessandro, Irina Korob'ina, and Ivan I. Leonidov. 2009. *Ivan Leonidov, 1902-1959.* Milano: Electa Architettura.

Gozak, A., Andrei Leonidov, Catherine Cooke, and Igor Palmin. 1988. *Ivan Leonidov: The Complete Works.* New York: Rizzoli.

Leonidov, Ivan I., S. Khan-Magomedov, and Institute for Architecture and Urban Studies. 1981. *Ivan Leonidov.* Vol. 8. New York, N.Y.: Institute for Architecture and Urban Studies: Rizzoli International Publications.

Leonidov, Ivan I., Alessandra Latour, American Institute of Architects New York Chapter, and Studi Filosofici Istituto per Gli. 1988. *Ivan Leonidov.* New York, NY: New York Chapter / American Institute of Architects.

h: Distance to Horizon

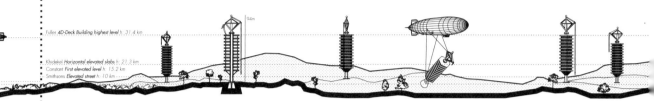

Fuller *4D-Deck Building highest level* h: 31.4 km
94m

Khidekel *Horizontal elevated slabs* h: 21.3 km
Constant *First elevated level* h: 15.2 km
Smithsons *Elevated street* h: 10 km

7

▌ BUCKMINSTER FULLER. AIROCEAN WORLD TOWN PLAN. 1927

The project for the 4D Tower seeks an alternative to urban expansion. It explores how a pre-fabricated, systemic method could be applied worldwide. As with the Russian projects of the 1920s, the intention is to maintain intact the surface of the earth but to use and redistribute the resources of the whole world equally among its population. To achieve this goal, Fuller proposes building 12 of these units in unpopulated, deserted areas, linking them together by aerial transport. They are built out of juxtaposing prefabricated horizontal decks that emphasize the scopic values of the new urban system.

ARCHIVE

Buckminster Fuller Archive at Stanford / MIT.

BIBLIOGRAPHY

Fuller, R. B. 1950. *Comprehensive Designing*. Cambridge, Mass.

———. 1954. "Fluid Geography: A Primer for the Airocean World.: *North Carolina State School of Design Journal*, 41–48.

———.1969. *Operating manual for spaceship earth*. Carbondale: Southern Illinois University Press.

———. 1969. *Planetary Planning - 1: Excerpts from the Jawaharlal Nehru Memorial Lecture*.

———. 1973. *Earth, inc*. Garden City, N.Y.: Anchor Press.

Fuller, R. B., James Meller ed., and James Meller editor. 1970. *The Buckminster Fuller Reader*. London: Jonathan Cape.

Hatch, Alden. 1974. *Buckminster Fuller: At home in the Universe*. New York: Crown Publishers.

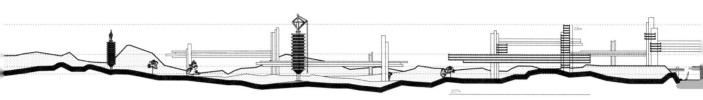

22

▌ LAZAR KHIDEKEL. ELEVATED CITY. 1927

In line with the post-revolutionary Russian sentiment, Khidekel creates an entirely new urban system, a new framework for a socialist way of life that extends urbanization across the Russian territory. The project has a strong architectural character, consisting of a system of interconnected, elevated bars superimposed on the existing terrain. The natural geography remains untouched. By radically differentiating between an untouched ground and an aerial city, Khidekel evokes contemporaneous explorations about aerial and extraterrestrial living. The alternative world is achieved by elevating the raised line to the height of the skyline and looking down at the ground and the horizon.

<u>ARCHIVE</u>

Familiar Archive New York.

<u>BIBLIOGRAPHY</u>

Garrido, Ginés. 2013. "Ciudades Aéreas: Visiones of Lazar Khidekel." *Arquitectura Viva*, n.153, p.58-61.

Khidekel, Mark. 1989. "Suprematism and the Architectural Projects of Lazar Khidekel." *Architectural Design*, v.59 n.7-8. p.iii-iv.

Khan-Magomedov, S. 2008. *Lazar Khidekel*. Moscow: Moskva Russkiĭ avangard.

Khan-Magomedov, S. and Catherine Cooke. 1987. *Pioneers of Soviet Architecture: The Search for New Solutions in the 1920s and 1930s*. New York: Rizzoli.

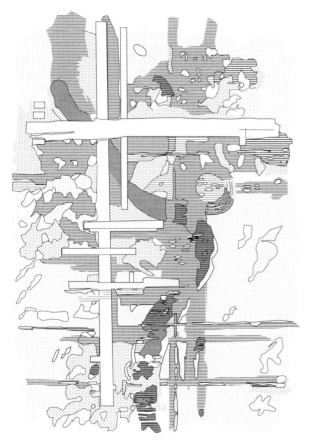

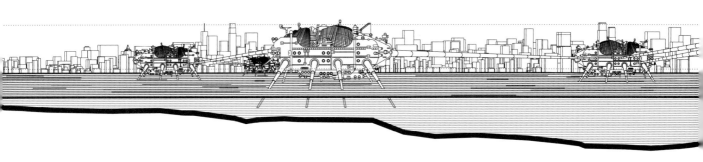

▌ ARCHIGRAM. WALKING CITY. 1964

The nomadic lifestyle of modern society is here adopted by the city itself. The city walks. It moves from one location to another and occasionally stops to refill. People work, live, and play in these moving cities, so everybody effectively moves while remaining in place. There are no borders anymore as no one is tied to place. Walking City covers the same horizontal expanse of the earth as current sprawl not by inhabiting it but by moving across it. In that sense, the horizon is made visible and accessible by taking the whole city to an elevated plain.

ARCHIVE

Archigram Archive: http://archigram.westminster.ac.uk/. The original is held within the Deutsche Arkitectur Museum collection.

BIBLIOGRAPHY

Cook, Peter, ed. *Archigram. Magazine for new ideas in architecture*. Vol 1-9 (1961-1970). London.

Cook, Peter. 1973. *Archigram*. New York: Praeger Publishers.

———. 1991. *Archigram*. Basel and Boston: Birkhäuser Verlag.

Crompton, Dennis, ed., and Archigram (Group). Archives. 2012. *A guide to Archigram 1961-74 = ein archigram-program, 1961-74*. Second, revised edition. New York: Princeton Architectural Press.

Crompton, Dennis, Peter Cook, Archigram (Group), and Cornerhouse (Gallery: Manchester, England). 1999. *Concerning Archigram*. 4th ed. London: Archigram Archives.

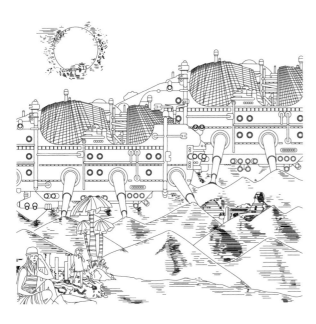

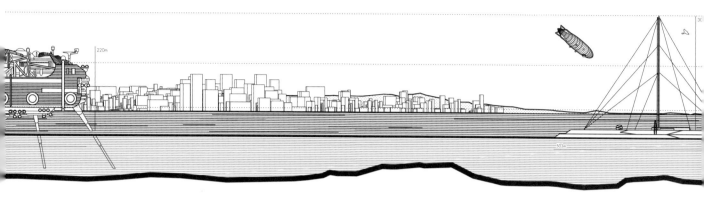

3

| IVAN LEONIDOV. COLUMBUS MONUMENT. 1929

Leonidov proposes a World Culture Center that brings together all the achievements of world history explaining them through communications and media. The system of communications includes an airport, a port, visual and acoustical media, culminating in an Institute of Interplanetary Communication. Through these systems, the Monument continuously receives information from and broadcasts it to several cities of the world. The Memorial is a sort of island. Its superior platform is located 20 meters above sea level in order to facilitate the perception of the surrounding geography and, especially, of the horizon at sea.

ARCHIVE

Original lost. Published in SA, n.4, 1929.

BIBLIOGRAPHY

Khan-Magomedov, Vieri Quilici, and Massimo Scolari. 1975. *Ivan Leonidov*. Milano: F. Angeli.

De Magistris, Alessandro, Irina Korob'ina, and Ivan I. Leonidov. 2009. *Ivan Leonidov, 1902-1959*. Milano: Electa Architettura.

Gozak, A., Andrei Leonidov, Catherine Cooke, and Igor Palmin. 1988. *Ivan Leonidov: The Complete Works*. New York: Rizzoli.

S. Khan-Magomedov, and Institute for Architecture and Urban Studies. 1981. *Ivan Leonidov*. Vol. 8. New York: Institute for Architecture and Urban Studies: Rizzoli International Publications.

Alessandra Latour, American Institute of Architects New York Chapter, and Studi Filosofici Istituto per Gli. 1988. *Ivan Leonidov*. New York: New York Chapter / American Institute of Architects.

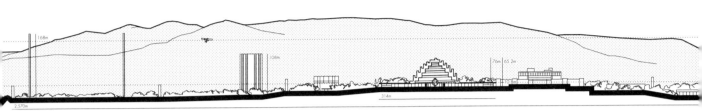

2

▌ LE CORBUSIER. MUNDANEUM. 1929

For Paul Otlet, its main promoter, the aim of the Mundaneum is to create an almost sacred place in which the world's civilizations could be brought together as one totality. Using both written and visual displays, the Mundaneum shows in a single location the discovery of the world's territories and their conquest by humankind, the development of human settlements, and the processes by which humankind came to live together as one community. The main building is intended to occupy the center of a projected World City, located outside Geneva. In their dimensions and positions, all the buildings are strongly associated with the surrounding geography. The Mundaneum itself takes the form of a ziggurat whose continuous horizontal surfaces create a system of external raised grounds that link the planetary intellectual project with the perception of the physical and human geography of the Alps.

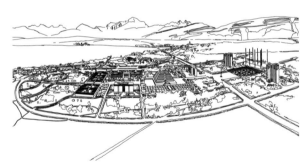

ARCHIVE

Foundation Le Corbusier

BIBLIOGRAPHY

Baird, George, and Karel Teige. 1974. "Documents: Karel Teige's 'Mundaneum,' (1929) and Le Corbusier's 'In Defense of Architecture' (1933)." *Oppositions* 4 (10): 79-108.

Le Corbusier and Fondation Le Corbusier. 1984. *Villa Savoye and other buildings and projects, 1929-1930*. Vol. 7. New York: Paris: Garland; Fondation Le Corbusier.

Le Corbusier, Pierre Jeanneret, and Willy Boesiger. 1935. *Oeuvre Complète*. Zürich: H. Girsberger.

O'Byrne Orozco, Maria Cecilia. 2004. "El museo del Mundaneum: Génesis de un prototipo." *Massilia* 3: 112-35.

h: Distance to Horizon

Haller *Central tower observation deck* h: 90.1 km

Le Corbusier *Radio Centric City* towers h: 67.2 km

Friedman *Bridge level* h: 44.2 km

The three routes: 1,500m

Linear Industrial City: 3,080m

17

LE CORBUSIER. THREE HUMAN ESTABLISHMENTS. 1945

Le Corbusier classifies three forms of settlement that could redress the urban chaos: radio-concentric commercial cities, linear industrial cities, and a network of agricultural villages. This taxonomy highlights the way these three forms of settlement "geo-architecturally" occupy the territory by directly linking to natural resources and forms of production. Each of the three establishments evokes a different horizontality of the territory juxtaposed to create a conceptually connected and harmonious world.

<u>ARCHIVE</u>

Foundation Le Corbusier. Paris.

<u>BIBLIOGRAPHY</u>

Cohen, Jean-Louis. 2008. "Interurbanités: Processus dialogiques à l'oeuvre [Interurbanities: Dialogical processes at work]." *Cahiers De La Recherche Architecturale Et Urbaine* (22) (02): 99-118.

Le Corbusier. 1945. *Les Trois Établissements Humains*. Paris: Denoël.

———. 1946. *Oeuvre Complete. 1938-1946*. Erlenbach-Zurich: Les Editions d'architecture.

———. 1959. *L'Urbanisme Des Trois Établissements Humains*. Paris: Édition de Minuit.

Saddy, Pierre. 1987. "Le ricchezze della natura = les richesses de la nature." *Casabella* 51 (531) (1987): 42.

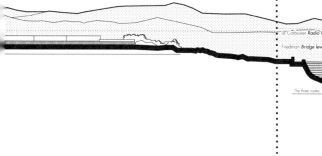

[Occupation naturelle du territoire]

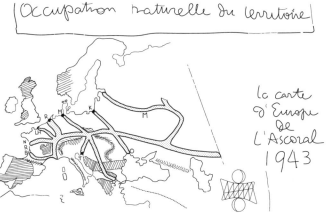

La carte
d'Europe
de
L'Ascoral
1943

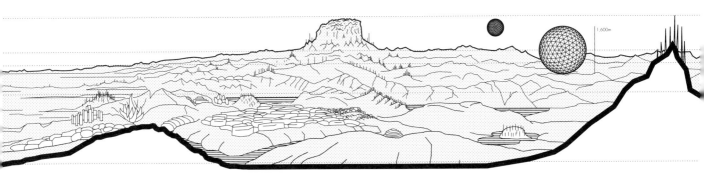

4

FULLER AND SADO. CLOUD 9. 1960

Cloud 9 takes to the extreme Fuller's exploration of geodesic structures and his interest in totally controlled environments to reconsider the different forms of human occupation of the earth. The project turns the geodesic domes into spheres to create mobile airborne habitats. These are meant to levitate by heating the internal air above the exterior temperature. The spherical form of the project and its orbital movement around the earth, mirrors the finite and fragile conditions of Spaceship Earth.

<u>ARCHIVE</u>

Buckminster Fuller Archive at Stanford / MIT.

<u>BIBLIOGRAPHY</u>

Fuller, R. B. 1950. *Comprehensive Designing*. Cambridge, Mass.

———. 1954. "Fluid Geography: A Primer for the Airocean World.: *North Carolina State School of Design Journal*, 41–48.

———.1969. *Operating manual for spaceship earth*. Carbondale: Southern Illinois University Press.

———. 1969. *Planetary Planning – 1: Excerpts from the Jawaharlal Nehru Memorial Lecture*.

———. 1972. *Floating Cities*.

———. 1973. *Earth, inc.* Garden City, N.Y.: Anchor Press.

Fuller, R. B., James Meller ed., and James Meller editor. 1970. *The Buckminster Fuller Reader*. London: Jonathan Cape.

Hatch, Alden. 1974. *Buckminster Fuller: At home in the Universe*. New York: Crown Publishers.

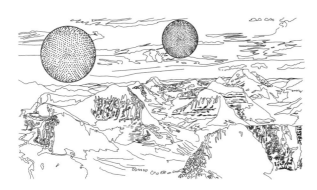

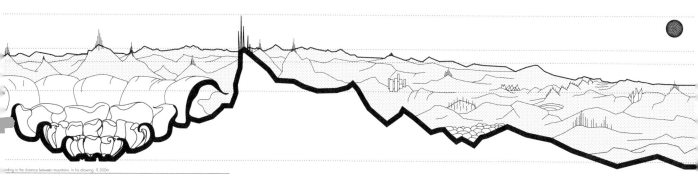

ording to the distance between mountains, in his drawing: 9,300m

10
| FRITZ HALLER. TOTALE STADT. 1968-1975

Haller's Total City is a grid that operates at different scales from building, to city, to the whole territory of the earth.

The development of the grid transcends (and modifies) geographical and political location. Its aim is to facilitate the re-occupation of the entire planet by more rational means than the existing ones in order to overcome the ecological and organizational dangers of overpopulation. For Haller this implies concentrating the population in just a few, densely populated nuclei. They are surrounded by the hinterland they require for agricultural production so that the rest of the earth can recuperate its natural state. The city is a new horizontal system often requiring landform modification. Its main buildings provide a view of the territory outside it.

<u>ARCHIVE</u>

ETH Zurich.

<u>BIBLIOGRAPHY</u>

Haller, Fritz. 1968. *Total Stadt: Ein Modell / Integral Urban: A Global Model.* Olten: Walter Verlag.

———. 1975. *Total Stadt: Ein Modell / Integral Urban: A Global Model.* Olten: Walter Verlag.

———. 1980. *Space Colony.*

Stalder, Laurent. "No limits to growth. The Global and Interplanetary Urban Models of Fritz Haller." *AA Files* 66 (2014): 145-152.

SCALE **1/175.000**

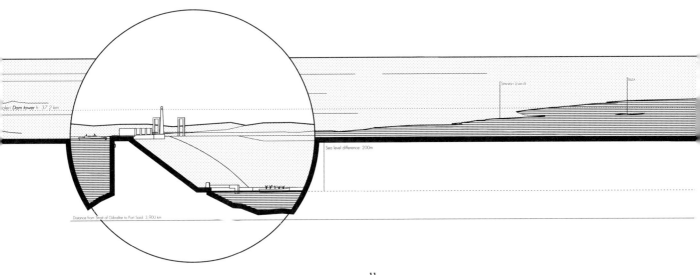

Dam tower h: 37.2 km.

Spanish Levante

Ibiza

Sea level difference: 200m

Distance from Strait of Gibraltar to Port Said: 3,900 km

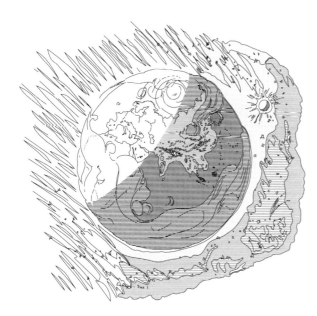

▌BRUNO TAUT. ALPINE ARCHITECTURE. 1919

Designed in the aftermath of WWI, Alpine Architecture proposes the collective construction of a new urban formation in the Alps as a symbol of a pacified European continent. The project presents a new understanding of the urban form that, detached from its historical relation to the city, could be re-projected onto the geographic space. The project forms a cohesive whole with the rest of Taut's graphic works; namely, The World Builder, The Dissolution of the Cities, and The City Crown, all of which recover the connection between humanity and the earth. The fusion between the ground and the skylines generates a strong awareness of the thickness of the inhabited world.

ARCHIVE

Deutsches Architekturmuseum / Architekturmuseum München / Stiftung Archiv der Akademie der Künste Berlin.

BIBLIOGRAPHY

Scheerbart, Paul. Taut, Bruno. 1972. *Alpine Architektur. Glass architecture*. New York: Praeger.

Solà-Morales Rubió, Ignasi and Bruno Taut. 1982. *Constructor del Mundo. La arquitectura del expresionismo*. Vol. no. 7.27; 2. Barcelona: Escola Tècnica Superior d'Arquitectura de Barcelona.

Taut, Bruno. 1918. "The Earth. A Good Home." *Oppositions*: 1978 Fall: 87-89.

———. 1919. *Alpine architektur: In 5 teilen und 30 zeichnungen des architekten*. Folkwang: Hogeni.

———. 1920. *Der weltbaumeister: Architektur-schauspiel für symphonische musik, dem geiste paul scheerbarts gewidmet*. Hagen i.W.: Folkwang-Verlag.

———. 1977. *Die Stadtkrone*. Nendeln, Liechtenstein: Kraus Reprint.

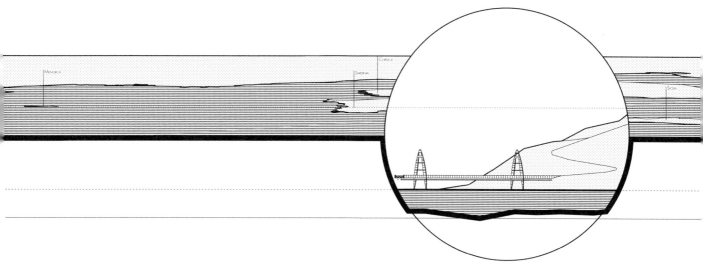

16

❙ HERMAN SÖRGEL. ATLANTROPA. 1920-1952

In Atlantropa, the European subcontinent is united with Africa by emptying the Mediterranean enough to create more land and land bridges. This connection is enhanced through communication networks and shared energy resources. Two giant dams produce hydroelectric power and lower the level of the Mediterranean Sea. They are placed in Gibraltar and Port Said. Two others are placed on the Dardanelles and in the Congo River. The new land is used for settlement and agricultural production. Unambiguous in its colonialist intent, the project guarantees the status of Europe among competing powers, converting Africa into an enormous source of materials and energy. The new but sunken ground line exposes continuity where the horizon could not.

<u>ARCHIVE</u>

Deutsches Museum. Munich.

<u>BIBLIOGRAPHY</u>

Cerviere, Giacinto and Yona Friedman. 2007. "Atlantropa-Projekt." *Domus* 900: 74-81. Print.

Christensen, Peter. 2012. "Dam Nation: Imaging and Imagining the 'Middle East' in Herman Sörgel's Atlantropa." *International journal of Islamic architecture* 1.2: 325-46. Print.

Sörgel, Herman. 1938. *Die Drei Grossen "A"; Gross Deutschland Und Italienisches Imperium, Die Pfeiler Atlantropas*. München: Piloty & Loehle. Print.

Voigt, Wolfgang. 1998. *Atlantropa. Weltbauen Am Mittelmeer: Ein Architektentraum Der Moderne*. Hamburg: Dölling und Galitz. Print.

SCALE **1/6.500.000**

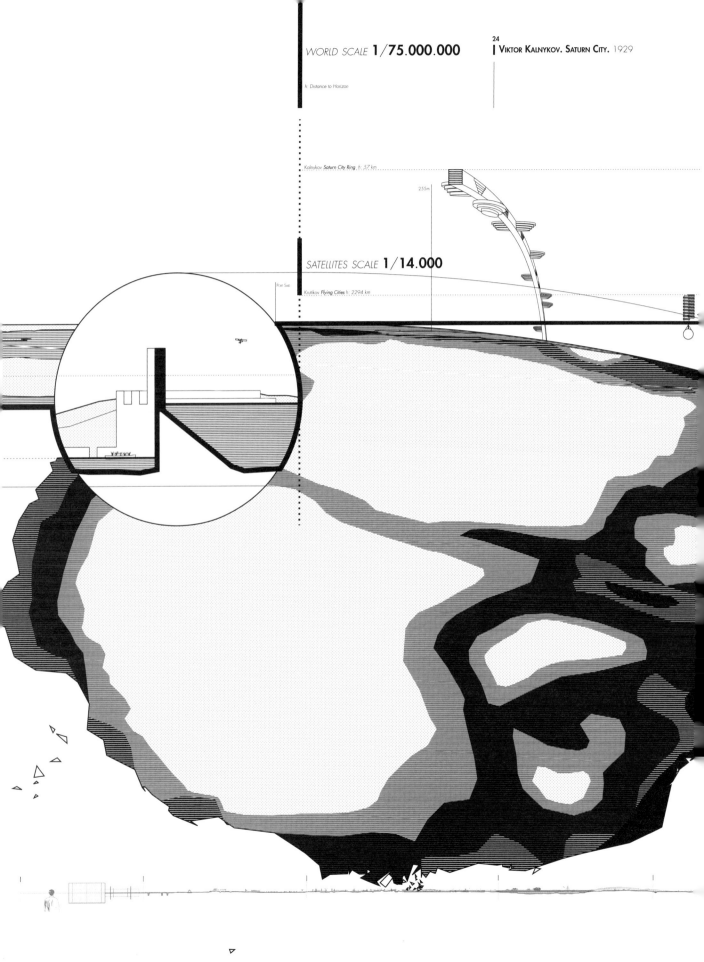

h: Distance to Horizon

Kalnykov *Saturn City Ring* h: 57 km

255m

SATELLITES SCALE **1/14.000**

PORT SAID

Krutikov *Flying Cities* h: 2294 km

. Ecumenopolis. 1967   25
| Giorgy Krutikov. Flying City. 1929

WORLD SCALE 1/55(

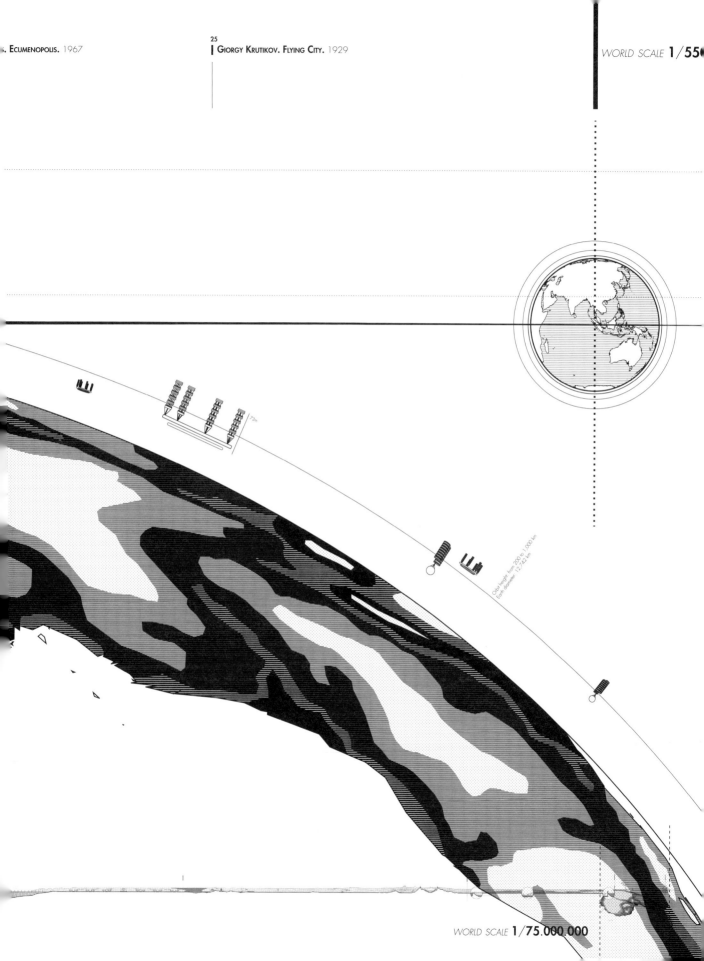

Orbit height from 200 to 1,000 km
Earth diameter 12,742 km

73m

Micro, Partial, Parallel, (In)Visible

Roi Salgueiro Barrio

I

We owe to Manfredo Tafuri the recognition of the importance of the world scale for architectural modernity, but also a severe criticism of the consequences of the discipline's involvement in the production of that scale. From his seminal 1969 article, "Toward a Critique of Architectural Ideology," Tafuri's critique of the historiography of modernism and of modernism itself derived from the understanding that the global scale had been the essential, implicit referent for architectural modernity. Behind this global referent lay, for the author, a dominant factor: capitalism, whose overarching influence had made architecture's entire development into a merely ideological attempt to resolve "the imbalances, contradictions and delays typical of the capitalistic reorganization of the world market."[01] This architectural reaction to the world market was more than a simple internalization of an external global sphere. It had directed the efforts of architectural and urban culture towards the construction of a multitude of "hypotheses of the global renovation of the physical arrangement of territory" that, as Tafuri noted in *The Sphere and the Labyrinth*, constituted a long chain of ineffective propositions, impeded by the very institutions of capitalism itself.[02]

Tafuri's reservations about architecture's endorsement of the world scale and its involvement in territorial organization did not stem simply from his identification of this scale with capitalism at large. His conception of criticism as a means of demystifying the universal character of categories such as "architecture" and "city" shares in a rejection of totalities that is also characteristic of later postmodern critiques of grand narratives.[03] In fact, "totality" itself represents a category in deep conflict with Tafuri's conception of architecture. For him, the architectural object was fundamentally an *exception* to the totality of social and spatial fields, standing in contrast to their hegemonic homogeneity. As he articulates with precision in his analysis of Hilberseimer's *Grosstadt Architektur* (1927), architecture's oppositional capacity is impeded when architecture addresses the totality, when it becomes subsumed within the global schema it itself has to generate. Tafuri shows how Hilberseimer's attempt to fuse architecture with the totality of the city transforms the former into a mere unit of the latter, its condition as object abandoned in favor of its new status as a partial element within an overall "process."[04]

This privileging of process, which comprises both the management of social relations and their spatial organization within an expanding territory, implies a radical disciplinary transformation. It promotes a predominantly organizational logic in which any exploration of architecture's own formal language becomes irrelevant; technical rationality prevails, and architecture is converted into pure, abstract labor. The integration of architecture in a broader totality leads, in this view, to a neglect of the discipline's position as a cultural artifact. Furthermore, it has a consequence that Tafuri believed had remained unnoticed, but which undermines the very object of the discipline, that is, the loss of architecture's cognitive value: the "utter refusal to consider architecture as an instrument of knowledge."[05] It is not strange, then, that in synthesizing the diverse forms of territorial organization conceived during modernity Tafuri detects a continual tendency to create a new technical agent, albeit one that is "the traditional architect only in the less significant cases."[06]

Architecture's exceptional oppositional capacity, its linguistic or formal significance, and its role as cognitive instrument conform the triad of interrelated values severely compromised by the global scale. Seen in this light, the planetary scale constitutes a notable challenge for architectural culture, a challenge that the discipline rejected by falling into a profound self-reflexive retreat which not only coincided with—and occasionally followed—Tafuri's critique, but also with the post-1970s historical period, in which the importance of the global scale was reinforced on every front, from the urban to the environmental and the political, and so on.

Tafuri closed "Toward a Critique of Architectural Ideology" with a critical question about his own project, wondering whether it would constitute an avant-garde or a rearguard. Retroactively, it can be said that the consolidation of the global scale during the last 40 years has developed hand in hand with a general abandonment of the exploration of how architecture can address this scale using its own instruments. This disciplinary void has promoted attempts to respond to the current concern with territorial and global questions—manifest in the multitude of inquiries focused on the Anthropocene, socio-economic globalization, or planetary urbanization, to name only a few—precisely by furthering the disciplinary transformation Tafuri rejected. Where Tafuri detected and criticized the inclusion of the object as a unit within a major process, now the interest in processes has extended to a more systemic consideration: within contemporary conceptual frameworks interested in studying the connections between architectural, territorial and global questions, such as landscape, resilience, metabolism, and theories of urban complexity, architecture is often re-conceptualized, at best, as a medium to manage both material and immaterial flows or, at worst, as a process in itself.[7]

Unavoidably, the rationality of such tendencies has been criticized from a Tafurian perspective. The value of the exceptional architectural artifact as a vehicle of knowledge provides a crucial dimension, for instance, to Pier Vittorio Aureli's call for the recovery of architectural autonomy. His vindication of architecture's exceptionality is a direct critique of the "cognitive metabolism" that characterizes the accounts of contemporary urbanization that cannot grasp

Ivan Leonidov, Columbus Memorial, 1929. Collage (original lost).

the urban beyond its appearance of incessant change and which, from that perspective, conceive the role of spatial disciplines through notions of landscape or network.[08] Understood as an autonomous artifact, architecture appears anew as an exception to the totalizing—now planetary—urban process.[09] For Aureli, autonomy provides a way of recovering the political role of architecture—a role situated importantly in the realms of representation and cognition. Instead of addressing totality by participating in the processes that generate it, the exceptional architectural object allows us to understand—and criticize—the whole by turning it into the referent to be negated by the object's singularity. Moreover, Aureli vindicates autonomy for its ability not only to confront the global urban process but also to counteract "cognitive frameworks such as vision, scenario, and utopia, which often reduce the world to simplistic and totalizing representations."[10] The singular, autonomous object contradicts both the totalizing aspirations of the process and the often-reductionist view of the global.

II

Tafuri and Aureli have pointed out how architecture's involvement in the global scale tends to situate the discipline between the Scylla of the process and the Charybdis of epistemological reductivism. Their response to these pitfalls by no means denies architecture's responsibility in the articulation of the territorial and, at least in Tafuri's case, of the global. Yet, their response posits this participation according to a unique vector. Tafuri preserves the global scale as a necessary horizon for architectural practice through a

movement from the particular to the universal. Only this direction, in his view, grants architecture its singularity, its capacity of linguistic exploration, and its cognitive value.[11] Aureli's approach to territoriality also adopts this direction, with the added goal of recovering architecture's political role.

While sharing Tafuri and Aureli's concerns, what follows explores the value of the direction these two authors have neglected. That is, it explores the possibility of also approaching the global scale through the *a priori* ideation of a totality (and eventually, the design of that totality) and through the incorporation of these meta-geographical and universalist positions into singular objects derived from it. By introducing this alternate direction, it is possible to engage in a more in-depth interrogation of the relations that might exist between architecture and the global scale. Previous architectural attempts to define totality have certainly encountered the pitfalls Tafuri and Aureli identify, yet they have also indicated the means to escape them, demonstrating that architectural exceptionality is not the only way of confronting the process-based understanding of the discipline. In fact, associating architecture with meta-geographic conceptions has propelled a continuous investigation of architecture's formal language, as well as its capacity to serve as a cognitive tool. Moreover, it has allowed architects, as Tafuri desired, to explore the relationship between the discipline's linguistic or formal dimension and the extra-linguistic—which is to say, social and political—realm.[12]

To understand the relationship between the architectural definition of totality, cognitive aims, and formal investigation, this section of the paper presents a provisional categorization of the epistemological positions that characterize the projects selected in the research The World According to Architecture, which will be complemented in the next section by some synthetic examples of different design praxis informed by such positions. The World According to Architecture has an initial historic component aimed to determine which projects have explicitly addressed the scale of the world. In this regard, it confirms that, from the birth of modern urban planning in the mid-19th century until the 1970s, the definition of the global scale was a constant concern for architectural culture, manifest in the design of planetary proposals, but also in addressing totality through interventions at other scales. The research also comprises an analytical component, aimed at understanding the disciplinary transformations implied by works that address the global scale, as well as the mechanisms through which those works were conceived. Yet, the formal mechanisms were not addressed directly. The variety of formal strategies employed to design specific global propositions was considered only after defining the epistemological positions that could lead to them. These positions were grouped into five categories,

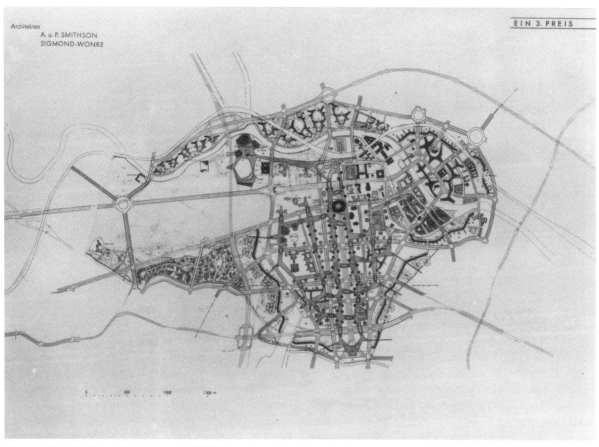

Architekten
A. u. P. SMITHSON
SIGMOND-WONKE

Alison and Peter Smithson, Berlin Haupstadt, 1957. Plan.

which are here reduced to four: the micro, the partial, the parallel, and the (in)visible.

As cognitive positions, the micro, the partial, the parallel, and the (in)visible are mediations—conceptual guidelines to approaching totality, which then privilege different design questions. Iteratively, the projects grouped within each of these categories construct a certain physical framework for the comprehension of the whole that is directly determined by the epistemological position from which the project derives. This transition from the epistemological to the formal is perfectly captured by Fredric Jameson's observation that "the social totality is always unrepresentable, we can count at most with maps and models that allow us to read its tendencies."[13] His remarks suggest, on one level, that we can only access totality through cognitive mediations, through epistemological positions that we have to elaborate and examine, not least because they have profound pre-formative implications—that is, they orient the way we intervene in the world.[14] On a second level, Jameson's observation implies that, in the construction of these epistemological positions, we constantly depend on formal operations. His statement suggests that not only does the global not preclude the

formal, but that it also opens up a specific question about the ultimate possibilities of formal definition. Seen from an architectural perspective, rather than an unavoidable descent into process management accompanied by the vanishing of the object, the global fosters an interrogation of the status and limits of architectural form. It implies an inquiry into where architecture's boundaries may reside, acknowledging that if the status of those boundaries is problematic, it is all the more necessary to discover what their roles and possibilities are. This interrogation of architecture's physical and disciplinary limits is what we find in the best examples of projects distributed among the categories of the micro, the partial, the parallel, and the (in)visible.

The micro (from *microcosm*) explores how architecture's historical role as a medium for cosmological representation was redirected toward the representation and production of the planetary scale. Projects in this category work from the assumption that the global scale can be apprehended by producing encapsulated, synthetic versions of the wider world, which is often referred to by analogy. Enclosed and potentially autonomous from its context, each microcosm can act like a monad. It can create a particular, interior vision

197

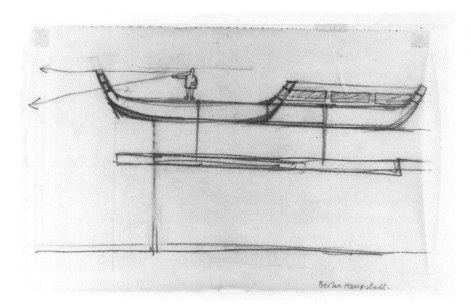

Alison and Peter Smithson, Berlin Haupstadt, 1957. Typical detail section through pedestrian net platform. Opposite page: Yona Friedman, *Paris Spatiale*, 1959. Bird's-eye view of the plan.

of the world, isolated and possibly divergent from those that other microcosms may generate. As a result, the multiplication of microcosms fosters a pluralistic scenario: a diversity of world images.

A lineage of microcosms goes from Patrick Geddes's Outlook Tower (1892)—a building whose different floors reflect a conception of the world as a succession of nested scales—to Archigram's Soft Scene Monitor (1968)—whose multiple screens give form, on the contrary, to the fragmentary and trans-scalar world produced by mass-media—passing through Ivan Leonidov's Columbus Monument (1929), Le Corbusier's Mundaneum (1929), and Buckminster Fuller and Shoji Sadao's Cloud 9 (1960). All of these works construct and magnify the cognitive tension between the limits of a specific location and the comprehension of the world at large, between the architectural object and the totality. Consequently, an inquiry into how the micro operates seeks to understand how the scale of the world can be addressed through singular and delimited objects. Through the micro it is possible to investigate how architectural techniques of separation from a given context and negation of the exterior are used to establish relations with a different scale. It also permits us to investigate what forms of framing, representation, and projection are used to address the external sphere and what relationships architecture may establish with the diverse non-architectural technologies that can facilitate these representations. The aforementioned lineage of microcosms simultaneously explores how architecture and diverse technologies of visualization and communication can be integrated and what specific dimensions of the global can be apprehended by architectural means—two investigations all the more pertinent now that digital technologies grant immediate access to a great variety of global representations. In this regard, the value of the micro has to be considered not only for its capacity to represent the global sphere in the architectural interior, but also for the formal operations that characterize micro objects and how their autonomy can be used to eventually organize urban and territorial systems.

The epistemological rationale of partial strategies is typological. Primarily, partial projects proceed by classifying the elements that constitute the world, looking for points in common rather than exceptional characteristics. Based on these classifications, they define parts or prototypes that act as representative segments of the broader totality; in doing so, they might be considered the visual equivalent of the synecdoche. The possibility of repetition of these partial elements and the resulting promotions of sameness are seen as positive attributes—as tools to comprehend how the totality is articulated and to contribute to its organization.

Partial strategies characterize the attempt to understand the totality of a territorial system by defining a prototypical section—as in Arturo Soria y Mata's Linear City (1882) and Alison and Peter Smithson's Golden Lane (1952-53); a building typology—as in Buckminster Fuller's 4D Tower (1927) and Leonidov's Club of a New Social Type (1929); or a global urban model—as in Fritz Haller's Totale Stadt (1968–75). Partiality is the category that resonates most closely with Tafuri's analysis of Hilberseimer, in that through the repetition of the prototype, partial projects can generate territorial processes. Yet, beginning with the necessity of selecting the elements that can represent a world system, this category also opens up specific questions about the role of architecture as an instrument of knowledge: What are the architectural forms of classification of the world? Can the potential repetition of the partial element be used to understand and enhance differences? What role does singularity play, if it is still preserved, within a prototype?

Parallel projects explore the capacity of physical distance to differentiate between subject and object, creating a necessary cognitive separation between them. Through this exploration of distance, parallel projects aim to facilitate the perception of the planet as a unitary object. In different degrees, they approach what, in 1987, Frank White termed the *overview effect*—the cognitive shift astronauts experience when seeing the earth from outer space.[15] In design terms, this attempt to construct the planet as object is systematically pursued by separating the intervention from the terrain, so that in this category every proposition becomes, literally, a layer parallel to the earth.

This dispositive has an additional consequence. It implies a differentiation between the earth system and the proposal that has facilitated the recourse to parallel projects in order to design alternatives to existing social modes of inhabitation. Together, the separation from the Earth and the difference between earth system and project tend to convert these parallel projects into utopias. This is the case with extra-atmospheric visions such as Viktor Kalnykov's Saturn City (1929) and Gyorgii Krutikov's Flying City (also 1929), but also with projects that maintain closer contact with the Earth, such as Lazar Khidekel's Elevated City (1927), Yona Friedman's Spatial City (1959), and Constant's New Babylon (1959–74). We should not allow the utopianism of these projects, however, to overshadow other aspects that these projects allow us to explore, which can be translated onto a variety of scales of operation. Parallel projects let us reflect on the spatial value of the sectional organization of the planet. Following their inquiries, it is possible to observe the effect produced by different levels of vertical separation from the Earth and how operating on each of these levels allows for different forms of reconfiguring the way the world is structured and perceived. Additionally, the intrinsic separation of these projects from the terrain leads to considering autonomy as architecture's initial condition, Earth and project as two different entities, and to exploring the relationship that can exist between them, drawing on that initial separation.

The final category, (in)visible, joins two differentiated but synergic approaches. From geographic conditions to forms of settlement to territorial or political relations, visibility aims to highlight certain features of the world and make them knowable. This cognitive purpose is mostly pursued by cartographic means and gestalt images that isolate the selected features in order to render them visible. This representational process is based on the contrast between figure and background, so that visibility depends on a simultaneous erasure—on the invisibility of other phenomena.

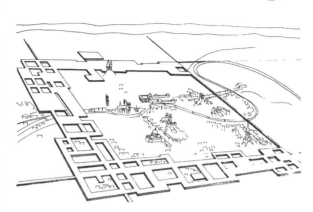

In its extreme form, the category of the (in)visible accesses totality through the procedure Jameson defines as *world reduction*; that is, "a principle of systemic exclusion, a kind of surgical excision of empirical reality, something like a process of ontological attenuation in which the sheer teeming multiplicity of what exists, of what we call reality, is deliberately thinned and weeded out through an operation of radical abstraction and simplification."[16]

The projects in this category translate the visible/invisible dialectic from cartographic representation to design. The projects that attempt to "make visible" bring to light a specific feature to the detriment of other conditions in the world, converting it into the main design principle. This operation characterizes, for instance, Le Corbusier's Three Human Establishments (1945), where the interest in visualizing European physical geography and the economic structure of the territory leads to a definition of the territorial system based uniquely on three types of settlements. It also characterizes projects such as Herman Sörgel's Atlantropa (1920–52), Fuller and Sadao's Dymaxion Map (1943–54), Yona Friedman's Bridge Cities (1963), Constantinos Doxiadis's Ecumenopolis (1967), and Saverio Muratori's territorial studies (also 1967). The projects that "make invisible"—Bruno Taut's Alpine Architecture (1919), Mikhail Okhitovich's disurbanist theory (1929), Rudolf Schwarz's proposals in *The Construction of the Earth* (1945), Yves Klein and Claude Parent's Air Architecture (1958–61), Paolo Soleri's Archology (1969), or Superstudio's Supersurface (1971)—take the previous operation further and propose to act against—and eventually eliminate—those attributes which contradict the construction of a particular vision of the world.

The central question raised by the category of the (in)visible concerns the possible relations between territorial interpretations, their cartographic mediations, and architectural production. The study of this question allows us to explore design positions ranging from the total assimilation

199

Roi Salgueiro Barrio

Yona Friedman, Seven Bridge Towns to Link Four Continents, 1963. <u>Opposite page</u>: *Le Monde en Projection Polaire*.

of cartography and project—as in Muratori's identification of the act of reading with the act of designing—to the recognition that the limitations and ideological biases of cartographic knowledge enable us to understand the critical tension between the architectural project and the cartographic image. In another direction, this category also allows us to examine how architectural conceptions of totality have led designers to conceive specific forms of cartographic visualization, and their roles either as mere cognitive instruments or as dialogical tools that open up the discussion about specific territorial conceptions.

III

The previous section focused on the cognitive operations that characterize the categories micro, partial, parallel, and (in)visible. Yet, a critical analysis of the categories also requires considering the transition from the general approach to totality to the variety of designs that each category includes. This transition allows us to analyze how these cognitive positions contributed to determining which

architectural strategies were pertinent, in a given historical moment, to confronting the global scale. In other words, it reveals how a determinate approach to totality led to the definition of diverse forms of spatial intervention. Although presenting the full range of formal options is beyond the scope of this essay, I would like to conclude with four examples of this movement from the epistemological to the formal in each category. My goal is to show how the consideration of a planetary totality allowed architects to address specific spatial and historical conditions, and how the interest in the global induced a constant interrogation of the possibilities of architectural, urban, and territorial form.

The attempt to produce the planetary scale from the architectural object structures Ivan Leonidov's work from the late 1920s. His interest in defining a universal urban system that could give a spatial dimension to the internationalist ambitions of post-revolutionary socialism motivated a strict investigation of the architectural object's autonomy.[17] Leonidov understood that communication media allowed for the integration of the planetary scale. Based on this consideration, instead of conceiving the architectural object as an assemblage of conflicting parts—as the constructivists had done in order to create an architectural equivalent of the metropolitan experience—he decomposed the object into a multitude of autonomous, pure, geometrical pieces: planes, prisms, domes, pyramids, always mutually distanced.[18] Each of these pieces was conceived as a microcosm. They were autonomous social cells aimed at producing the global scale by concentrating external information and disseminating internal information. From a formal standpoint, their abstract geometry was a tool for their universal applicability, and their isolation and radical autonomy were tools for negating architecture's historical role as a medium for enclosing space.[19] As a result, the use of microcosms was a means to restructure the urban system through the autonomy of the architectural object and to favor a-territoriality, in place of the territorial demarcation characteristic of existing urban forms.

This very notion of architectural autonomy was challenged in the early 1950s by the Smithsons, who considered it an insufficient response to a world where the urban had become a global condition.[20] For the Smithsons, the architectural, urban, territorial, and global scales had become spatially interlinked and permanently in contact. The architects addressed their consequent interest in defining an architectural system that could mediate between these diverse scales by using a partial strategy: defining a sectional template that condensed and vertically stratified the land uses and forms of transportation and communication representing the possible organization of the world.[21] The sectional logic of this interrelation was markedly infrastructural and, in fact, supported a discourse based on the notions of change, growth, and networks. At the same time, the section reversed the indeterminate nature of the network by relating architecture to its environmental conditions. In this sense, the partial strategy allowed for a mediation between universality and the specificity of contextual conditions, producing formally differentiated "clusters" or islands (as in their Berlin Hauptstadt project), from which to understand the structure of the surrounding territory.

Although he shared the Smithsons' concern with the global scale and he dealt with the same socio-spatial conditions, Yona Friedman dismissed their investigation of a new architectural model and sought instead to redefine the city as a whole. With the Spatial City, Friedman pursued that redefinition through a parallel strategy in which the structural spatial grids that Konrad Wachsmann had defined were appropriated, de-contextualized, and, once augmented, converted into an urban artifact. This elevated artifact orchestrated the two types of vision Friedman considered necessary to facilitating the development of a new social and ecological contract: the vision of others from a

strictly individual perspective and the vision from outside.[22] If the former was, for Friedman, the basis of a new form of collaborative social organization, the latter was the tool for transforming the fragmentary perception of the Earth into a comprehensive view. The progressive elevation of the point of view allowed Friedman to use the Spatial City: first, as a means to frame existing cities, defining them as single, delimited entities; then, as a tool to transform the European territorial structure, converting it into a system of 120 spatial cities; and, finally, as a way to consolidate the Earth as a "terrestrial infrastructure," or spatially unified whole, in his Seven Bridges to Link Four Continents, a project that would unite the different continents into a single land mass.[23]

Lastly, Saverio Muratori's understanding that once civilization reaches its planetary spatial limits, evolution can only be internal motivated his insistence on defining territory as an architectural construct and as the key operative scale for spatial articulation.[24] This instrumentalization of territory required making the geographical support of civilization visible by cartographic means. Muratori maintained an essentially determinist position, according to which geography informs and should guide the formal structures of human settlements. As a result, cartographic representations act as a visual guide to reverse the deleterious effects of contemporary urbanization. These representations made the existing urban condition invisible", showing instead how the link between geographical conditions and settlement

201

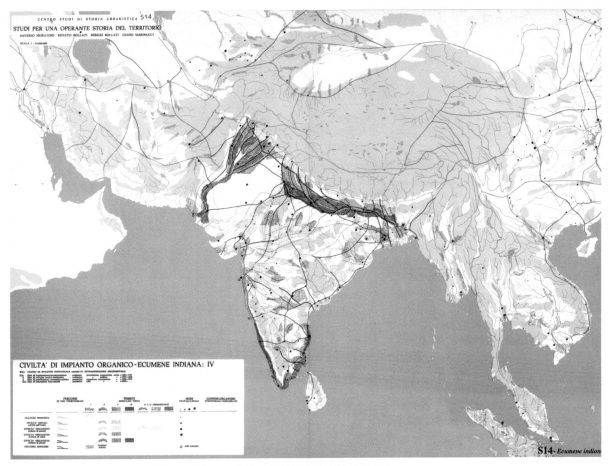

Saverio Muratori, *Civiltá d'Impianto Organico- Ecumene Indiana: IV*, E 1: 10.000.000, Folio S14.

patterns have historically created specific territorial types. The recovery of these types as guides for urbanization became a form of combating global spatial homogeneity, redefining the world as a puzzle composed of differentiated territorial pieces.[25] Moreover, the typological conception of territory was internally strengthened, each territory defined through its characteristic architectural types.[26]

The aforementioned works by Leonidov, the Smithsons, Friedman, and Muratori are just an ideologically disparate sample of how micro, partial, parallel, and (in)visible strategies were used to transition from meta-geographic conceptions to an elaboration of disciplinary instruments at the architectural, urban, and territorial scales. Additionally, by conceiving a planetary totality, each of these projects offers, if not a direct political proposition, a critical response to a different reality.

The ultimate goal in studying the categories of the micro, partial, parallel, and (in)visible and the projects they contain, is to reconsider architecture's critical capacity to respond to the global scale. These categories are an approximation of the rationalities that have guided architecture's

relation to the global. Without a doubt, they imply their own deficiencies and contain possible points of complicity with some of the phenomena Tafuri pertinently denounced. Exploring the ways in which architecture can reposition its participation within the diverse processes of global structuring now at play will require both a critical reading of the positions themselves and of the forms in which these epistemological positions were deployed. Their value is not prescriptive; on the contrary, they are conceived as objects of analysis and critique. Yet, the fundamental proposition they contain can be maintained: there are diverse forms of mediation between the global and the architectural, forms of mediation that allow us to simultaneously explore the conditions of social totality and the capacity of architectural language to respond to them, that encourage both the comprehension and production of the global scale. In this sense, the micro, parallel, partial, and (in)visible are tools to understand that, borrowing from Tafuri, it is by considering totality that architecture can explore which linguistic aspects can address the extra-linguistic realm.

The research project The World According to Architecture is being conducted at the Massachusetts Institute of Technology under the direction of Dean Hashim Sarkis. A fragment of this research was shown at the Yale University School of Architecture from September 3 to November 14, 2015 and will also be exhibited at the Lisbon Triennale and at the School of Architecture of São Paulo in 2016. I would like to thank Dean Sarkis, Gabriel Kozlowski, and Adrià Carbonell for providing critical feedback on this paper.

01. Manfredo Tafuri, "Toward a Critique of Architecture Ideology" ("Per una critica dell'ideologia architettonica"), *Contropiano* 1 (January–April 1969), rpt. in *Architecture Theory Since 1968*, ed. K. Michael Hays (Cambridge, MA: MIT Press, 1998), 32.

02. Manfredo Tafuri, *The Sphere and the Labyrinth: Avant-gardes and Architecture from Piranesi to the 1970s* (Cambridge, MA: MIT Press, 1987), 20. Originally published as *La sfera e il labirinto: avanguardie e architettura da Piranesi agli anni '70* (Turin: Giulio Einaudi editore, 1980).

03. See Manfredo Tafuri, *History of Italian Architecture, 1944–1985* (Cambridge, MA: MIT Press, 1989), 132. Originally published as *Storia della architettura italiana, 1948–1985* (Turin: Giulio Einaudi editore, 1986).

04. Tafuri, "Toward a Critique of Architecture Ideology," 22.

05. Tafuri, "Toward a Critique of Architecture Ideology," 23.

06. Tafuri, *The Sphere and the Labyrinth*, 21.

07. On theories of urban complexity, see for instance: Michael Batty, *The New Science of Cities* (Cambridge, MA: MIT Press, 2013); Roger White, Guy Engelen and Inge Uljee, *Modeling Cities and Regions as Complex Systems. From Theory to Planning Applications* (Cambridge, MA: MIT Press, 2015). For a critical approach to resilience and metabolism see, respectively: Ross Exo Adams, "Scales: Planetary Bodies"; Lafarge Holcim Forum 2016, "Infrastructure Space"; and Daniel Ibañez and Nikos Katsikis, ed., *New Geographies* 06: *Grounding Metabolism* (2014).

08. Pier Vittorio Aureli, "Toward the Archipelago: Defining the Political and the Formal in Architecture," *Log* 11 (Winter 2008): 111–13.

09. Neil Brenner and Christian Schmid, "Planetary Urbanization," in *Urban Constellations*, ed. Matthew Gandy (Berlin: Jovis, 2011), 10–13.

10. Aureli, "Toward the Archipelago," 114.

11. Tafuri, "Toward a Critique of Architecture Ideology," 25–28; and Tafuri, *History of Italian Architecture*, 149–69.

12. Tafuri, *The Sphere and the Labyrinth*, 15.

13. Fredric Jameson, *Archaeologies of the Future: The Desire Called Utopia and Other Science Fictions* (London: Verso, 2005), 14.

14. On the necessity of this critical examination, see: Giuseppe Dematteis, "Sull Crocevia della Territorialità Urbana," in *I Futuri della Città. Tesi a Confronto*, ed. Giuseppe Dematteis, Francesco Indovina, Alberto Magnaghi, Elio Piroddi, Enzo Scandurra, and Bernardo Secchi (Milan: Franco Angeli, 1999), 117–18. On the necessity of models as cognitive tools, see Steven W. Horst, *Cognitive Pluralism* (Cambridge, MA: MIT Press, 2016).

15. Frank White, *The Overview Effect: Space Exploration and Human Evolution* (Boston: Houghton Mifflin, 1987).

16. Jameson, *Archaeologies of the Future*, 270.

17. See, in this respect: Moisei Ginzburg's appreciation in Selim Omarovic Khan-Magomedov, "Ivan Leonidov, un Architetto Sovietico," in *Ivan Leonidov, 1902–1959,* ed. Alessandro De Magistris and Irina Korob'ina (Milan: Electa architettura, 2009), 24; El Lissitzky, *Russia: An Architecture for World Revolution* (Cambridge, MA: MIT Press, 1984). On the theme of Leonidov's dissertation proposal, "Architecture and the Design of Inhabited Areas in the Conditions of Contemporary Society Using the Most Advanced Technical Possibilities," see: Ekaterina A. Barabanova, "Igarka, la Costruzione di una Città nell'Estremo Nord dell'Unione Sovietica," in De Magistris and Korob'ina, ed., *Ivan Leonidov, 1902–1959*, 73.

18. Virili Quilici, introduction to *Ivan Leonidov*, ed. S. O. Khan-Magomedov (New York: Institute for Architecture and Urban Studies, 1981), 5.

19. Ivan Leonidov, "Notes on the Problem of a Memorial," in *Ivan Leonidov*, ed. Khan-Magomedov, 50.

20. Alison Margaret and Peter Smithson, "Urban Re-identification," in *Ordinariness and Light: Urban Theories, 1952–1960, and Their Application in a Building Project, 1963–1970* (London: Faber, 1970), 163.

21. Alison Margaret and Peter Smithson, *Urban Structuring: Studies of Alison & Peter Smithson*, ed. Peter Smithson (London: Studio Vista, 1967), 28.

22. Yona Friedman, "Architecture and Urban Design from a Particular Point of View" and "Seen from Outside," in *Arquitectura con la Gente, por la Gente, para la Gente / Architecture with the People, by the People, for the People: Yona Friedman*, ed. María Inés Rodríguez (New York: Actar, 2011), 54–55, 92–93.

23. Yona Friedman, *Utopies réalisables* (Paris: Union Générale d'Éditions, 1976).

24. Saverio Muratori, *Civiltà e territorio* (Rome: Centro di Studi di Storia Urbanistica, 1967), 28 and 491.

25. Carlo Ravagnati, *L'invenzione del territorio: L'atlante inedito di Saverio Muratori* (Milan: F. Angeli Ravagnatti, 2012), 93–101.

26. Ibid., 55, 119.

Image Credits

197, 198: Alison and Peter Smithson Archive. Courtesy of the Frances Loeb Library, Harvard Graduate School of Design.

199, 200, 201: Courtesy of Yona Friedman.

202: Courtesy of Biblioteca Civica d'Arte Luigi Poletti, Modena.

Roi Salgueiro Barrio

The City of
Seven Billion

**Joyce Hsiang
& Bimal Mendis**

1. The World is an Island

The Earth floats on water.

—Thales of Miletus

The earliest conception of the world was as a metaphysical island. The oldest preserved map, from about 600 BCE, depicts the world as a flat disk encircled by water, with Babylon at its center. Although its geographical features imply an understanding of the earth as circular, the primary purpose of this map—with its representations of imaginary beasts and supernatural heroes—was mythological.

At around the same time, the Greek philosopher Thales of Miletus (about 624–546 BCE) sought to rationally (rather than supernaturally) understand the world by explaining the relationship between land and water. Thales described the world as a compact mass, floating in the middle of an all-encompassing and infinitely vast ocean. In aphorisms such as "All is water" and "The earth floats on water," his conception of the world survives.[01]

A pupil of Thales, Anaximander (about 610–546 BCE), extended the work of his teacher shortly thereafter. He applied what is considered to be some of the earliest scientific thinking to the representation of the world as an island and is credited with creating its first map, as well as attempting to construct its first globe. Anaximander sought to describe the world as the separation of land from water—that is, as a bounded mass of land within a mass of water. While no physical document or facsimile remains, his description survives through written descriptions of his map of the inhabitable world, what the ancient Greeks termed *ecumene*. Depending upon the source, Anaximander's conception of the ecumene is described as the flat top of a cylinder three times wider than tall, either surrounded by or floating above water—an island within or above an ocean—with Greece at the center.[02]

At this early time in history, the conception of the world was inseparable from the idea of the island. The end of the earth—the edge of its geography and geology—was the start of the ocean. The physical limit set by the geographical boundary between land and water coincided with its epistemological boundary: what was beyond this limit was the boundless. The inhabitable world emanated outward from that what was considered the center of the "known world," be that Babylon or Greece.

Today, the ancient metaphor of the world as an island reasserts itself. Once again, it is invoked to delineate the known from that which lies beyond epistemological bounds. As we enter the Anthropocene, however—an epoch in which the world is profoundly and perhaps irrevocably transformed by human activity—and we witness a limitless urbanization that defies political fault lines from a continuous, thickening stratum over the earth's surface, plunging into oceans and reaching toward outer space, the metaphor invites further speculation. What is known or unknown, inhabited and uninhabited, can no longer be clearly distinguished through spatial and geographic means such as a two-dimensional closed figure floating on water, or a singular volume hovering in space.

The metaphor of the world as an island and the concept of the limits or bounds of the "known" or "inhabitable" world have regained potency as a means of confronting the inhabited world as a city, or *ecumenopolis*, as in the interpretation of architect and town planner Constantinos Doxiadis (1913–1975).[03] Whereas the cosmological conquest of space exploration has hurled astronauts, spaceships, and probes as far as 11.3 billion miles away, and the GPS-enabled navigation of quotidian life has tethered us to a swarm of satellites orbiting Earth's atmosphere, the terra firma beneath our collective feet remains a relatively unknown underworld, untransgressed beyond a mere 7.6 miles. We have, quite literally, barely begun to scratch the earth's surface. What then lies beyond, outside, or exterior to the "known world" within this new reality? The spatial definitions and cartographic practices of the "world as an island" invite not only reexamination but reinvention.

2. The Terrestrial and Celestial

Here people say there is an island but this is false and I won't put one here.

—Vincenzo Coronelli

In his essay "The Traveler in the Map," the Italian writer Italo Calvino describes his encounter with the great globes of cartographer Vincenzo Coronelli (1650–1718), shown at the Centre Pompidou in Paris in 1980 as part of the exhibition "*Cartes et Figures de la Terre*" ("Maps and Figures of the Earth"). The twin spheres depicted the terrestrial and the celestial. Such a pairing was not new. As Calvino explains, the "spheres of the firmament and our terraqueous globe are put side by side in many Oriental and Western representations."[04] This had become an established convention by the 17th century, when Coronelli's globes were unveiled, and it gained popularity in the centuries that followed. Calvino continues,

> Two gigantic spheres, each 12 meters in circumference—
> a globe of the earth and one of the sky—are the high point
> of the exhibition and occupy the whole of the 'Forum' of
> the Pompidou Center. These are the largest globes ever
> constructed, and were commissioned by Louis XIV from
> a Franciscan monk from Venice, Vincenzo Coronelli. . . .
> The great marvel is the earthly globe, in dark brown and
> ocher colors.[05]

Similar to the elemental division of land and water implied by Anaximander's conceptions of the world, this pairing of globes sets forth a division between land and air, imparting both a mythological and a material quality to the skies through the depictions of celestial bodies and heavenly constellations upon a solid orb. In Greek mythology the Titan Atlas stood at the end of the earth, bearing the heavens on his shoulder. He held earth and sky apart from each other. Rather than a vast, empty expanse, the sky was a rigid substance—a vast dome, tangible and firm. The heavens had weight, materiality. Rather than airy and infinite, they were solid and finite according to these ancient worldviews.

Today, this firmament is carved into diverse strata of occupation and control. Air rights crisscross the sky and divide it into parcels. On any given day, approximately eight million people (a population equivalent to that of New York City) inhabit the atmosphere, flying as high as six miles above the earth's crust. Hundreds of thousands of aircraft routinely circle the world, transporting nearly three billion passengers a year.[06] The footprint of urbanization goes beyond the two-dimensional, constituting a volume rather than an area.

What then are the limits of this volumetric city, if not the boundary between land and water, the urban and the rural, the terrestrial and the celestial? Some might say the Kármán line: at an altitude of approximately 62 miles above sea level, this line forms the internationally accepted boundary between the earth's atmosphere and outer space and is arguably the ultimate edge of the earth as a physical planet. And yet, humans transgress this frontier, time and time again. Nested together at incremental altitudes are increasingly dense spheres of human occupation and control: commercial aircraft at six miles, stealth aircraft at 12 miles, weather balloons at 25 miles, commercial shuttle prototypes at 68 miles, space stations and space shuttles at 200 to 400 miles, low-orbit satellites at 440 miles, medium orbit satellites at 12,500 miles, and high-orbit geostationary satellites at 22,000 miles.

The terrestrial world as it is known and inhabited is inextricably linked to a vast and viscous cloud of celestial equipment, the fixtures of a city whose edges extend far beyond the outermost threshold of the atmosphere. Technologies that enable people to occupy these cosmological strata also afford the vantage points from which to witness how humankind has transformed the surface below. The world as a city of seven billion people thickens in varying and shifting vertical gradients, stretching toward the bottom of the oceans and the far reaches of the solar system. Signs of human life, if not actual human figures, are ubiquitous, permeating through land, water, air, and outer space. Perhaps this city, the "City of 7 Billion," is now larger than the earth itself.

<u>Left and opposite page</u>: enlarged section (fragments).

3. A Return to Sphaerography

> Now Globes must be temples themselves, as well by the
> magnificence of proportions as by the beauty of work-
> manship and the scrupulous care of scientific drawing.
>   —Élisée Reclus

More than a century ago, French geographer Élisée Reclus
called for the development of a new science—sphaerography—to counter the popularity of map making. In his address to the Royal Geographical Society of London in 1898,
Reclus states, "There is only one way to represent truly the
surface of the Earth. Curves are to be translated in curves; a
sphere or fragment of a sphere must be reproduced by another sphere or fragment of sphere."[07] Sphaerography, Reclus argued, represented the logical and the most important
mode of geographical work to develop. Although it had
not "kept pace with the other, cartography," he presumed
it would "be a real revolution when it has taken in science
and practice the paramount place that it deserves."[08] Reclus's
project of building a giant globe in relief, initially at a scale of
1:100,000, remained a lifelong (unrealized) dream.[09]

Reclus's urgent call for the construction of huge globes
was neither unique nor the first. The *Geographica* of Strabo
(about 64 BCE–after 21 CE) describes the first constructed
terrestrial globe: the globe of Crates of Mallus from the 2nd
century BCE. Crates's was a terrestrial globe depicting the
known world. Strabo instructs:

> But since there is need of a large globe, so that the section
> in question (being a small fraction of the globe) may be
> large enough to receive distinctly the appropriate parts
> of the inhabited world and to present the proper appear-
> ance to observers, it is better of him to construct a globe
> of adequate size, if he can do so; and let it be no less than
> ten feet in diameter. But if he cannot construct a globe of
> adequate size or not much smaller, he should sketch his
> map on a plane surface of at least seven feet.[10]

For the Greek geographer and historian, maps were a necessary evil resulting from the constraints of scale, whereas
globes were the ideal medium. They needed to be no fewer
than 10 feet in diameter: significantly smaller than Reclus's
great 420-foot-diameter globe, although created in response
to the same concerns.

Whereas two-dimensional maps are inevitably a compromise between area, shape, and bearing, the globe's fidelity
to the earth's geometry brings with it a likeness or simulacrum
that can powerfully convey information more accurately. The
larger the globe, the larger the resolution of information it
could convey. A globe could never be big enough, it seems (at

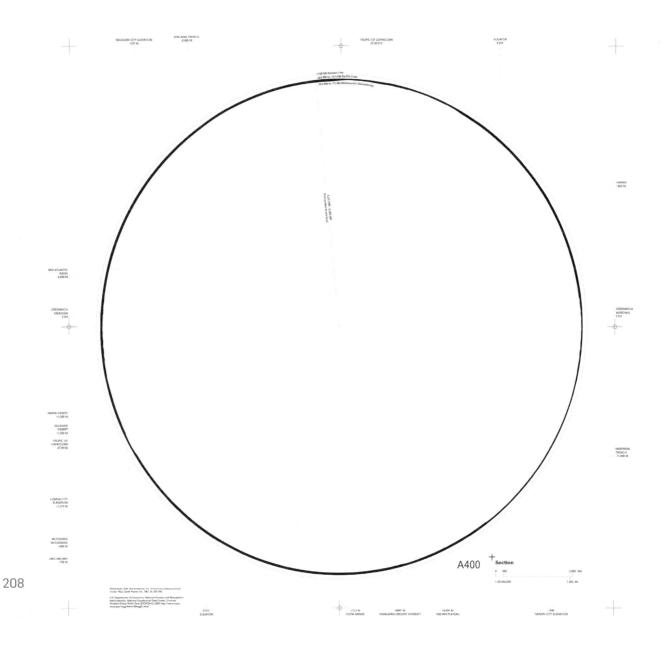

NEUQUEN CITY ELEVATION
+337 M

ATACAMA TRENCH
-8,085 M

TROPIC OF CAPRICORN
23°26'0"S

EQUATOR
0'0'0"

+100 KM Karman Line
+8.8 KM to ~10.9 KM Earth's Crust
~10.9 KM to ~11 KM Mohorovičić Discontinuity

6,331 KM - 6,384 KM
Earth's Outer Core to Earth's Inner Core

HAWAII
+923 M

MID-ATLANTIC
RIDGE
-2,500 M

GREENWICH
MERIDIAN
0'0'0"

GREENWICH
MERIDIAN
0'0'0"

NAMIB DESERT
+1,000 M

KALAHARI
DESERT
+1,000 M

TROPIC OF
CAPRICORN
23°26'0"S

MARIANA
TRENCH
-11,000 M

LUSAKA CITY
ELEVATION
+1,279 M

MUCHINGA
MOUNTAINS
+690 M

LAKE MALAWI
-700 M

A400

Datesoutce: A.M. and Anderson, D.L. Preliminary reference Earth
model. Phys. Earth Planet. Int., 1981 25, 297-356.

U.S. Department of Commerce, National Oceanic and Atmospheric
Administration, National Geophysical Data Center. 2-minute
Gridded Global Relief Data (ETOPO2v2), 2006. http://www.ngdc.
noaa.gov/mgg/fliers/06mgg01.html.

Section
0   500   2,500 KM
                                     1,200 MI
1: 20,000,000

0'0'0"
EQUATOR

+712 M
VIDYA RANGE

+8847 M
HIMALAYAS (MOUNT EVEREST)

+4,500 M
TIBETAN PLATEAU

+540
TIANJIN CITY ELEVATION

Global relief section.

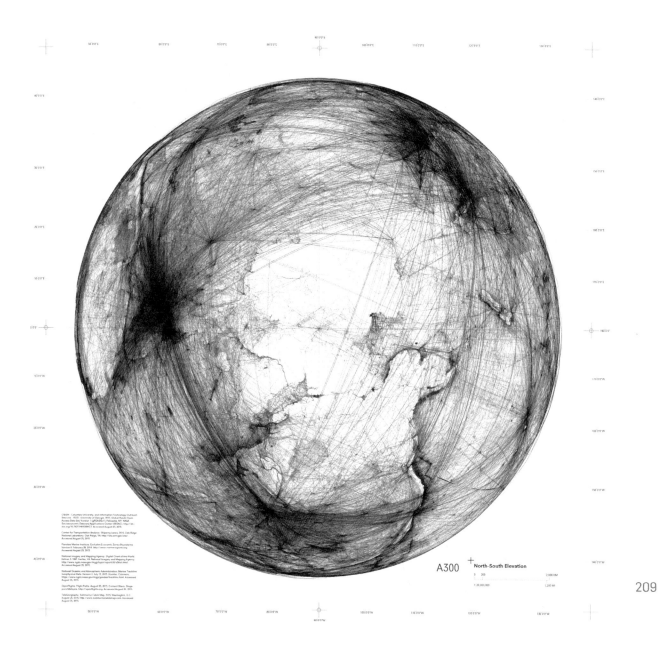

North-South Elevation

1: 20,000,000   1,200 MI

North-south elevation (shipping lanes, exclusive economic zone boundaries, flight paths,
submarine cables).

least to Reclus), to capture or contain humanity's increasing knowledge of the earth's surface. And yet, that which literally resides within the mass of the earth remains, by comparison, untrodden and unknown, a featureless void.

4. Terra Firma/Terra Incognita

Ignoramus et ignorabimus (We do not know and we will not know).

—Latin maxim

It is rare to find a featureless map. "Ocean-Chart," an illustration for Lewis Carroll's 1876 "nonsense poem" *The Hunting of the Snark* created by Henry Holiday (1839–1927), shows the ocean as a single blank rectangle, its border bound by only a few mapping conventions. Carroll's "perfect and absolute blank" map shows nothing, therefore rendering itself useless for navigation. It is simultaneously absurd and realistic.[11] Carroll's fiction—as opposed to the fiction found in most other maps—lies in the presumption that in many parts of the world the surface of the earth is populated by nothing: neither landforms, nor dragons, nor other identifying features.

Geographical efforts are still today stamped with a caveat "of the known world." The earth is understood to the extent that humans have traversed it. Dry ground is continually eroded, filled, and moved, rendering satellite photos outdated as soon as they are taken. And the seafloor, beyond a blurred image, is as much as 99.95 percent uncharted. In reality, modern-day sphaerography is merely a stitched-together ball of uneven information.

To this end, Calvino's description of the exhibition "*Cartes et Figures de la Terre*" again comes to mind. "The earliest need to fix places on a map was linked to travel: it was a reminder of the successions of stops, the outline of a journey. It was thus linear in form and could only be made using a long scroll."[12] These lines of travel, both material and human, inscribe the ways people travel, communicate, and get to know the world; they represent the very contours and physical infrastructures of human existence. If it hasn't been traced, it cannot be known. Thus, these conduits to globalization and the ways we traverse them are fundamental to delineating the world is it is known.

The sphere—continuous, whole, eternal—tricks the viewer into registering completeness. The earth is circumscribed by road networks, transmission lines, submarine cables, shipping lanes, and air routes. And yet, there are countless stories of unresolved quests around the globe: legends of disappearances within the Bermuda Triangle; Donald Rumsfeld's "known unknowns" in the search for Iraq's (nonexistent) weapons of mass destruction; the 2014 disappearance of Malaysia Airlines Flight 370. It is still possible to "fall off the face of the earth." Early globe makers painted sea monsters in parts of the ocean they could not observe directly or approximate. Better to be cautious than clueless.

Any understanding of the urbanized sphere must admit its gaps. Even the surfaces we claim to know should be read with suspicion. The lattices and pockmarks on the surface of the urbanized globe—the unknowns of the earth's crust—are as distinctive as they are vast. They serve as an important corollary to what is known.

It is therefore equally imperative to frame the urbanized sphere through the things that remain unknown—the terra

<u>Above</u>: Site plan (global roads and railroads).

incognita—as it is through the known world, and to foreground the unknowns and not be fearful of them, as if they were marked with dragons or monsters. According to Calvino, Coronelli inscribed his great, wondrous globes with quips such as, "I found I had a space to fill so I inserted this caption."[13] Perhaps if framed with a bit of humor and vitality, and certainly with pleasure and excitement, we might all look at the unknown anew.

If the "City of 7 Billion" merges the terrestrial and celestial spheres in grasping humanity's ever widening sphere of habitation, the unknown no longer simply resides beyond this sphere but rather now exists within it. The "Sphere of the Unknown" is the ever-expanding city. It is less about what is known of the world than about what remains unknown—about an absolute and almost perfect blank.

01. We know of Thales mostly through the writings of other philosophers such as Aristotle, who cites principles by Thales, but do so without necessarily stating a source. See Aristotle's *De Caelo* 294, where he writes, "Others say the earth rests upon water. This, indeed, is the oldest theory that has been preserved, and is attributed to Thales of Miletus." For a full translation of De Caelo, see J. L. Stocks, *The Works of Aristotle Translated into English*, De Generatione et Corruptione (Oxford: Clarendon Press, 1922).

02. See Christoph J. Scriba and Peter Schreiber, "5000 Years of Geometry: Mathematics in History and Culture," (Heidelberg: Springer Basel, 2015), 31–32; and Denis Cosgrove, "Apollo's Eye, A Cartographic Genealogy of the Earth in the Western Imagination" (Baltimore: Johns Hopkins University Press, 2001), 36.

03. Constantinos A. Doxiadis, *Ecumenopolis: The Inevitable City of the Future* (New York: W. W. Norton, 1974).

04. Italo Calvino, "The Traveller in the Map" in *Collection of Sand Essays*, trans. Martin McLaughlin (Boston: Mariner Books, 2014), Kindle edition, 20.

05. Ibid., 19–20.

06. World Bank, "Air Transport Passengers Carried," data, 2012, provided by the International Civil Aviation Organization, Civil Aviation Statistics of the World and ICAO staff estimates, http://data.worldbank.org/indicator/IS.AIR.PSGR/countries/1W?display=graph.

07. Élisée Reclus, "A Great Globe," paper read at the Royal Geographical Society, London June 27, 1898, published in *The Geographic Journal* 12, no. IV (October 1898): 402–06.

08. Ibid., 403.

09. See G. S. Dunbar, "Élisée Reclus and the Great Globe," *Scottish Geographical Magazine*, 90, no. 1 (1974): 57–66, DOI: 10.1080/00369227408736269.

10. Strabo, *The Geography of Strabo*, vol. 1, trans. Horace Jones (London: William Heinemann, 1917), bk. 2, chap. 5. These dimensions, Strabo writes, "In length apparently, thus the scale would suit 70,000 stadia, the length of the inhabited world." While it is important to note that Anaximander too made forays into globe construction, it is unclear whether those globes were terrestrial or celestial.

11. Lewis Carroll, "Fit II—The Bellman's Speech," in *The Hunting of the Snark* (London: MacMillan and Co, 1876), Google eBook, 15–17.

12. Calvino, 16.

13. Ibid., 20.

Image Credits

206–210: Courtesy of the authors.

Joyce Hsiang & Bimal Mendis

A Microcosm on a
Sheet of Paper

**Design Earth
(Rania Ghosn & El Hadi Jazairy)**

Love Your Monsters

In 1682 an icy celestial body crossed the sky following the same path as others visible in 1531 and 1607. Using the law of universal gravitation developed by his friend Sir Isaac Newton, Edmond Halley showed that all three appearances were actually of the same comet, traveling around the Sun in a long orbit and returning every 76 years. He predicted that the comet would reappear in 1758. The periodic comet did indeed return, in 1759—a little late, having been slowed down by Jupiter's strong gravitational pull. It also returned in 1835, 1910, and 1986.

The reactions provoked by the appearance of Comet Halley shifted over the centuries. Until the late 17th century, it was widely believed that the "long-haired star" was a portent of impending disaster (a word whose etymology goes back to *astèr*, or star). The discovery of the regular motion of the comet vacated its ominous meaning. More recent observations further normalized the comet as just another member of the solar system, like the Moon and Mars, ripe for exploration. In the comet's last sojourn through the inner solar system, five space probes flew through its tail, closely observing its jets of evaporating material and snapping thousands of photographs as they swept by, in anticipation of a future of near-Earth object mining.

In 2062 the Halley Armada project will initiate its mission to land a spacecraft on the comet and experiment in a closed ecological system with in-situ resource utilization. This comet mining mission benefits from the regulatory framework established by the Outer Space Treaty and the Moon Agreement.[01] These United Nations-sponsored agreements paradoxically treat outer space as the common heritage of mankind—a *res communes* territory in which space mining and the extraction of natural outer-space resources are allowed and where private property and exclusive ownership rights over those resources, when removed from their natural place, are granted. Scientists are thrilled about this cosmological assignment. To astronomers a comet is a flying natural history museum filled with precious artifacts. Like a cosmic refrigerator, it is stocked with the leftovers of creation—the odd bits and pieces of simple, unused matter dating from the moment when the Sun and its attendant planets assumed their present form. By plowing into Halley's cold heart and sifting through its dust and gases, the Halley Armada will explore conditions that have persisted for over five billion years.

The armada will launch when Comet Halley approaches the earth in 2062. Its mission patch reads, "Love Your Monsters" and "Care for Your Technologies as You Do Your Children."[02] The space probe will be composed of 30 modules, each enveloped in a soft membrane and host to a living, hairy palpal bulb. Landing in the comet's Central Depression, the modules will implant their feeding stem to suck liquid from the comet's nucleus, which is mostly ice from water. In this primal moment of insemination, the parasites fleet leeches off the body of their host.

The formal configuration of the modules will respond to Halley's trajectory around the Sun and to the set of associated physical processes and chemical compounds across its expansive temperature range. The armada will reconfigure in relation to the comet's changing temperature milieu, between the perihelion and aphelion, between the closest and most distant points in the comet's orbit around the Sun. As this dirty snowball swoops toward the Sun, ice and frozen gases are vaporized on the comet's sunward surface. The energy liberated in this sublimation will inflate the membranes of each module, their surfaces harnessing light and heat in a process of artificial photosynthesis. The envelopes will collapse as the comet moves away from the Sun. The dormant cells will incubate, weave their shell, and assemble into one large, blue egg. Irritated by trillions of objects and icy debris at the fringes of the solar system, the egg will hatch a swarm of spider monsters beyond the Oort cloud. This cycle will repeat every 76 years, with interruptions and reformulations, until the comet eventually disintegrates into meteor clouds.

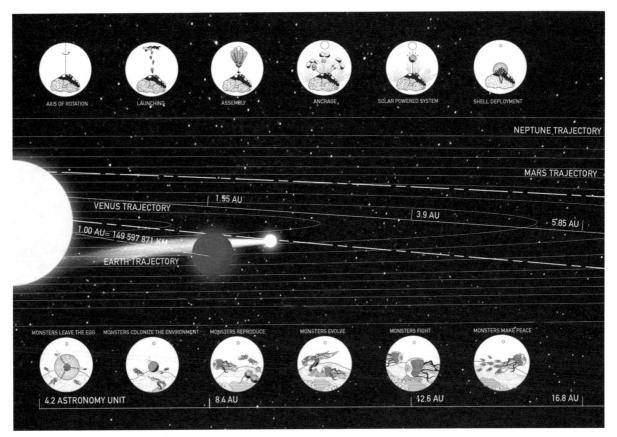

Trajectory of Halley's Comet across the solar system

How do we read this cosmic story? The short story above probes the politics and aesthetics of technology in the age of the (outer-space) environment. In response to the expansion of resource exploitation beyond the earth, the story stages the extraplanetary as a matter of concern for design, soliciting an architectural and geographic imagining of the cosmos. The extraplanetary also provides for a sustained rethinking of technology and politics on Earth and asserts the significance of speculative aesthetics in reimagining these relations.

Extraplanetary geographies counter an ecological worldview of the earth as an island by situating it its broader cosmographic dimensions. The iconic Apollo photographs "The Whole Earth," "Earthrise," and "22727" staged a world picture that was global and ecological, but they also outlined a conception of the earth as a stand-alone globe, detached from outer space.[03] We do not live on a "Blue Marble," however, insofar as that image of our planet symbolizes an objective and holistic Earth made visible by our own technological achievements. What is the new portrait of the earth? The industrial appendage of satellites and space junk and ongoing proposals for the development of extraplanetary mining indicate that the technological reshaping of Earth's systems is an

extraplanetary phenomenon, the response to which requires new concepts and imaginaries.

Outer Earth has been a sphere of human endeavor for well over 50 years. Indeed, since the development of the Cold War space programs, human activity has been shaping the nature of this extraplanetary condition. This has taken on new significance in light of the emergence of commercial actors speculating in off-sourced extractive industries. Planets and asteroids have become the next frontier in the quest to privatize resources, as the earlier conception of space as common property becomes subject to renegotiation.[04] In an epoch of extensive anthropogenic transformations, extraplanetary geographies have become a matter of crucial legal and political importance. How do we make sense of such technologies and scales as a question of design—that is, as a concern of, a site for, and an aesthetic of the architectural project?

To live in an epoch that is shaped by extensive extractive activities is to be confronted with the scale of the earth. In *Homo Geographicus* (1997), Robert Sack notes that "we humans are geographical beings transforming the earth and making it into a home, and that transformed world affects who we are." He adds that the consequences of our

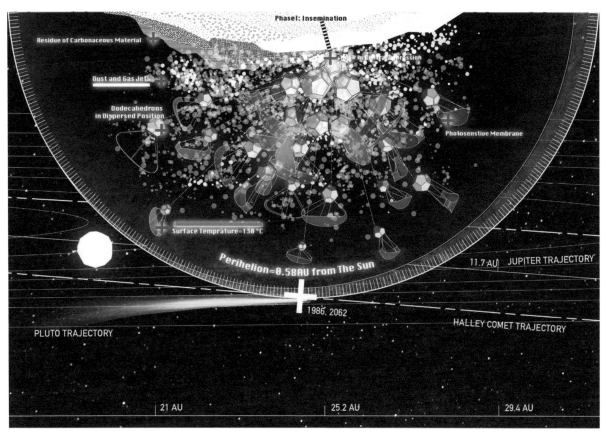

Image labels: Phase1: Insemination; Residue of Carbonaceous Material; Dust and Gas Jets; Dodecahedrons in Dispersed Position; Hole in Central Depression; Photosensitive Membrane; Surface Temprature=130 °C; Perihelion=0.58AU from The Sun; 1986, 2062; 11.7 AU JUPITER TRAJECTORY; HALLEY COMET TRAJECTORY; PLUTO TRAJECTORY; 21 AU; 25.2 AU; 29.4 AU

Phase 1: Insemination

geographical agency are more pressing because we are now "geographical leviathans."[05] Riding the wave of neo-Malthusian claims of material scarcity, a growing body of design projects attempts to reconcile the imperatives of the economy with a managerial, ecological ethics by further expanding into new "resource frontiers." Such a worldview defines the issues to be tackled as inherently "problems of the environment," the response to which generally take the form of additional environmental fixes. In this worldview, *homo geographicus* is *homo economicus*. Can the political arts, which include architecture, destabilize this taken-for-granted space of economy, with which ecology has come to ally itself?

First, a larger-scale framing of the question of resources favors a mode of practice that privileges not only a systemic approach to technology but also a model of the world that operates for the benefit of all its inhabitants. This integrated approach to the large scale was suggested by R. Buckminster Fuller in his *World Game* (1971) and *Operating Manual for Spaceship Earth* (1963).[06] World Game offered individuals or teams of players a tool to explore the use of resources available on Earth directed toward a better standard of living for humanity, and that by providing an inventory of the

world's vital statistics. According to its creator, the objective of World Game was to "to make the world work, for 100% of humanity, in the shortest possible time, through spontaneous cooperation, without ecological offense or the disadvantage of anyone."[07] The self-described "comprehensive anticipatory design scientist" aimed to reconnect the branches of specialized knowledge by designing a description of a new world. Fuller believed that humanity faced unprecedented threats in rising population rates and finite resources. He felt confident that scientists—in collaboration with engineers and architects, seated at the helm of the new "Spaceship Earth"—could correct its path.

In *Operation Manual for Spaceship Earth*, Fuller argued that Earth could no longer be thought of as a natural object: instead, it needed to be recognized as a huge, artificial construct—a spaceship. His world microcosms, which included his Dymaxion maps as well as World Game, came to stand in for the power of a rational, orderly, and wisely managed space colony.[08] The World Resources Simulation Center (a geoscope, or miniature Earth), for example, represented statistical knowledge in a managerial fashion. It was used to educate students and the public, and to make world planning possible. The implementation of this educational simulation

215

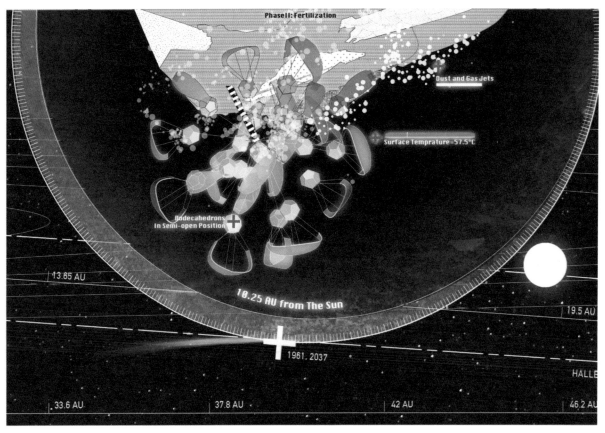

Phase 2: Fertilization

required compiling an expansive database of quantitative and qualitative statistics on the distribution of global resources, a model that cultivates and proliferates tools often associated with contemporary practices of "design research" on technological systems and world mappings.

The scale of Fuller's engagement with world resources extended beyond the earth. "Start with the universe," Fuller told us.[09] In *Comosgraphy* (1992), he looked into the conditions of the cosmos (he called this "cosmic fishing") and, in a forward-looking view, proposed reconfiguring our patterns of living by introducing new artifacts into the environment. He contended that nature was able to be so prolifically diverse in reproduction and variation because it models configurations and structural strategies requiring the least effort.[10] Grounded in triangles and tetrahedral (as is the carbon chemistry of all organic life), his "synergetics," or geometry of thinking, went to the very structure of matter and the shape-fitting cosmos at large.[11] Fuller also experimented, albeit modestly, with other forms of engaging large-scale questions. In *Tetrascroll: Goldilocks and the Three Bears, A Cosmic Fairy Tale*, Fuller narrates to his young daughter Allegra his ideas about the universe and man's place within it—"everything I think and feel in mathematics and philosophy and everything else."[12] The fairy tale gradually becomes a cosmic seminar, with Goldie leading the Polar Bear family in a sky-party teach-in somewhere in the universe.

Love Your Monsters, Bis

The technoscientific imagination so evident in Fuller's thinking has produced many Frankensteinian monsters, emblems of fear of the nature–technology entanglement and symbols of guilt over the unintended consequences of our ever-increasing environmental actions. In *Love Your Monsters* (2011), philosopher Bruno Latour deploys Victor Frankenstein's creature as a parable of political ecology. Latour observes,

> Written at the dawn of the great technological revolutions that would define the 19th and 20th centuries, Frankenstein foresees that . . . we have failed to care for our technological creations. We confuse the monster for its creator and blame our sins against Nature upon our creations. But our sin is not that we created technologies but that we failed to love and care for them.[13]

216

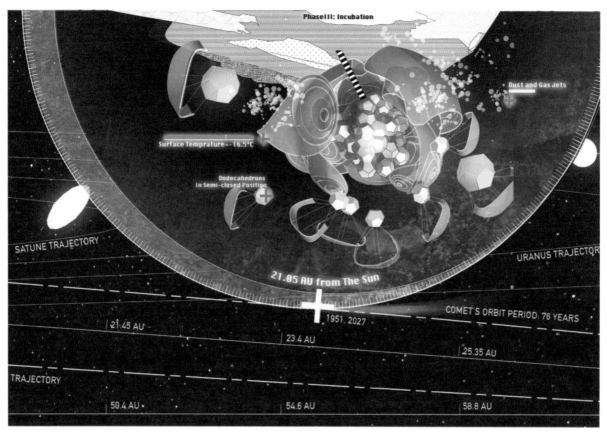

Phase 3: Incubation

"What, then," Latour asks, "should be the work of political ecology?" For him, it is the work of mixing many more heterogeneous actors, at a greater scale and at an ever-tinier level of intimacy with the new natures we are constantly creating.[14] Given that we cannot stop being involved in the world we create, political ecology has the obligation to internalize the externalities that it has viewed up until now as an outside world, and to engage our environmental technologies with patience and commitment. What we need is not to isolate once again the worlds of science and politics. Instead of distinguishing that which can no longer be distinguished, Latour invites us to ask these key questions: "What world is it that you are assembling, with which people do you align yourselves, with what entities are you proposing to live?"[15] In the words of Latour, the earth has become once again what he calls "our common geostory":

> The Earth is neither nature, nor a machine. It is not that we should try to puff some spiritual dimension into its stern and solid stuff—as so many romantic thinkers and Nature-philosophers had tried to do—but rather that we should abstain from de-animating the agencies that we encounter at each step. Geo-physiology as well as

geo-morphology, geo-physics, geo-graphy, geo-politics should not eliminate any of the sources of agency—including those generated by former humans, those I call Earthbound—if they want to converge toward a common geostory.[16]

A Portrait of the Cosmos

Although the extraplanetary might feel futuristic, the concern with outer space is an old geographical project that predates the disciplinary schism of astronomy, geography, and other sciences of the earth. Alexander von Humboldt's influential treatise *Kosmos,* published in five volumes between 1845 and 1862, had achieved a unitary worldview by drawing together a physical geography of the earth and outer space, of planets and cosmic nebulae. His "portrait of nature" presented a totality of the scales and sciences of the earth in an assemblage of astronomy, geography, and geology.[17] Although Humboldt's avowed task as "scientific traveler" was to accumulate information, his drawings assembled forms of knowledge that engaged the aesthetic experience of the reader or viewer. They made commensurability possible. Humboldt found the panorama to be a powerful experiential contraption, particularly as it staged the totality of nature

The image contains the following labels: Phase IV: Hatching, Dust and Gas Jets, Dodecahedrons in Compact Position, Surface Temprature=-178°C, Envelope Becomes A Shell, Messengers leave the belly of the monster, Aphelion=35 AU from The Sun, 27.3AU, 29.25 AU, 1948, 2024, 31.2 AU, 33.15 AU, 53 AU, 67.2 AU, 71.4 AU, 18°

Phase 4: Hatching

across spheres of knowledge and nested a range of scales—from the micro to the macro—within one another. The panorama also made such knowledge accessible to a broad public. Its architecture assembled in large cities different geographies and different zones of elevation. "People want to see," Humboldt noted, "and I show them a microcosm on a sheet of paper."[18] The panorama renders sensible the dimensions of the world and, through geographic representation, invites the reader to understand the earth and humanity's relation to it.

The short story that opens this essay weaves a few stories, concepts, and drawings together into a panorama, a cosmology that narrates a monstrous and mythological Earth and a cosmography that frames the planet within the surrounding constellations. Philosopher Donna Haraway reminds us, "It matters what stories we tell to tell other stories with; it matters what concepts we think to think other concepts with."[19] We might add that it matters what representations we draw to outline the world with. This short story counters a human-centered model of ecology by imagining the cosmos and our complicity in its production. In fact, the speculative attributes of design allow us to think—and feel—the environment, precisely because they can engage cosmic temporal and spatial scales while drawing together things such as life forms, orbits and trajectories, gases, sunlight, and geological strata. The feelings of wonder at the complexity and immensity of the cosmos are channeled into a tool for politics. In this respect fictional speculations are critical instruments to survey the consequences of environmental and technological futures, on earth as it is in heaven. The end of such stories is not another technological fix but the assembly of a political body that cares to speak to the earth's changing state. Each monster brings forth new possibilities for the meaning of difference, all the while engaging the most significant things that define us as humans on earth, which are stories. We have big environmental stories to tell, and these stories are political. "If you want to read it as such," as China Miéville recently quipped, "that's fantastic. But if not, isn't this a cool monster?"[20]

218

Design Earth project team for Love Your Monsters: El Hadi Jazairy + Rania Ghosn, with Jia Weng, Ya Suo, Sihao Xiong, Bin Zhang, Mingchuan Yang, Shuya Xu, Yinglin Wu, with initial contributions by Jennifer Ng, Larisa Ovalles, Cheng Xing.

01. The Outer Space Treaty, officially titled the Treaty on Principles Governing the Activities of States in the Exploration and Use of Outer Space, Including the Moon and Other Celestial Bodies, was finalized by the United Nations in 1966 to provide the basic framework for international space law. It entered into force in 1967. The Moon Agreement, or Agreement Governing the Activities of States on the Moon and Other Celestial Bodies, was reached by the UN General Assembly in 1979 and entered into force in 1984. The treaties limited the use of celestial bodies to peaceful purposes and forbade any government from claiming an extraterrestrial resource.

02. Bruno Latour, "Love Your Monsters: Why We Must Care for Our Technologies as We Do Our Children," The Breakthrough Institute, Winter 2012, http://www.bruno-latour.fr/sites/default/files/downloads/107-BREAKTHROUGH-REDUXpdf.pdf

03. Denis Cosgrove, Apollo's Eye: A Cartographic Genealogy of the Earth in the West (Baltimore: Johns Hopkins University Press, 2001). See also, El Hadi Jazairy, New Geographies 4: Scales of the Earth (Cambridge, MA: Harvard University Graduate School of Design, 2011).

04. See Fraser MacDonald, "Anti-Astropolitik Outer Space and the Orbit of Geography," Progress in Human Geography 31, no. 5 (2007): 592–615.

05. Robert Sack, Homo Geographicus (Baltimore: Johns Hopkins University Press, 1997), 1.

06. R. Buckminster Fuller, The World Game: Integrative Resource Utilization Planning Tool (Carbondale: World Resources Inventory, Southern Illinois University, 1971); R. Buckminster Fuller, Operating Manual for Spaceship Earth (New York: E.P. Dutton, 1963).

07. "World Game," Buckminster Fuller Institute, http://bfi.org/about-bucky/buckys-big-ideas/world-game.

08. See Peder Anker, "Buckminster Fuller as Captain of Spaceship Earth," Minerva 45, no. 4 (2007): 417–34.

09. "When I heard that Aunt Margaret said, 'I must start with the universe and work down to the parts, I must have an understanding of it,' that became a great drive for me," in R. Buckminster Fuller and Robert Snyder, R. Buckminster Fuller: An Autobiographical Monologue Scenario Documented and Edited by Robert Snyder (New York: St. Martin's, 1980), 12.

10. Scott Eastham, American Dreamer: Bucky Fuller and the Sacred Geometry of Nature (Cambridge, UK: Lutterworth, 2007), 17.

11. Ibid., 77.

12. Buckminster Fuller, Tetrascroll: Goldilocks and the Three Bears, a Cosmic Fairy Tale (New York: St. Martin's Press, 1982), interior cover.

13. Latour, "Love Your Monsters," 20.

14. Latour, "Love Your Monsters," 20.

15. Bruno Latour, Waiting for Gaia: Composing the Common World through Arts and Politics, November 2011, 7, http://www.bruno-latour.fr/sites/default/files/124-GAIA-LONDON-SPEAP_0.pdf

16. Bruno Latour, "Agency at the Time of the Anthropocene," New Literary History 45 (2014): 3.

17. Alexander von Humboldt, Cosmos: A Sketch of a Physical Description of the Universe (London: George Bell and Sons, 1883).

18. Quoted in J. M. Drouin, "Humboldt et la popularization des sciences," Revue du Musée des Arts et Métiers, no. 39/40 (2003): 60.

19. Donna Haraway, "Sowing Worlds: A Seed Bag for Terraforming with Earth Others," in Beyond the Cyborg: Adventures with Donna Haraway, ed. Margaret Grebowicz and Helen Merrick (New York: Columbia University Press, 2013), 138.

20. "The Believer—Interview with China Miéville," April 2005, http://www.believermag.com/issues/200504/?read=interview_mieville.

Image Credits
214–218, 220–221: Courtesy of Design Earth.

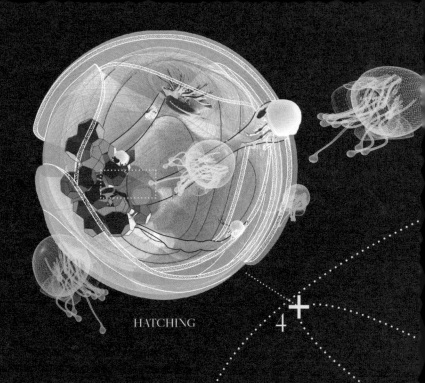

HATCHING

Uranus

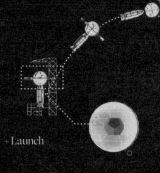

+Launch

Assemble

Merge

INSEMINATION

Land

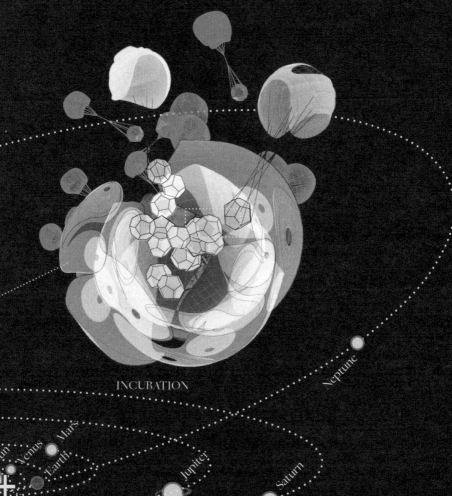

INCUBATION

Neptune

Mercury
Sun
Venus
Mars
Earth

Jupiter

Saturn

2

FERTILIZATION

Contributors

Stan Allen, FAIA is an architect based in New York. He is the George Dutton '27 Professor of Architecture, Architectural Design, at the Princeton University School of Architecture, where he is also the Director of the Center for Architecture, Urbanism, and Infrastructure. His buildings, projects, and essays have been widely published, most recently in *Stan Allen: Four Projects* (2016), part of the Source Books in Architecture series sponsored by the Knowlton School of Architecture at Ohio State University.

Anita Berrizbeitia is a professor of landscape architecture and the chair of its department at the Harvard University Graduate School of Design. Her research focuses on theories of modern and contemporary landscape design and on Latin American cities and landscapes. She is the editor, most recently, of *Urban Landscape: Critical Concepts in the Built Environment* (2015).

Daniel Daou is a doctoral candidate at the Harvard University Graduate School of Design. He holds masters degrees in city planning and architecture from MIT. His dissertation, *Synthetic Ecology: Urbanism after Nature*, retraces the rise of ecology as a cultural metaphor and critically revisits its influence on design. He has been a fellow of the National Fund for Arts and Culture and National Council for Science and Technology of Mexico, as well as the Harvard University Center for the Environment. The author of more than 60 essays, published in journals including *Thresholds*, *Lunch*, *Domus*, and *Arquine*, Daou has served on the editorial board of *New Geographies* since 2013 and is the co-editor of this volume.

Alexander Felson is an ecologist and landscape architect. At Yale University, where he is an associate professor, he founded the Urban Ecology and Design Lab and directs the joint program of the schools of Architecture and Forestry. His research integrates ecological knowledge and methods with urban design and land development strategies to shape human/natural systems. In 2016 Felson received a HUD National Disaster Resilience grant to develop projects on the Connecticut coast that will adapt to severe weather events caused by climate change.

Rania Ghosn is a partner at Design Earth and an assistant professor at the School of Architecture and Planning at MIT. Her work critically frames the politics and aesthetics of technological systems. Rania holds a doctor of design degree from the Harvard University Graduate School of Design, where she was a founding editor of *New Geographies* and editor-in-chief of *New Geographies 02: Landscapes of Energy*. She is the coauthor of *Geographies of Trash* (2015) and the recipient of an Architectural League of New York Young Architects Award (2016).

Laurent Gutierrez is an artist, architect, and cofounder of MAP Office. He earned a PhD in Architecture from the Royal Melbourne Institute of Technology. He is a professor at the School of Design at Hong Kong Polytechnic University, where he leads the Master of Design in Design Strategies program as well as the Master of Design in Urban Environments Design program. He also serves as the codirector of the Urban Environments Design Research Lab.

Stefan Helmreich is a professor of anthropology at the Massachusetts Institute of Technology (MIT). He is the author of *Alien Ocean: Anthropological Voyages in Microbial Seas* (2009), a study of marine biologists working in the microscopic world, the deep sea, and oceans outside national sovereignty, and *Sounding the Limits of Life: Essays in the Anthropology of Biology and Beyond* (Princeton University Press, 2016).

Susan Herrington is a professor in the School of Architecture and Landscape Architecture at the University of British Columbia. Her scholarship concerns landscape theory, history, and design, and children's landscapes. Herrington is the author of *School Yard Park: The 13-Acres International Design Competition* (2002), *On Landscapes* (2008), and *Cornelia Hahn Oberlander: Making the Modern Landscape* (2013), which won the J. B. Jackson Book Prize in 2015. Her book *Landscape Theory in Design* is slated to appear in 2017.

Joyce Hsiang is a critic at the Yale University School of Architecture and a principal in the firm Plan B Architecture & Urbanism. Her research includes the design of a sustainability index to manage urban growth, the WorldIndexer project to model the impact of global development, and the production of a parametric planning methodology for the Maldives. Hsiang received a Hines Research Grant for Advanced Sustainability in Architecture in 2009 and an AIA Upjohn Research Grant in 2010.

El Hadi Jazairy is a partner of Design Earth and an assistant professor of architecture at the University of Michigan. His research investigates spaces of exception as predominant forms of contemporary urbanization. El Hadi holds a doctor of design degree from the Harvard University Graduate School of Design, where he was a founding editor of *New Geographies* and editor-in-chief of *New Geographies 04: Scales of the Earth*. He is the coauthor of *Geographies of Trash* (2015) and the recipient of an Architectural League of New York Young Architects Award (2016).

Kees Lokman is an assistant professor at the School of Architecture and Landscape Architecture at the University of British Columbia. His research focuses on the relationships between landscape, infrastructure, ecology, and urbanism. His recent writings have appeared in the *Journal of Architectural Education*, *Topos*, *MONU Magazine*, and *Landscape Architecture Frontiers*. Lokman is the founder of Parallax Landscape, a collaborative platform that explores design challenges related to climate change, water and food shortages, energy extraction, and ongoing urbanization.

Robin Mackay is the director of the publishing and arts organization Urbanomic and chief editor of the journal *Collapse: Philosophical Research and Development*. He has organized collaborative projects with artists, including Florian Hecker, John Gerrard, and Pamela Rosenkranz. He has written widely on philosophy and contemporary art and translated a number of works of French philosophy, including Alain Badiou's *Number and Numbers* (2008), Quentin Meillassoux's *The Number and the Siren* (2012), and François J. Bonnet's *The Order of Sounds* (2016).

Bimal Mendis is an adjunct assistant professor, assistant dean, and director of undergraduate studies at the Yale University School of Architecture. He received the AIA Latrobe Prize in 2013 for his research on the "City of 7 Billion," which examines and models the condition of continuous urbanization at the global scale. His research also includes the design of a sustainability index to manage urban development, which was awarded a Hines Research Grant for Advanced Sustainability in Architecture 2009 and an AIA Upjohn Research Grant in 2010.

Jamie Mills is an artist, illustrator, animator, and lecturer currently based in York, UK. He is a member of the collaborative project Garden Book Club. His work examines shape, texture, and topology to elucidate and make sense of complex, shifting systems of growth, movement, and interaction. *New Scientist*, *NUT Magazine*, and *Wired UK Magazine*, among other publications, have featured his projects.

Timothy Morton is Rita Shea Guffey Chair in English at Rice University. A prolific writer, he has published more than 160 essays and 14 books, which include *Dark Ecology: For a Logic of Future Coexistence* (2016), *Nothing: Three Inquiries in Buddhism* (2015), *Hyperobjects* (2013), *Realist Magic* (2013), *The Ecological Thought* (2010), and *Ecology without Nature* (2007). In 2014, he gave the Wellek Lectures in Theory at the University of California, Irvine. He has collaborated on creative projects with Björk, Haim Steinbach, and Olafur Eliasson.

Mary Oliver is an American poet who has won the National Book Award and the Pulitzer Prize. The *New York Times* described her as "far and away, this country's best-selling poet." Recognized for the evocative use of natural imagery, Oliver's writing is firmly rooted in the romantic nature tradition. Poet Maxine Kumin noted that Oliver "stands quite comfortably on the margins of things, on the line between earth and sky, the thin membrane that separates human from what we loosely call animal."

222